The Perfect Yankee

1526529

The Incredible Story of the Greatest
Miracle in Baseball History

DON LARSEN

with
Mark Shaw

796.357
L 329

SAGAMORE PUBLISHING
Champaign, IL

Book design: Susan M. McKinney
Dustjacket and photo insert design:
    Michelle R. Dressen and Deborah Bellaire
Editors: Susan M. McKinney, Russ Lake
Proofreader: Phyllis L. Bannon

ISBN: 1-57167-043-2
Library of Congress Catalog Card Number: 96-68629

Printed in the United States.

This book is dedicated to the memory of
Jack Leer and Dr. Bill Howard,
two of the finest men who ever walked the face of the earth
and
my lovely wife Chris,
who never quits believing in me.

—Mark Shaw

Other Books by Mark Shaw . . .

Down for the Count

Bury Me in a Pot Bunker

Forever Flying

Acknowledgments

Working on this book has been a labor of love that I have shared with many people.

My heartfelt thanks go to Don and Corrine Larsen, who trusted me to help tell their story. They are humble people who have become special friends.

I also thank Donna Stouder, a gifted editor and writing partner who has become a reluctant baseball aficionado. And my lovely wife, Chris, who believed as I did that baseball fans all over the world should read about the miracle that occurred on October 8, 1956.

I'm also appreciative of the efforts of Frank Weimann, the tireless literary agent who found a home for the book at Sagamore Publishing. Their group of literary specialists, including Peter Bannon, Mike Pearson, Susan McKinney, Michelle Dressen, Deborah Bellaire, Dave Kasel, and Russ Lake have been most supportive of the book.

My thanks also go to Mark Alvarez and the Society of American Baseball Research (SABR) for not only including an article about Don Larsen in the 1996 edition of *The National Pastime* but for featuring a splendid portrait by Todd Reigle of Don on the cover.

I also thank Ken Birkemeier, a diehard Reds fan who provided valuable input with regard to early drafts of the book. And the Baseball Hall of Fame for their assistance in providing statistics quoted in the text.

My thanks also go to Hall of Fame broadcasters Vin Scully and Bob Wolff for their kindness. And to the irrepressible Yogi Berra for writing the foreword for this book.

I also thank my four children, Kimberly, Kevin, Kent and Kyle for their love and support. And my loyal canine pals, Bach, Snickers, Peanut Butter, Shadow, White Sox and Reggie Miller for their early morning companionship.

Above all, I thank the good Lord for watching over me. I truly believe I am the most blessed man on earth.

—Mark Shaw

Contents

Foreword

by Yogi Berra

Except for the day I was inducted into the Hall of Fame, there is no greater thrill I've had in baseball than catching Don Larsen's perfect game in the 1956 World Series.

Before that day, I had caught both of Allie Reynold's no-hitters, but he was far from perfect in both games. In fact, in one of them, I could have caused him a few problems when I dropped a ninth-inning foul ball hit by Ted Williams. I wanted to crawl in a hole after that error, but fortunately Ted hit another foul ball I caught near the Yankee dugout for the final out.

Allie was a successful pitcher who could be expected to throw a no-hitter, but no one would have expected that kind of pitching from Don Larsen. That's not to say that on any given day, he couldn't do it, but he was very inconsistent. Ol' Gooney Bird could throw with the best of them, but sometimes his mind didn't seem to be in the game.

Don did pitch well over the last four games of the '56 season. He threw a few low-hit games and seemed to be more confident. His success started when he used the no wind-up delivery. He told everyone he got the idea from the comic book "Ghoulies." I read lots of his comic books and never saw anything in there about the no wind-up, but that doesn't mean Don didn't.

That no wind-up kept me on my toes because I had to be ready for him to throw at any second. With the full wind-up, there's time to set, but when Don started his motion, I knew the ball was coming pretty quickly. I think batters had trouble with timing their swings until they saw him pitch that way several times.

The no wind-up really worked for Don, but he did have trouble in Game Two of the '56 Series. He had good stuff that day, but he was just missing strikes, and he got behind a lot of the Dodger hitters. After he walked four batters, Casey had enough and yanked him out.

In Game Five, Don had the best control of any pitcher I have ever seen. He could hit any spot he wanted to, and his fastball and slider were really moving around. He never waved off a pitch I called and hitters seemed off-stride all day.

I've seen lots of pitchers get through six or seven innings without giving up a hit, but along about the seventh inning I realized that Don might have a shot at a no-hitter. We only had a 2-0 lead, but he was concentrating on every pitch.

In fact, the only real bad one he had thrown to that point was the slider that Gil Hodges clobbered in the fifth inning. Mickey Mantle took care of that one with one of the best catches I've ever seen in left-center field.

Don really dominated the hitters in the seventh and eighth innings. The ball that Hodges hit in the eighth to Andy Carey was a blue-darter, but Andy was right on top of it. None of the Dodger hitters said too much. Carl Furillo told me "Larsen really has good stuff today." I nodded agreement.

The excitement when we began the ninth inning is hard to describe. Yankee Stadium was as loud as I'd ever seen it. The fans were all standin' and cheerin' from the moment Don took the mound. I tried to see if he looked like he was all shook up, but I didn't notice anything different when he threw the warm-up pitches.

My heart was poundin' when Carl Furillo stepped to the plate. He was a tough out and I hoped Don wouldn't make a mistake. He didn't, and both Carl and Roy Campanella went down on sliders that were as good as Don had thrown all day.

When Dale Mitchell stepped to the plate, I thought my eardrums were gonna burst from the crowd noise. I tried to give Don the pitching signs, but my hands were shaking when I did that.

We hadn't gone over the "book" on Mitchell since he wasn't a regular player, but I knew that fastballs and sliders were what I wanted Don to throw. Remarkably, Don's last few pitches were some of the best he threw in the game. I don't think Mitchell had ever seen Don's no wind-up, and so I figured his timing would be off if Don could just get the ball around the plate and not throw a fat one down the middle.

The key to the success of the no wind-up was that the ball just kinda came out of nowhere. The pitch was at the plate before the hitter thought it would be. Don's first pitch was just low, and Mitchell laid off. He was a smart hitter and he was trying to gauge the speed of Don's pitches.

The second pitch was a dandy slider and Dale took it for strike one. Don delivered another slider that Dale was way behind when he swung. Now it was one ball and two strikes and Don was just one strike away from perfection.

Pitch number three would have been strike three, but Dale fouled it off. The crowd was roaring, but Don stepped off the mound after I threw a new ball out to him. He played with his cap and the rosin bag, and I wondered whether he was ever going to throw the next pitch.

I only had a few seconds. I called for a fastball and Don threw a beauty. It was moving all over the place and Dale must have wondered whether to pull the trigger. At the last second he decided to swing, but then checked it.

There's been a lot of people over the years who have tried to spoil what Don did that day by saying the last pitch was a ball. I'm here to say that the pitch was right down the alley. Babe Pinelli made the right call. Besides, Dale Mitchell's checked swing went too far and he would have been called out anyway.

When I heard Babe say strr....iii...kke three, I felt like a kid on Christmas morning. I came out of my squat and ran toward Don. Then I leaped on him and hugged him like a brother. Don Larsen had pitched the only perfect game in World Series history and I was proud to be a part of it.

Very seldom does a day goes by that I don't think about Don's perfect game. It was a magical time for the Yankees and for me and I will never forget it. I'm pleased that Don asked me to write the foreword for his book and I know that anyone who reads it will enjoy reliving that special day when Don pitched his greatest game.

Author's note

by Mark Shaw

The good Lord has provided me with many wonderful experiences in my life, but none more memorable than the night I spent in April of 1996 with members of the 1956 New York Yankees and Brooklyn Dodgers. The occasion was a banquet honoring the 40th anniversary of the last Subway Series.

My sojourn to that evening began three years earlier when I read Mickey Mantle's best-selling book, *My Favorite Summer, 1956.* While the book chronicles Mantle's incredible triple-crown winning season, I was captivated when I read Chapter 13 entitled "Perfect."

Authors Mickey Mantle and Phil Pepe presented a vivid portrait of Mantle's image of Don Larsen's perfect game in the fifth game of the '56 Series. When I finished reading that account of Larsen's achievement, I knew I wanted to write a book about the incredible Walter Mitty feat.

One month later, I sat in Don Larsen's living room at his home in Morgan Hill, California. Don and his gracious wife, Corrine, and I talked for a full afternoon. They showed me a bulging scrapbook filled with hundreds of articles and pictures from the perfect game. I also saw the silvered glove, shoes and cap Don used to no-hit the Dodgers on October 8, 1956. A congratulatory letter from President Dwight D. Eisenhower hung on the wall.

I found Don Larsen to be an incredibly humble, unassuming man. I literally had to pull information out of him, a process that continues to this day. Here was a man who had pitched arguably the greatest game in baseball history, and he honestly didn't think it was that big a deal.

When our meeting was nearly over, Corrine asked me if I wanted to see Don's baseball collection. My eyes lit up while she headed for the garage. When Corrine returned, she held a dilapidated, dusty light blue laundry basket filled with baseballs, some still in wrappers.

My hands literally shook when I started picking up the treasured mementoes. I held balls signed by Mickey Mantle, Satchell Page, Babe Ruth, Joe DiMaggio, Ted Williams, Whitey Ford, Willie Mays, Jackie Robinson, Henry Aaron, Yogi Berra, Duke Snider, Casey Stengel, and many others.

"Don," I said, "you've got your grandson's education in this laundry basket. You might think about putting them in a safer place."

Don's casual attitude about the baseballs was comparable to his feelings about the perfect game. While I sensed his pride about the performance, I began to understand that his inability to become a great pitcher in the years following 1956 had unfortunately diminished the achievement.

Over the past 24 months, I have worked with Don to recreate his miracle on the mound. Numerous drafts of the book were written, but it was not until this past winter that I felt comfortable with the text. Telling the story in Don's own humble way was of paramount importance as was my intention to bring to life the ballplayers, managers, coaches, and umpires who were a significant part of the perfect game. I also wanted to honor other pitchers who have achieved perfection and provide a glimpse of yesteryear when baseball was not only a game, but a part of the American experience.

When I arrived in New York in April to work with Don and hopefully interview members of the '56 Yankees and Dodgers, I had no idea what was in store for me. The players were guests of the Downtown Athletic Club, most famous for its annual presentation of the Heisman Trophy.

The first words out of Don's mouth that day were, "You've got to meet Rudy Riska." He rushed me up the elevator to Rudy's office. Riska is a bespectacled gentleman and former Yankee farmhand with swept-back silver and black hair, a deep New York brogue, and a smile that fills his face. He has been the executive director of the Heisman ceremony for 35 years.

I had planned to stay at another hotel, and I did not have a ticket to the evening banquet honoring the Yankees and Dodgers. Ten minutes later, Rudy saw to it that I had a complimentary room at the Downtown Athletic Club and a ticket at his table for the dinner. He even arranged for the Club to loan me a sport coat.

My fantasy voyage into the past began when I stood and listened to Don talk baseball with Hall of Famer Enos Slaughter, player/

manager Hank Bauer, and former Yankee lefty Tommy Byrne. Then an ageless character named Mickey McDermott, of Red Sox fame, walked up.

"Watch out," Don said, "all left-handers are goofy." Byrne gave him an incredulous look, as if to say, "Larsen, you're calling someone goofy?"

Along came former Dodger pitcher Clem Labine, and behind him, Yankee pitcher Bob Grim. Pitcher Ralph Branca followed as did former Dodger infielder "Handsome" Ransom Jackson. Later, Yankees Moose Skowron and Johnny Kucks, Dodger outfielder George Shuba, and the great Bobby Thompson were among the players I met.

As I listened to these ballplayers talk about the game they love, I began to sense a camaraderie among them that is deep and fraternal. Later, under a cloud of liquor that loosened their lips, I listened as Don, Hank Bauer, Bob Grim, Mickey McDermott, Moose Skowron, and Tommy Byrne talked about old times as if they had happened yesterday.

Stories about Ted, Joe D., the Mick, Mel Parnell, Charlie Keller, Tommy Heinrich, Whitey, Casey and Pee Wee filled the air. Images of baseball's glory days told by the men who were there.

Listening to Don debate Hank Bauer and Moose Skowron about their recollections of Casey and Mickey and watching Tommy Byrne show how he threw a pitch *behind his back* to Pee Wee Reese made me long for those lost days. Heart-warming stories made their way into the conversation too, especially when Bauer, the crusty ex-Marine, told how Mickey Mantle broke down and cried every time he talked to a crippled kid.

The stories went on for hours. Many times, five or six ballplayers talked at the same time, interrupted often with bursts of laughter as they recounted the baseball they knew in the fifties.

When I left them, still talking and laughing, my mind was exploding with the wonder of what I had witnessed. I came away believing that I had heard and seen baseball in its purest form, told by men who played not for million-dollar salaries, but because they just loved the game.

This book is written in that spirit with the hope that Don Larsen's story brings back memories of all that is great about baseball. In a day and age when many modern ballplayers have forgotten the rich heritage of the game, I hope *The Perfect Yankee* will stand as a monument to players like Don and his contemporaries who gave their hearts to baseball.

Introduction

To attempt to explain what transpired on October 8, 1956 in the fifth game of the 1956 World Series, one need consult *Webster's Dictionary*. It defines the word "miracle" as "an extraordinary event in the physical world which surpasses all known human or natural powers and is ascribed to as a supernatural cause [and] considered a work of God."

By all accounts, the no-hit, perfect game pitched by Don Larsen in the '56 World Series qualifies as a true miracle. Only the Good Lord knows why it happened. Or why an unlikely baseball player like Larsen was chosen to perform it.

Super-human feats depicted in such films as *Field of Dreams* or *The Natural* pale in comparison to what Larsen achieved. It is arguably the greatest Walter Mitty performance in the history of sport for the odds against an inconsistent, obscure pitcher like Larsen throwing a perfect game in the World Series were truly astronomical.

In fact, an evaluation of the facts surrounding the perfect game make it difficult to believe it ever happened. When baseball traditionalists debate the great performances in the history of the game, Larsen's miracle is often forgotten. It's as if it couldn't have occurred because no one could have done what he did on that October day against the power-packed defending World Championship Brooklyn Dodger team.

Analyzing what many baseball experts have dismissed as a fluke starts with Larsen himself. Always considered a pitcher with "promise," the gangly right-hander had lost a major league, leading twenty-one games for the Baltimore Orioles in 1954. Brought over to the Yankees as a "throw-in" in the infamous eighteen-player trade between ball-busting general managers Paul Richards and George Weiss after that season, Larsen was a Jekyl and Hyde pitcher who alternated steady performances with ones where he didn't throw a strike for a week.

Larsen's 1956 season with the Yankees had begun when "Gooney Bird," as he was known to his teammates, wrapped his sports car around a telephone pole in spring training. That was in keeping with his label as a fun-loving ball player whose off-field antics and party-boy reputation (his favorite expression was "let the good times roll") made teammates, his manager Casey Stengel, and various sportswriters who covered the team question his maturity and dedication to the game.

The fact that Larsen pitched at all in Game Five was a shock in itself. Stengel had unceremoniously yanked him after just two innings in Game Two when he walked four of the first nine batters to face him. Stengel and pitching coach Jim Turner had Johnny Kucks, Bob Turley, Tommy Byrne and Larsen to choose from to start Game Five. But the nod went to Larsen based on what Stengel later said was a "hunch."

Putting the erratic Larsen against any opponent was risky at best, but the team he faced in Game Five was one of the finest in baseball history. They were Walter Alston's Bums, the defending champion Brooklyn Dodgers, sporting such great players as Duke Snider, Jackie Robinson, Gil Hodges, Roy Campanella, Pee Wee Reese, Don Newcombe, and a side-winding, crafty, brush-back pitching artist named Sal "The Barber" Maglie.

To be sure, Larsen versus Maglie was a definite lop-sided mismatch. Although Larsen had pitched well in his last few outings during the regular season, Maglie was a tireless legend whose no-hitter against the Philadelphia Phillies just weeks before the Series and his superb performance in Game Two of the Series marked his return to prominence as one of baseball's elite pitchers. If anyone should have pitched into baseball immortality on that fateful Sunday in October, it was Sal Maglie.

To face the crusty Dodger veteran in any game would have been a formidable task for Larsen, but their battle would come in pivotal Game Five of the '56 Series. With victories tied at two apiece, and the Yankees forced to play the final two games in the unfriendly confines of Ebbets Field (they had lost their last five games there), the mighty Bronx Bombers, led by Mickey Mantle, Yogi Berra, Billy Martin, and Whitey Ford, faced a do-or-die situation in Game Five. If they lost, Brooklyn could wrap up the Series in game six or seven and the men in pinstripes would be second fiddle to their hated cross-town rivals for the second year in a row.

As if by divine intervention, the man who faced the Yankees in the pressure-packed Game Five was armed with a new, unconventional weapon. Just four games before the end of the regular season, he surprised everyone with a no wind-up, quick-as-a-wink, buggy-whip delivery designed to catch batters off-guard. Curious sportswriters were informed by the Yankee pitcher, a comic book aficionado, that the "Ghoulies" had sent him the radical idea.

Adding to the almost mythical atmosphere that surrounds Larsen's miracle was the fact that he *predicted* a no-hitter the night before the game. A few minutes before midnight on the 8th of October, he was riding in a taxicab in New York City with famous *Mirror* sportswriter Arthur Richman.

Less than 13 hours before Game Five, the "night marauder" had partied for hours in some of the Big Apple's most notorious watering holes. Even though there was little chance Larsen would be allowed to pitch in the critical game, he had a premonition. He told Richman, "Tomorrow, I'm gonna throw a no-hitter." He then swaggered out of the cab toward his hotel room.

Don Larsen's preposterous, against-all-odds prediction would be the first of many mind-boggling events that surrounded his performance the next day. Yankee third baseman Andy Carey's father also felt something in the air on the night before the fifth game. He purchased two newspapers at a Times Square novelty shop with the mock headlines "Gooney Birds Pick Larsen To Win Fifth Game," and "Larsen Pitches No-Hitter." He did so as a joke, not knowing if Larsen would even pitch the next day.

Certainly none of the 64, 519 fans in the stands at Yankee Stadium were aware of Larsen's prediction or Carey's father's mock headlines when Game Five began. From the first inning on, however, they realized the Yankee right-hander was a different pitcher from Game Two.

Unlike his previous start, Larsen had pinpoint control. He was the master of a weaving fast ball, a darting curve, and a deadly slider. Of the 97 pitches he threw, an astounding 70 were strikes.

On a day when he could do no wrong, Larsen was also backed up by outstanding plays in the field. Gil McDougald, Billy Martin, and Mickey Mantle, who made what he called the greatest catch of his illustrious career, cemented the Dodgers' fate with sterling defensive efforts

Adding to the mysticism surrounding the game were two Dodger attempts at home runs that would go foul by inches. Right-field umpire Ed Runge called them both. A veteran man in blue, Runge had managed one of Larsen's summer league baseball teams in San Diego. He was there only because two extra umpires were added for the World Series.

The powerful Dodger lineup had blasted opponents into oblivion during the regular season. Now they could only manage to hit ten balls out of the infield. Even Larsen's bad pitches were either fouled off or hit just off the sweet spot into the gloves of perfectly positioned players.

For some reason, the Dodgers never attempted to bunt their way on base. Manager Walt Alston chose to utilize just one pinch hitter, and only Jackie Robinson tried to shake up Larsen's rhythm by stepping out of the box during his third at-bat.

Even though six umpires were assigned to the Series, the veteran Babe Pinelli umpired Game Five. He was calling his final game behind the plate after twenty-two seasons. Not one of his calls was protested, and except for the foul ball decisions by Runge, there were no close calls in the game.

Even Larsen's offbeat antics couldn't jinx the miracle. There was the long-established superstition against discussing no-hitters during a game. Despite that, he told Mickey Mantle midway in the 7th inning, "Look at the scoreboard. Wouldn't it be something? Two more innings to go." Needless to say, Mantle walked away from him.

Nothing could stop Larsen. He continued to mow down the Dodgers inning after inning. His incredible, once-in-a-lifetime array of pitches baffled the Dodgers and never permitted anything close to a hit. He was ahead on the count to a phenomenal 23 out of 27 batters. Only one, Pee Wee Reese, gained a count of three balls.

It took just over two hours for the miracle perfect game to occur. There is no question that the skies opened up and the Graces perched themselves squarely on Don Larsen's shoulders.

To this day, the incredible feat still remains an anomaly. In a sporting world filled with the improbable, Larsen's achievement ranks with the great underdog efforts of all time. From relative obscurity, he leaped to instant fame by establishing a record that has never been matched in 537 World Series games played (1903, 1905-1995).

That's because for one day, Don Larsen was the best there ever was and perhaps the best there ever will be. Here is his story, told by *The Perfect Yankee*, the man who pitched the greatest game in the history of baseball.

Prologue

The match-up between my club the New York Yankees and our arch-rivals, the Brooklyn Dodgers in Game Five of the 1956 World Series featured two teams who had completely dominated baseball during the seven-year era from 1949-1956.

Consider:

A) The Yankees won the World Championship *five* out of the *seven* years preceding 1956, and the Dodgers were the defending world's champions from 1955;

B) Together the two teams collectively won *11* league pennants in the 7 years up to and including 1956;

C) The Dodgers won 93 games in 1953, 98 in 1954, and 92 games in 1955. In 1956 they won the 1956 National League pennant with a .604 winning percentage (93-61) over such powerful teams as the Milwaukee Braves (Hank Aaron, Eddie Matthews, Joe Adcock, Warren Spahn, and Lew Burdette), the Cincinnati Reds (Ted Kluszewski, Frank Robinson, and Wally Post), and the St. Louis Cardinals (Stan Musial and Ken Boyer);

D) The Yankees won 99 games in 1953, 103 in 1954, and 96 games in 1955. In 1956 they won the 1956 American League pennant with a .630 winning percentage (97-57) over such great teams as the Cleveland Indians (Early Wynn, Herb Score, and Rocky Colavito), the Chicago White Sox (Nellie Fox, Billy Pierce, and Minnie Minoso) and the Boston Red Sox (Jackie Jensen, Ted Williams, and Mickey Vernon);

E) In Game Five of the 1956 Series, the Dodgers featured:

1) Four regulars who would be inducted into the Hall of Fame (Duke Snider, Jackie Robinson, Pee Wee Reese, and Roy Campanella);

2) Manager Walter Alston, who would also became a member of the Hall of Fame;

3) A starting pitcher (Sal Maglie) who won 119 major league games and pitched a no-hitter during the 1956 regular season;

4) A starting lineup that had a total of *71* years of major league experience led by Pee Wee Reese with fourteen;

5) Four men in the starting lineup who hit more than *20* home runs in 1956 (Duke Snider 43, Gil Hodges 32, Carl Furillo 21, and Roy Campanella 20);

6) *Eight* starting players who drove in at least *40* runs during the regular season led by Snider 101, Hodges 87, and Furillo with 83;

F) In Game Five of the 1956 World Series, the Yankees featured:

1) Three members of the starting lineup who would be inducted into the Hall of Fame (Mickey Mantle, Enos Slaughter, and Yogi Berra);

2) Manager Casey Stengel, who would be inducted into the Hall of Fame, and coach Bill Dickey, who was already a member;

3) A starting lineup that had a total of *72* years of major league experience, led by Enos Slaughter with *16*;

4) Three men in the starting lineup who hit more than *20* home runs in 1956 (Mantle 52, Berra 30, and Bauer 26);

5) *Seven* starting players who drove in at least *40* runs during the regular season led by Mantle 130, Berra 105, and Bauer 84.

Since both teams were laced with powerful hitters, chances for low-hit, low-run games were slim. The odds became even greater when the likelihood for a no-hitter or perfect game were thrown in.

Statistics indicate that through the end of the 1995 season there were a total of 138,794 games played in the major leagues. 71,208 of those games have been played in the American League (1901-1993) and 67,586 in the National (1896-1993).

To date, only *214* games have been officially recognized as no-hitters while just *14* games have been designated as perfect (no runs, no hits, no errors, no walks, and no hit batsman). While a no-hitter is rare, approximately once in every 700 games, the perfect game comes along just once in every *11,500* or so games played.

Odds against a no-hitter or perfect game being pitched were high enough for regular season games, but they jumped off the chart when the potential for one in a World Series game was figured in. Especially the match between the Dodgers and our club in the pivotal fifth game of the 1956 Series. The chances of anyone pitching a perfect game under such conditions was unthinkable.

Game Five of the '56 Series was being played at the end of a tumultuous year filled with friction and conflict on the national and international scene. The Fall Classic would in many ways allow people to take a deep breath and escape for a moment into the comfortable and exciting American tradition of crowning the world champion of baseball.

When the year began, we were still concerned about whether their beloved war hero and President Dwight D. Eisenhower would recover from the heart attack he suffered in 1955. And if he did recover, would he decide to run for the presidency again? If not, who would challenge the Democratic nominee Adlai Stevenson and his running mate, Estes Kefauver. Kefauver had defeated the up

xxiii

and coming John F. Kennedy for their party's vice-presidential nomination.

Nineteen fifty-six also marked an attempt, not unlike the one in 1992 regarding Vice-President Dan Quayle, by disgruntled Republicans to dump Vice-President Richard Nixon from the ticket. It was unsuccessful and in November, Eisenhower and Nixon were re-elected.

In the summer months of 1956, the country was rocked by violent racial confrontations in the South. Young civil rights leader Martin Luther King continued to press for equality for African Americans and confrontation greeted him at every turn.

In 1956, Nikita Khrushchev rose to power in the Soviet Union and Winston Churchill bowed out in England. President Gamal Abdel Nasser of Egypt confronted the world with the closure of the Suez Canal. The United States and other countries had to mobilize forces to reopen the critical waterway.

In sports, 1956 was a year in which the Soviet Union won the medal count at both the summer and winter Olympics, but Bill Russell led the United States Olympic basketball team to the gold medal. Twenty-one-year-old Floyd Patterson defeated Archie Moore to win the Heavyweight Boxing Championship of the World, while former champion Joe Louis had to wrestle no-name Cowboy Rocky Lee just to pay his back taxes.

In the entertainment field, *My Fair Lady* made its debut on Broadway, while the legendary producer Cecile B. DeMille brought *The Ten Commandments* to the big screen. Grace Kelly left motion picture stardom to become a fairy tale princess in Monaco. Kim Novak and William Holden starred in *Picnic*, and producer/director John Huston brought *Moby Dick* to theaters around the world.

James Dean, Elizabeth Taylor, and Rock Hudson starred in *Giant*, and blond bombshell actress Marilyn Monroe's films grossed more than $50 million. Liberace charmed sold-out audiences at London's Royal Festival Hall, while Elvis Presley captivated the American music scene with his own special brand of "shakin'-hips" rock and roll.

At the top of the television charts in 1956 were "The Ed Sullivan Show," "The Sixty-Four Thousand Dollar Question," "The Perry Como Show," "I Love Lucy," and "December Bride."

Since the 1956 Series would be played in one metropolitan area, the already strong neighborhood rivalries in and around New York City and Brooklyn steamed to a fever pitch. Everyone chose sides and began to anticipate rooting their favorite team to victory.

Harvey Frommer, in his book *New York City Baseball* describes it best.

> Loyalty to the team became virtue. Hatred of the opposition was expected. Whole families rooted for one club. A non-conformist who switched allegiance provoked family rifts and worse. A resident of one borough who mistakenly displayed fondness and affection for a team from another borough courted ostracism, even violence.

To be sure, the great cross-town Yankee-Dodger rivalry was always a heated one, but never more than when the two great clubs came face to face six times in the eight years that the Yankees won the American League crown between 1947 and 1956.

In 1947, the Yankees won the championship in a Series that featured Floyd Bevens's near no-hitter. The Yankees prevailed again in 1949, when they beat the Jackie Robinson-led Dodgers. In 1952, Billy Martin's sensational catch of a pop-up saved Game Seven of the Series for the Yanks.

The Dodgers had another powerful club in 1953, led by Roy Campanella, but the Yankees again pummeled their "Subway Series" rival in six games.

After a one-year departure from the Series, the clubs clashed again in 1955. The Dodgers finally broke and won their very first world championship by beating our club in seven games. We were seeking revenge in 1956, refusing to play second fiddle to a bunch of Bums.

—1—

The 1956 Dodgers

THAT BROOKLYN DODGER TEAM I faced in the Fifth Game of the 1956 World Series was a spirited one. Several times they were bridesmaids to the championship, but the Dodgers had finally broken through in 1955 and won it all.

That had been Walter Alston's second year as manager for the Dodgers. The pieces had come together to produce what veteran Dodger announcer Vin Scully called "perhaps the most balanced Dodger team in their long history."

To most baseball experts, Alston, the Dodger's low-key, pear-shaped manager, was a flat-out baseball genius. He ended up a success in spite of the fact that he almost never became manager of the Dodgers.

The Brooklyn Dodgers had won the pennant in 1953 under manager Chuck Dressen. Most baseball people felt he had done a great job. They also thought he had a smooth relationship with Dodgers' management. That apparently ended when Dressen pressed for a long-term contract; Walter O'Malley, the Dodgers' owner, refused to make the commitment.

Disappointed at the Brooklyn team's second successive World Series loss to us, O'Malley decided it was time for a managerial change. His choice was a simple, soft-spoken man from the small town of Darrtown, Ohio.

Born December 1, 1911, Walter Emmons "Smokey" Alston had joined the Dodgers organization in 1946. A graduate of Miami University (Ohio) in 1935, Alston became very familiar to most of the Dodgers' minor league hopefuls by successfully managing at the Triple A level both at St. Paul and Montreal.

Alston's roots with the Dodgers were deep. In fact, I learned later that he had been signed off of the Miami campus for the club by Frank Rickey, Branch's brother.

Baseball records indicate that the unassuming Alston, the son of a tenant farmer, had a brief baseball career as a player first with Greenwood of the Class C East Dixie League and then with Huntington, West Virginia, of the Mid-Atlantic League, where he batted .326 and led the league with 35 homers.

At 24, Alston reported to the St. Louis Cardinal team as a first baseman, but sat on the bench while playing behind Johnny Mize and Rip Collins, two fine ballplayers. In fact, Manager Frankie Frisch never played Alston at all until the very last game of the 1936 season.

Alston's minor league career included stops at Rochester, Houston, Portsmouth, and Columbus. He was released by Rochester in 1944.

My understanding was that Alston almost gave up baseball. Then Branch Rickey called and offered him a player/manager job at Trenton in the Inter-State League. Alston did well there, and then managed at Nashua, Pueblo, and St. Paul. Two firsts and two seconds at Montreal of the International League, signaled the Dodgers that he was ready to manage in the majors.

George "Shotgun" Shuba, later an outfielder for the Dodgers, played for Alston at Montreal. While the Skipper was known to be mild-mannered, George told me Alston had a temper. "Our club was leading the league, but we lost a few games. Walter came into the clubhouse, picked up a huge oak chair and busted it into a zillion pieces. We started winning after that. Later, I saw him stop our team bus after a loss and challenge anybody to come outside and fight him. Nobody did."

When Alston was announced as the new Dodger manager in November 1953, few, including me, knew who he was. In fact, headlines across the country the next day read "Alston (Who's He?) to Manage Dodgers."

In later years, Dodger players and ex-players told me Walter Alston was one of those managers who treated everyone alike. Superstar or raw rookie made no difference to him. He commanded the respect needed to lead the Dodgers to one successful season after another.

In a great book entitled *Alston and the Dodgers,* Dodgers general manager and longtime friend of Alston, Buzzie Bavasi, described the Dodger manager:

> Walter Alston's the most honest manager I've ever known. He plays no favorites. He levels with you at all times. He isn't afraid to tell off a star, when necessary. He doesn't hesitate to get on the big, highly paid guys with the talent, but he can be very gentle and understanding with the young fellows. He works with the kids, sympathizes with them, and brings them out.

In a recent interview, Dodger broadcaster Vin Scully presented another view of Walt Alston. "Walt was miscast. He should have been born in another time period; he would have been comfortable back in the days of the old west riding shotgun on a stagecoach."

Walter Alston went on to manage the Dodgers through the 1976 season when he was replaced by Tommy Lasorda. Over 23 seasons, his record was 2,040 wins, 1,613 losses and five ties. Most everyone who knew him would agree with my opinion that the game has never known any more of a true gentleman than ol' Smokey.

The 1955 Dodgers had been led by catcher Roy Campanella, who had an MVP year after coming back from a hand injury that restricted his playing time in 1954. He hit .318 and directed a Dodger pitching staff that topped the heap in the National League.

Campanella hit 32 home runs in 1955. Duke Snider led the club with 42. Gil Hodges had 27, Carl Furillo 26, and infielder Don Zimmer 15. The Dodger team had a season high total of 201 home runs, 26 more than our club had in the American League.

Roy Campanella batted in 109 runs that year. Snider led the pack in the Junior Circuit with 136. Gil Hodges and Carl Furillo added almost 200 more to his total. I can't even imagine what it would have been like to pitch to that lineup every day.

While the team was power-laden, versatility was a real key to the Dodger success. Hodges played first base and the outfield, Junior Gilliam second and right, Jackie Robinson third, second, first, and the outfield, and Don Zimmer second, short, and third.

The Dodger pitching staff was anchored by burly Don Newcombe. Watching him pitch made me wonder how he ever lost a game. His fast ball was overpowering and he could change speeds with the best of them. He had bounced back from a disappointing 9-8 in 1954 to go 20-5. Carl Erskine won 11 games, Billy Loes 10, and Clem Labine 13 with 11 saves out of the bullpen.

Also on that 1955 Dodger team were future greats Sandy Koufax, who went only 2-2 but struck out 30 in just 12 games, tall, lanky, flame-thrower Don Drysdale, and a journeyman pitcher named Tommy Lasorda. Lasorda appeared in four games, had no won-loss record, and an astronomical 13.50 E.R.A.! I wish I'd had a chance to bat off of him.

I remember reading the newspaper article about the 10-game winning streak the Dodgers began with in 1955. Their hot streak continued when they won 22 of their first 24 games to lead the National League by $12\frac{1}{2}$ games in July. The team faltered in July and August, but they still beat the pre-season favorites, the Milwaukee Braves, by $13\frac{1}{2}$ games. And then they defeated our club in the World Series in seven games.

The lineup for the 1956 Dodgers was very similar to the 1955 breakthrough championship club, although Brooklyn made some off-season moves to strengthen the team. In the winter, they traded infielder Don Hoak for "Handsome" Ransom Jackson, a third baseman with the Cubs. Pitcher Billy Loes was traded to Baltimore, and pitcher Russ "The Monk" Meyer ended up in Chicago. Outfielder Gino Cimoli was brought up from Montreal, and infielders Charlie Neal and Chico Fernandez joined the club to bolster the infield corps.

Two important players were absent from the Dodger lineup. Left-hander Johnny Podres, the star of the 1955 Series, was called up by the Navy prior to the season. Then the team lost utility infielder Don Zimmer when he was hit in the face by a fast ball from Cincinnati pitcher Hal Jeffcoat.

Every member of Alston's 1955 blockbuster starting lineup was back in full force in 1956. Hodges was at first, Gilliam at second, Pee Wee Reese at short, Robinson at third, and Sandy Amoros, Snider, and Furillo in the outfield. Roy Campanella was behind the plate. Randy Jackson spelled Robinson at third and hit a respectable .274 in 101 games. Gino Cimoli, Charlie Neal, and Rube Walker contributed to the effort as well.

Robinson also played first, second, and left field. Gilliam would often shift to left field where he platooned with the Cuban-born, 1955 Series miracle-catch man, Amoros. It was a tough group, all tried and true professionals.

More than anything, it was the Dodgers' pitching staff in 1956 that stacked the deck in their favor. Don Newcombe, Carl Erskine, and Roger Craig were dependable starters. Clem Labine would again anchor the bullpen, backed up by Ed Roebuck. Drysdale and Koufax got in a few appearances, and Don "The Weasel" Bessent, a character if there ever was one, and left-hander Ken Lehman saw action as well.

Don Newcombe, who was a great pitcher *and* hitter, had the best season of his career. He won the Cy Young Award and the MVP by going 27 and 7. Carl Erskine and Clem Labine pitched in with 23 victories between them. When ageless Sal Maglie joined the team on May 15th, that put the Dodgers over the top.

How the Dodgers got Maglie is quite interesting. When Johnny Podres left for the service, the Dodgers needed a dependable starting pitcher. Cleveland put Maglie on waivers, and the Dodgers decided to take a chance on him even though many baseball experts thought he couldn't pitch anymore.

Donning a Dodger uniform let lightning out of a bottle. The Sal Maglie of old suddenly reappeared, and he won 13 games for the Dodgers. Better than that, Sal won two extremely important games late in the season. He also pitched a no-hitter against the Phillies in September.

The race for the National League Pennant in 1956 was between the Dodgers, Braves, and Cincinnati Reds. The Reds had set a National League record for most home runs by a club. Birdie Tebbetts's young team was led by big Ted Kluszewski, who hammered 35 home runs and knocked in 102 runs. Frank Robinson (38 homers in his rookie year), one of the finest players I ever saw, Wally Post (36), Gus Bell (29), and Ed Bailey (28) added to the Red's firepower. Brooks Lawrence won 19 games, and the "old left-hander," Joe Nuxhall, won 13 to spearhead the pitching staff.

Joe Adcock clobbered 38 home runs and had 103 R.B.I.'s to lead the Milwaukee Braves. Sluggers Eddie Mathews, Johnny Logan, and a young Hank Aaron, who hit .328 with 26 homers and 92 R.B.I.'s added to the Braves' punch. Warren Spahn, the future Hall of Famer who ended up with more victories than any left-hander in the history of baseball, and Lew Burdette keyed the pitching staff for the Braves, who won 92 games under managers Charlie Grimm and Fred Haney. I was glad I didn't have to pitch against those two ball clubs. They had some dynamite hitters.

I remember clearly that the pennant chase went down to the final day. I was pulling for the Dodgers because we wanted a return match.

Milwaukee led by one game with three to play, but on the last weekend of the season, the Braves dropped two of three games to St. Louis, while the Dodgers swept the Pirates to win the pennant.

The newspapers in New York quoted the Dodgers as being supremely confident as they headed into the Series. "We're not about to let the Yankees beat us," Walter Alston told a reporter. "We like being called World Champions."

2

The 1956 Yankees

THE NEW YORK YANKEES of 1956 faced great obstacles. Our club was plagued with a bellyfull of injuries, starting the first day of spring training.

I'd seen Mickey Mantle injured a few times my first year with the club, but the hamstring injury he sustained in the final month of the 1955 season was awful. When training camp opened for the 1956 season, Mickey was still hobbling.

The newspapers said Casey Stengel counted on Gil McDougald as our starting shortstop, but he fell on a slick driveway in Miami and damaged his knee. Then Norm Siebern fractured his knee cap when he hit the concrete wall at our spring training facility, Al Lang Field. And Bob Cerv, the former University of Nebraska fullback, pulled a muscle in his stomach. To top it off, catcher Elston Howard broke a finger.

I thought we were snakebit, but despite temporary setbacks, our club was as tough as ever. Especially Mickey, who recovered from his injury and had what he later called his finest year. I'd say so. He won the Triple Crown by batting .353, slugged 52 home runs, and led the league with 132 runs batted in.

To the left of Mantle in the outfield was my close buddy, feisty Hank Bauer. His fielding was flawless. Hank always made good contact with the bat, which made him the perfect lead-off hitter.

To Mantle's right when World Series time came was Enos "Country" Slaughter, a lifetime .300 hitter. At 39 years old, he had enjoyed one of his finest years in 1955. He had hit .322 in 108 games with Kansas City before being traded back to the Yankees in a late August 1956 waiver deal.

The infield was a versatile one, allowing Casey to move our players around according to the strengths of the opponent. Mickey's roommate and buddy, fiery Billy Martin, was a mainstay at second base. He shared playing time with Jerry Coleman.

Twenty-three-year-old Jerry Lumpe had beaten out future Hall of Famer Luis Aparicio as the top shortstop in our farm system while at Birmingham. He started the year as our shortstop. When Jerry made eight errors in nine games, Gil McDougald took over.

Joe Collins and Bill "Moose" Skowron, also known as "Popeye," shared the first base job. California native Andy Carey spent most of his time at third. Billy Martin also could play third, as could McDougald, giving Stengel many options.

Of this group, "Moose," who attended Purdue University (he said he was a P.E. student —"physical engineering") on a football scholarship, was the target of most of the practical jokes on the team. An easy-going guy for a big fellow, he bitched and moaned privately about the lack of playing time, but publicly he was the gentle giant.

My teammates were tough on "Moose." His nickname didn't refer to his size or to the animal. He told me it came from the name "Mussolini," which is what his grandfather called him when he was a young boy. I never got a straight answer as to why. Some say Moose has a face only a mother could love, but his smile lights up a room.

Another pal of mine, a ballplayer named Rocky Bridges, had similar facial features. George Shuba told me Pee Wee Reese once said to Rocky, "Does that face hurt you?" Bridges replied, "You're no Mona Lisa," apparently believing that Mona was some sort of a beauty.

It was a rare day when Moose Skowron, a pizza and Pepsi freak, wasn't the brunt of a practical joke. The pranks were so predictable that he was forced to check all his personal possessions carefully before he used them. A favorite trick was to pack Moose's shoes with some gooey concoction like shaving cream. He'd fuss and fume when we pulled one over on him, but Moose wasn't a fool, and sometimes I think he tolerated the foolishness just to lighten up things around the clubhouse.

Moose Skowron was a lot like Mickey Mantle in one respect: he thought he should get a base hit or even a home run every time he went to the plate. That caused him great frustration, but as the years progressed, he developed a more relaxed attitude and became an All-Star from the 1957 season through 1961. He ended up with a .282 lifetime batting average. Now he owns a successful restaurant in Chicago called "Call Me Moose."

Catcher "Yogi" Berra was starting his tenth season as a Yankee. Arguably the best in the game, except for possibly Campanella, Berra was a master at handling pitchers. He was also a great hitter. Casey always batted him in the number four slot behind Mantle, giving the opposing pitcher no chance to pitch around Mickey.

Our pitching staff in 1956 was one of the best in baseball. Most of the pitchers were young and new to the club, but one of us always seemed to come through.

Whitey Ford peaked in 1956, and with Bob Turley, Tom Sturdivant, Tom Morgan, Johnny Kucks, Bob Grim, Tommy Byrne, and me, our club had a dependable staff that kept all opponents in tow. Added to the mix was my roommate Rip Coleman, who had an unhittable heater when he could find the plate.

Left-hander Tommy Byrne was a one-in-a-million ballplayer. A quiet, shy fellow off the field, he was the daffy kind of pitcher who drove everyone nuts. I loved to watch him pitch.

While warming up for an inning, Tommy would often use a double wind-up, or he'd clown around by throwing the ball from behind his back. Anything to affect the batters' sense of time and confuse them.

He called that pitch his "kimono" (wrap-around) pitch. Recently Tommy showed Hank Bauer, Bob Grim, and Moose Skowron and me how he threw it. He looked like a pretzel after he was through. Tommy told us he fired the kimono pitch to Pee Wee Reese in spring training one year. Tommy said Pee Wee froze when the pitch crossed the plate and gave him a look as if to say "What was that?"

Tommy played with everyone's minds. While he won some important ball games, it seemed he was always just one out from disaster. He was in perpetual motion on the mound, always fidgeting with his uniform, his hair, his cap, or the ball.

He was every fielder's nightmare. They never knew when or if he was going to throw the ball toward the plate. I remember seeing Casey's face turn beet red when Tommy casually tossed the ball up and down into his glove while he stood on the mound glancing around the ball park.

Tommy Byrne liked to talk to the hitters, trying to distract them or discover any advantage. One player who Tommy used to infuriate was Ted Williams. Right before he stepped to the plate, Tommy would bring up the delicate subject of Ted's estranged wife.

On one occasion, Tommy jawed with Hank Bauer when he was still with the Browns. He told Hank a slider was coming. Hank fouled off the first one. "Let's try another one," Tommy said. Hank hit it into the left field stands. As Hank rounded second, Tommy yelled, "Now that's the way to hit a f_____ slider."

Tommy Byrne had three stints with the Yankees, the last when he rejoined the club in 1954. At age 32, he would only go three and two in '54, but in 1955, Tommy had won 16 games and lost only five.

He also pitched the best game of his career against Johnny Podres in Game Seven of the '55 Series. Unfortunately, that was the day Podres stopped us with a brilliant performance, and the Dodgers won the game 2-0 to capture the World Championship.

We also had a left-hander on the '56 team named Maurice Joseph "Mickey" McDermott. I always thought lefties had a screw loose and Mickey was no exception. His "off-field" antics have been compared to mine, but he was in a different league.

At the beginning of the season, Norm Siebern, Tony Kubek, and Bobby Richardson were sent to Denver of the American Association. Only Norm became a member of our World Series team. Ed Robinson fell behind Joe Collins and "Moose" Skowron at first, and he was sold to the Athletics in mid-season.

Three rookies made the 1956 team. Tommy Carroll was just nineteen, but with the new league rule regarding "bonus babies," the club had to keep him. I never thought he was a favorite of Casey's, and Tommy was teased mercilessly by most of my teammates. Some resented the big bonus money he'd gotten from the Yankees, especially because most everyone felt he would never be much of a big leaguer.

Tommy had quite an ego, and that got him in real trouble later in the season in Kansas City. It happened after he bragged about his blazing running speed with a few of the veterans before a game against the Athletics. One was Hank Bauer. A bet was made for a hundred bucks that Carroll couldn't beat Bauer in a foot race.

To Tommy's dismay, Hank crushed him in the 50-yard race. Then Carroll was challenged by 35-year-old Joe Collins, who also out-ran him. Next up was a 40 yarder against, of all people, Yogi Berra. Yogi turned on the speed and nipped Carroll at the wire. I thought Tommy was gonna have a heart attack, but he wasn't through yet.

Other players enticed the $300 loser into a match with me. I had just been called up from Denver and I was in great shape. Taking me on was a mistake, because next to Mickey Mantle, I was probably the fastest man on the team.

As expected, I annihilated Tommy. When the race was over, I saw that Casey had watched the whole show. He just stood there and shook his head in disbelief.

Big Frank Leja, a first baseman with potential power, also made the 1956 Yankees. But the man who got the most fanfare was our new catcher, Elston Howard.

I understood that general manager George Weiss had once made the statement that he would never allow a Negro to wear a Yankee uniform. True to his word, the Yankees had never invited a black player to spring training, even though everyone knew many had been suggested to them by their scouts through the years.

In 1954, Elston had been converted from outfield to catcher. He was only 25 and had had such a spectacular year that it was tough for even Weiss to deny his potential. At Toronto, he had batted .330, hit 22 home runs, and knocked in 109 runs. He was named the league's Most Valuable Player.

George Weiss finally gave in and invited Howard to spring training. He made the club. God never put a nicer guy than Ellie on the face of this earth, and I was pleased that he was part of our team. Elston Howard had appeared in 97 games in 1955, and batted .290. In 1956, he hit .262 in 98 games.

In 1956, we opened the season against the Washington Senators. Mickey Mantle hit two powerful home runs, each traveling farther than 460 feet. Mantle's tape-measure blasts were the talk of the early season, especially at Yankee Stadium where the fans loved him.

Yogi Berra joined Mantle to supply the power for our club in May when the Cleveland Indians were our main competition. He responded by hitting 12 home runs. His batting average was close to .350. I loved to watch Yogi hit. He was a pitcher's nightmare.

It was May l6th when we took over first place. We never relinquished it again. Even though I helped out later in the year, it was Bob Turley, Tom Sturdivant, Tom Morgan, and Johnny Kucks, along with Whitey Ford, who carried the pitching for the club during much of the regular season.

Nicknamed "Plowboy" by Yankee broadcaster Mel Allen for the way he loped to the mound, Tom Morgan had a brutal sinker that enabled him to become a top reliever. He appeared in 41 games for our club in 1956, garnering six victories and 11 saves. That was an outstanding number in those days.

Quick-pitching Johnny Kucks was a favorite on "getaway day" (final game of a road trip). That was because he took so little time to throw his pitches. When Tommy Byrne struggled, Johnny replaced him in the starting rotation and never looked back. By season's end, he had 18 victories and just six defeats. This was in spite of a fierce temper that made him his own worst enemy when he wasn't pitching well. Nineteen fifty-six was his dominant year in baseball. He never regained the form he showed that year.

Our team increased its lead to $9\frac{1}{2}$ games shortly after the All-Star game. In August, we faltered a bit, but maintained a safe margin. Besides Mantle's assault on the Triple Crown, a highlight of the season was that the club hit 190 home runs. That broke the American League record set by the Yankees with Joe DiMaggio and Lou Gehrig in 1936.

Whitey Ford was superb down the stretch. He won 10 of his last 11 decisions. Bob Turley, Tom Sturdivant, and I contributed as well. We won going away, the final margin being nine games. Based on the strength we had, the club was more than ready to take on the Dodgers.

Our confidence grew because we had manager Casey Stengel in our corner. Many times during a game, I'd glance over at Casey. After all, it was his belief in me that made me a Yankee.

My respect for Casey was immense. When someone believes in you, no matter who the detractors, that forms a bond that is like no other. Casey and I had that bond. It meant a great deal to me, especially in view of the incredible managing record that Casey recorded in his tenure with the Yankees.

Born July 30, 1889 (some say it was 1890), to Louis and Jennie (Jordan) Stengel of Kansas City, Missouri, Charles Dillon (Casey) Stengel was the youngest of three children. I was told that Stengel almost became a dentist, but finally decided that he might be better suited to the baseball field than the dentist's chair.

Ironically, after stints at Kansas City in American Association ball, Kankakee in the Northern League, Maysville in the Blue Grass League, Aurora in the Wisconsin/Illinois League, and Montgomery in the Southern League, Stengel joined the Brooklyn Dodgers in 1912. Over the next twelve years, he hit over .300 three times and ended up with a lifetime .284 batting average.

Already possessed of the nickname "Casey" (legend has it he was named after *Casey At The Bat,* which was a popular poem at the time), Stengel participated in three World Series, one with Brooklyn in 1916, where he went 4 for 11, and two with New York in 1922 and 1923, where he was a combined 7 for 17.

In 1934, Casey Stengel was hired for his first managerial position by Brooklyn. Without many top players, Casey's record was 71-81 in 1934, and 70-83 in 1935. Another losing season followed in 1936 (67-87). Stengel was giving no indication that he would be the kind of manager who could lead a club to five consecutive World Championships in later years.

After uninspiring seasons as a manager of several clubs, Casey Stengel was introduced to the media as the new skipper of the New York Yankees on October 13, 1948. Newspaper reports said he was expected to bring organization to a club that had little order under previous manager Bucky Harris.

One of my favorite descriptions of Casey appears in the book, *The Bronx Bombers* by authors Bruce Chadwick and David Spindel. They also discussed Stengel's impact on the Yankees:

> Though the Yankees had dominated the major leagues during the '30s and '40s, the team didn't really become a dynasty, an invincible force, until the arrival in 1949 of an unlikely character named Charles Dillon Stengel, known to history as Casey. Already fifty-eight years old if not exactly over the hill, he brought baggage with him more fit for a vaudeville act than the nation's finest baseball team. He had an extra large set of ears on an extra large head on a body that always seemed smaller than its listed 5 feet, 11 inches. Stengel was a cartoon of a man, known best during his playing days for coming to bat and doffing his cap to reveal a bird under it ... Fans, writers, and players regarded him

first and foremost as a clown—which he certainly looked like, with that rubbery face, big ears, and too-large uniform always dangling from his aging frame.

Casey Stengel had a certain way of phrasing things that kept everyone on their toes. The press dubbed it "Stengelese." It was the first foreign language I'd encountered before I was introduced to "Berraisms" from Yogi Berra later on.

In *The Bronx Bombers*, the authors described a famous Stengel quote:

> When asked about platooning, Stengel said, "What's the secret to platooning? There's not much to it. You put a right-hand hitter against a left-hand pitcher and a left-hand hitter against a right-hand pitcher and on cloudy days you use a fast-ball pitcher."

Sounds logical to me. No wonder we got along so well.

Casey Stengel was blessed to have some great ball players already set in the Yankee lineup when he took over. Mixing and matching his lineups, he won pennants and World Championships in 1949 and 1950.

In 1951, Casey Stengel assembled what many called the "first instruction school" in baseball history by bringing together such great baseball men as Frank Crosetti, Ed Lopat, Bill Dickey, and Ralph Houk.

To this group, Casey added several other coaches. These men were assigned the task of developing the skills of the young Yankee prospects. This innovative "instruction" technique paid off big for our club, since Mickey Mantle, Gil McDougald, Tom Morgan, Bob Grim, and Tony Kubek became regulars on the future Yankee teams and led the club to its greatness in the 1950s.

In the years 1951, 1952, and 1953, the Yankees steamrolled to pennants and three more World Championships. They lost the American League pennant to Cleveland in 1954, despite winning 103 games, but returned to the World Series in 1955 against the Dodgers.

I believe Casey Stengel's success at managing was due to his skill at keeping everybody on the ball club happy. We were always ready to go the extra mile for him, starters and fringe players alike.

Similar to the successful modern managers such as Sparky Anderson, Tony LaRussa, or Jim Leyland of the Pirates, Casey was good at spotting "team" ball players. The greatest example of that type of player was Charlie Silvera. He would have run through a wall for Casey.

Time and time again I saw evidence of Casey's abilities as a motivator. He encouraged us to be the best. He was also a true believer in working players hard in spring training. He then presumed we would perform up to his expectations during the regular season.

Casey Stengel always dwelled on the positive, even when the club was going through hard times. In fact, Casey never called team meetings when we were in the midst of a losing streak. Because of our winning tradition, he expected us to win, and believed that we would individually figure out what we were doing wrong, correct it, and then get back to winning again.

Leonard Koppett, in the excellent book, *The Man In The Dugout*, told it like it was:

> Like McGraw, but to a lesser degree, Casey wasn't concerned about hurting a player's feelings by a sarcastic or sharp criticism in the dugout, in front of others. But he stuck to a pattern. When the club was losing, he wouldn't criticize much. When it was winning, he became almost intolerably edgy and nasty, trying to forestall a letdown.

As crazy as that sounds, that strategy worked, because Casey had the respect of his players. After all, who could argue with a man who led his club to five successive World Championships? That respect allowed Casey to chastise us for poor play when we were in the middle of a winning streak, because he felt that was when he could best gain our undivided attention.

I think former American League president Dr. Bobby Brown, who played third base for the Yankees before attending medical school, summed it up best when he told the *San Francisco Chronicle's* Art Rosenbaum in 1956 that:

> Stengel's funny at times, but he's no clown. I think his instinct borders on the genius. A good manager draws the best from all players, good or mediocre, and Casey is a remarkable psychologist.

Further insight into the managing success of Casey Stengel, whose face was described by sportswriter Jimmy Cannon as having the "look of an eagle that had just flown through a sleet storm," is presented in *The Man In The Dugout*. Author Koppett, a highly respected former sportswriter and columnist for the *New York Times* and the *Sporting News*, dissects Stengel's ability to manage:

> [Stengel] displayed methods they weren't used to—lots of platooning, hunches that violated orthodox logic, incomprehensible chatter, and a taste for kooky publicity. Somehow the players believed in Casey by the end of his third year of managing even though they didn't understand what he was doing, and shook their heads at crazy moves that seemed to turn out right by sheer luck.

Many times I'd see Casey pinch-hit for the pitcher in early innings when we had runners on base. That drove some of the pitchers nuts, but Casey believed in getting runs early. Most times that strategy worked.

While many people thought Casey was a fool, his fresh outlook on life allowed him to see things others never even noticed. He had a great instinct for the game and he could outfox the best of 'em.

While Casey was masterfully skilled in handling all of our players in 1956, an important part of the team's success centered around the coaches. They included pitching coach Jim Turner, third base and batting coach Frankie Crosetti, and Hall of Famer Bill Dickey.

Frank Crosetti was a quiet man who worked the Yankee infielders hard in spring training. He served as Casey's eyes and ears when he wasn't around. He also became a very good third base coach.

Crosetti began his major league career with the 1932 Yankee team that featured Babe Ruth, Lou Gehrig, and Bill Dickey. Frank was a three-position player for the club (shortstop, second, and third). He was a steady and durable player for the Yanks during his sixteen-year playing career.

"The Crow," as he was known, was never a great for-average hitter, but he was dependable. His occasional bursts of power made opposing pitchers take notice. His best hitting year was probably

1936, when he played exclusively at shortstop. That year he hit .288 with 15 home runs and 78 runs batted in for a World Championship team led by Gehrig, Joe DiMaggio, and Bill Dickey.

As a player and coach, Frank Crosetti's value is symbolized by the fact that he cashed *twenty-three* World Series checks. When his playing career ended in 1948, he joined the Yankees as coach.

A native of Bastrop, Louisiana, Bill Dickey was elected to the Baseball Hall of Fame in 1954. Dickey began his big league career with the Yankees during the 1928 season, when he appeared in 10 games and batted 15 times. In 1929, though, he became the regular Yankee catcher. He played alongside Babe Ruth and Lou Gehrig and compiled a .324 batting average in 130 games. In 1930, Dickey not only watched the Babe swat 46 home runs, but continue to show promise by batting .309.

Bill Dickey batted over .300 for the next four seasons before leveling off at .279 in 1935. He, Lou Gehrig, and future coaching pal Frank Crosetti led the Yankees to the World Championship.

Nineteen thirty-six was also the year that Joe DiMaggio made his debut for the Yankees, and Gehrig had an MVP year. But it was Dickey who made the difference when he hit a career high .362, with 22 home runs and 107 runs batted in.

One hundred and three more RBI's came from Dickey in 1937, but Joe DiMaggio stole the show with 46 homers and an astounding 167 runs batted in. The Yankees won their second straight World Championship. They went on to win two more in succession with Bill Dickey as the mainstay of the offense and a steady force behind the plate.

I still regret that I never saw Bill Dickey play, but I know from what other players have said he was something to behold. He was a devoted coach, working around the clock with Yogi Berra and the other catchers in spring training. I can still see him 15, 20 feet away from Berra, blistering him with harder-than-hell line drives with a fungo bat.

The coach I worked with most was Jim Turner. He may be the finest pitching coach who ever lived. Of course, nobody can teach speed or a wicked curve ball, that comes naturally. But Jim taught all of us how to throw to a variety of hitters and how to adjust our pitching style to different game situations.

Besides talking with us individually about pitching, Jim Turner also worked with Stengel by looking at a respective pitcher's records with different clubs. Together they would schedule us to pitch against teams we'd had the best luck with in the past. For me that meant Boston, Baltimore, and Detroit.

Nicknamed the "Milkman," the mild-mannered Turner, a native of Antioch, Tennessee, began his career with Boston in 1937. When he was a 30-year-old rookie, he won 20 games and had the lowest earned-run average in the league. He spent three seasons with Boston and three with Cincinnati, where he pitched with mixed results before coming to the Yankees in 1942.

In ten seasons in the majors, Jim won only 69 games and lost 60 while appearing in 231 games. He appeared in 88 games for the Yankees in his four seasons with them as a player, winning 11 and losing nine. Jim's knowledge of "how to pitch" was a lot more important than any statistic. As Casey's pitching coach, he was responsible for keeping the Yankee pitching at the top of the league.

Leonard Koppett, in the book *The Man In The Dugout* talked about Casey's relationship with Jim Turner.

> He [Casey] brought in Jim Turner, who had pitched for him in Boston after having McKechnie's tutelage, as his pitching coach— and put him in charge, as if pitching were a sub-department of the ball club. The pitchers were "his" to look after—not just their mechanics and their training and their rotation, but their problems and desires as a group. Turner was their delegate to the central brain trust, protecting their "interests," as well as their foreman. Then, having given Turner this responsibility, Stengel deferred to his judgment most of the time.

Even though we had Casey and his coaches to guide and prepare us for the last Subway Series ever played, we all knew that the match with the Dodgers was going to be a rough one. Of course, there was no shame in losing the Series, since many great ball players never played on a championship team. But in the Yankees organization, runner-up was a dirty word.

My teammate Andy Carey recently summarized our feelings as we went into the 1956 series.

> We were determined not to lose. What made us so good was that if the big guns weren't hitting . . . someone would pick up the slack. It was a team effort and every time we went into the seventh, eighth, or ninth inning, it just happened. Other teams expected to get beat by us, and we obliged them. Brooklyn would be no different.

3

1956 World Series

Games 1-4

WHEN I STROLLED INTO THE YANKEE STADIUM clubhouse on the morning of October 8th, there were less than six hours left before the start of the Fifth Game of the 1956 World Series. Of the 19 players who could have stolen the spotlight that afternoon, I may have been the most unlikely.

Prior to the World Series, my overall record in three major league seasons was 19-35. Most baseball experts said I was a pitcher with "promise," whatever that meant.

By all rights I should never have even pitched for our club in that pivotal fifth game in the 1956 Series. Despite some idle boasting to the contrary, even the remote possibility of pitching a perfect game, or a no-hitter, or a shutout, or even a low-hit game never crossed my mind. In fact, I didn't expect to pitch at all. And for good reason.

In the second inning of Game Two at Ebbets Field, Yankee manager Casey Stengel had crossed the chalk-line and replaced me with Johnny Kucks. I thought my pitching days for the Series were over. I had been given the extraordinary opportunity to start a World Series game, and I had not only disappointed Casey, who had shown great faith in me, but my teammates as well.

Game Two was vitally important, since our club lost Game One to the Dodgers, 6-3. Ace southpaw Whitey Ford, called by Casey

Stengel, "my professional," had taken the mound to open the Series for us. There was good reason to feel confident since he had been by far our best pitcher during the regular season.

In Ford's previous three seasons, his victory totals were 18, 16, and 18. He'd topped that with 19 victories and only six defeats in 1956. In addition to those impressive numbers, Whitey was the best clutch pitcher in baseball.

When "The Chairman of the Board," as he was called, started Game One, the demons of Ebbets Field were looming large against him. The distance from home plate to the left field measured just 343 feet. Only a 9-foot 10½ -inch wall stood ready to defend against the home run.

The deepest part of center field measured 403 feet from home plate. There was a 40-foot high screen that guarded Bedford Avenue, but it was only 297 feet away from home plate. There they had the famous Abe Stark Company sign. If a player hit the sign, he won a suit of clothes. You could read the sign from home plate. Moose Skowron said recently the fences were so close, "I could piss 'em over at Ebbets Field."

Long regarded as a shaky place for a left-handed pitcher to feel safe and secure, Whitey fell prey to the strange bugaboos of the Dodgers' home park. He didn't last through the third inning.

I remember that game vividly. President Dwight Eisenhower threw out the first pitch. Whitey was then staked to a lead in the top of the first inning when Mickey Mantle hit a two-run homer over the right-field screen.

We had a great start to the series, but then Whitey couldn't contain the hard-hitting Dodgers. They scored on home runs from first baseman Gil Hodges and third baseman Jackie Robinson and cuffed him for five runs in just three innings. Johnny Kucks and Bob Turley followed Whitey to the mound. They slowed the Dodgers down, but our hitters couldn't solve the mystery of Sal Maglie. He threw a 6-3 complete game win, despite giving up a homer to Mantle and then one to Billy Martin.

When I took the mound for Game Two of the Series, I felt extra pressure. Prior to the Series, Boston Red Sox slugger Ted Williams had told the press: "I think the pitching of Don Larsen will make the difference in the Series. I know he gave me all kinds of trouble … I only got a couple of hits off him last season. [Larsen] is the toughest pitcher I had to face because of the no wind-up delivery."

Ted had been a Marine pilot in the Korean War. Ironically, his wing commander was future astronaut John Glenn. Mickey McDermott told me recently that Ted Williams was the man John Wayne wanted to be. Mickey also said that while he and I were distracted by "off-field" temptations, Ted was so focused as a hitter that it was scary.

Of course, I was both amazed at, and flattered by Williams's comments about my pitching. During my entire career, there was no other quote that I'm more proud of. To have Ted Williams say that I was a "tough pitcher" is the ultimate compliment, because I consider Ted Williams the greatest pure hitter I ever saw in my thirteen big league seasons.

It's hard to explain, but for whatever reason, I had good luck against Williams. I enjoyed the match-ups we had, even though he was such a fearsome figure at the plate.

The only bad thing about pitching to Ted was that if he let the pitch go by it was most always called a ball. He knew the strike zone so well that I felt the umps were letting him umpire.

If Williams took a couple of pitches, they were usually called balls even if they were close. That meant I was behind in the count. That also meant that most times I had to bring one in to Williams, and then watch out because he'd usually paste it somewhere.

Ted Williams hit the ball harder than anyone I ever saw play. He was awesome to watch, even in batting practice. One time he hit a vicious liner at me that blackened both of my knees.

I pitched against Williams, Mantle, Mays, Harvey Kuenn, Al Kaline, and the other great hitters of the day. Of that group, I'd say the one thing that made Ted the best hitter was his incredible eyesight. I never saw him swing at bad pitches. Somehow he could tell what kind of pitch I was throwing the instant the ball left my fingers.

My pitching opponent in Game Two was big Don Newcombe, the 27-game winner for the Dodgers in 1956. Because rain postponed Game Two by a day, Newcombe had an extra day of rest coming back from the Dodgers' pennant-clinching victory against Pittsburgh the previous Sunday.

In preparation to face the hard-throwing Newcombe, Casey made lineup changes from Game One. He benched third baseman Andy Carey and first baseman Bill Skowron. Billy Martin moved over to third base, and Jerry Coleman took over at second. Joe Collins, an experienced left-handed hitter, played first base.

Our club took a 1-0 lead in the top of the first when Collins singled "Country" Slaughter across, but in the bottom half I walked lead-off hitter Junior Gilliam. Pee Wee Reese then popped to Gil McDougald on a hit and run, and Gilliam just made it back to first. I then issued a walk to center-fielder Duke Snider. That meant there were two on and only one out. Fortunately, Billy Martin bailed me out by taking Jackie Robinson's sharp ground ball and turning it into a double play.

My Yankee teammates tried to make it easier for me by coming up with five runs in the top of the second.

Billy Martin started the inning out with an infield single when Junior Gilliam couldn't quite come up with his grounder beyond second base. Jerry Coleman sacrificed Martin to second, and I helped my own cause with an RBI single to left, scoring Martin with the second run.

Gil McDougald then singled to right, and I ended up on second base. Enos Slaughter was up next, and when he forced McDougald at second, I moved on to third.

Newcombe then intentionally walked Mickey Mantle to load the bases, and Yogi Berra was up next. He responded by hitting a Newcombe fast ball over the right-field wall for a grand slam home run.

Ed Roebuck replaced the disappointed Newcombe, who never had much success in the postseason, and Joe Collins grounded out. The score after the first inning and a half was Yankees 6, Dodgers 0. I had a big smile on my face when I headed for the mound to begin the bottom half of the inning.

With that kind of lead, any pitcher knows the object is to throw strikes and stay away from the dreaded base on balls. I can say for a fact that that's easier said than done.

Gil Hodges began the second inning for the Dodgers with a single to right. I might have gotten out of the inning, but left-fielder Sandy Amoros hit a grounder to first baseman Joe Collins. Collins fielded the ball cleanly, but dropped it in his haste to try to force Hodges at second.

Joe Collins wasn't immune to making errors that season, and according to Mickey Mantle in his book *My Favorite Summer 1956,* second baseman Billy Martin knew the reason why. Mantle wrote:

> Billy used to say Collins had the shortest arms in baseball. When Billy made a bad throw [to first], he'd get on Joe for not coming up with the ball, and he'd go around mimicking him by pulling his arms up and shortening them by a few inches. It used to make Collins madder than hell.

To me, errors were unavoidable. I never let them bother me. I just tried to go on about my business and get the next man out.

Despite Joe's error, I still could have recovered, but then I hurt myself by walking my third batter of the game, right-fielder Carl Furillo. That filled the bases. Later, Hank Soar, the home plate umpire for Game Two, told reporters, "Larsen was just missing the plate." What's that about close only counts in horseshoes?

I had excellent stuff that day, so it was very disappointing that my control was off. Casey Stengel always said that when a pitcher doesn't have control, he's pitching to the hitter's strengths. If he has control, then he pitches to their weaknesses. Ol' Casey was right about that.

With the bases loaded, the chances for the Dodgers to get back into the game loomed large. I tried to gather myself as the great Dodgers' catcher Roy Campanella came to the plate.

Yogi Berra called for a fast ball, and I threw a good one, almost too good. But Campy hit a first-pitch liner to Enos Slaughter in left.

The ball was deep enough for Gil Hodges to tag up at third and score the first Dodgers run, making the score Yankees 6, Dodgers 1. Ironically, next up was pinch-hitter Dale Mitchell, who batted for pitcher Ed Roebuck. Fortunately, I got the former Cleveland Indians hitter to pop-up to Billy Martin in foul territory. I was one out away from ending the inning without any further damage.

With two on and two out, my control let me down once again. I walked Junior Gilliam to fill the bases with Dodgers. After ball four, I saw Casey coming from the dugout. I knew I was through for the day, and maybe for the Series. Casey didn't like walks. That was always my Achilles' heel, even though I tried every method known to man to cut down on them.

My box score for one and two-thirds innings of work showed only one hit given up, but I had walked four batters. I'd survived the bases-loaded situation with Roy Campanella at the plate, but apparently Casey had seen enough. He thought that my lack of control was a sign of trouble.

Stengel replaced me with right-hander Johnny Kucks, but he didn't fare too well either. Pee Wee Reese greeted him with a single, scoring Amoros and Furillo. That was all for Kucks, who was replaced by Tommy Byrne as the Yankees still held a 6-3 lead. Duke Snider put an end to that lead by blasting a Byrne fast ball over the right field wall for a three-run homer to tie the game. The Dodgers went on to win, 13-8.

Inside the clubhouse, I was angry and disappointed. As usual, I kept most of the fury inside of me. I was mad at Casey for taking me out, but mostly I was upset that I had walked so many batters. I knew Casey had a lot of faith in me, and I had let him down.

In fact, even after the series, Stengel's praise of me was pretty qualified:

> Larsen has everything going for him, except maybe himself. He can run, he can hit, he can bunt, he can throw. He's been a fella who should be able to pitch good—but he don't always pay attention to business.

Ted Williams echoed those thoughts. He told a reporter I was one of the greatest natural athletes he'd ever seen. He said the only thing I lacked was discipline. Those comments always caused me concern, but there was no doubt that in Game Two I had been extremely focused. Maybe it was nerves, or the fact that Ebbets Field intimidated me, but I just couldn't find the plate on a consistent basis.

That evening, I was still mad as hell. I'd blown a big chance to help our club, and now we were down two-zip to the Dodgers. Mickey Mantle said later that we just weren't keyed up for the first two games. He thought we'd had it too easy in the regular season, and figured we'd waltz all over the Dodgers. Losing those first two games got our attention, but I was convinced I'd be banished to the bullpen for the rest of the Series. That was my mindset as we headed to majestic Yankee Stadium for Games Three and Four.

Babe Ruth hit the first home run in Yankee Stadium when it opened for business on April 18, 1923.

The triple-decker, oval-shaped stadium seated just over 67,000. Beyond the grandstands, thousands of fans stood and watched the games. Some could see the giant horseshoe playing field from the 161st Street elevated subway line platform; others perched on the roofs of houses nearby.

I loved to pitch in Yankee Stadium because the dimensions made it nearly impossible for a home run to be hit to the center-field bleachers. They were 461 feet away from home plate. Right and left-field home runs were more prevalent since the measurements were 296 feet and 301 feet, respectively.

The rain that postponed Game Two of the 1956 Series for a day actually provided our down-in-the-dumps club with a huge break. Whitey Ford, who hadn't made it past the third inning in Game One, could now come back and pitch Game Three.

And what a game he pitched. Before an overflow home crowd of 73,977, Whitey got his revenge on the Dodgers by pitching a masterful game. He scattered eight hits and struck out six to win 5-3. It was his fourth World Series triumph and third over the Dodgers, all at Yankee Stadium.

The game turned out to be a great pitching duel between Whitey and young Roger Craig of the Dodgers. Brooklyn led 2-1 in the sixth inning. Then Enos Slaughter drove a 3-1 pitch into the right field stands. It was his third World Series homer. That blast scored Bauer and Berra ahead of him and gave us a 4-2 lead. Whitey never relinquished it; he pitched a complete 5-3 game winner.

Now behind 2-1, we returned to Yankee Stadium to square the Series in Game Four. The Dodgers chose right-hander Carl Erskine from Anderson, Indiana, for this critical game. He had set a World Series record with 14 strikeouts in the third game of the 1953 Series. Erskine would face Tom "Snake" Sturdivant, our former infielder turned Yankee right-hander from Oklahoma City.

Tom's best pitch was a fast ball, but he had a pretty good knuckle ball as well. Many people don't know it, but Mickey Mantle liked to fool around with the knuckler. He threw some great ones in batting practice that were unhittable.

That pitch was something I could never master. I tried, but the results were embarrassing. It would either flutter up toward the plate and flatten out or fall short of the plate and bounce up.

The best I ever saw with the knuckler was Hoyt Wilhelm. In fact, he pitched a no-hitter against me when he was with Baltimore. General Manager Paul Richards bought Gus Triandos an oversized catcher's mitt so he could at least try to knock down the bobbing pitch if he couldn't catch it.

That day against us, I pitched one hit ball through seven innings. Hoyt was unbelievable, though. None of my Yankee teammates got a hit.

Attempting to hit that pitch was awful. Everyone tried to get up in the front part of the batter's box and try to swat it before it began to dance. But Hoyt was a master, and the bottom would fall out. Hitters returned to the bench shaking their heads. I thought guys with short swings had a better shot at the knuckler. My big swing never had a prayer.

In Game Four, Tom Sturdivant came up with a strong performance, mixing up fast balls and sliders with the knuckler. He held the Dodgers to just six hits, beating Erskine and relief pitchers Ed Roebuck and Don Drysdale. Mickey Mantle and Hank Bauer contributed home runs before 69,705 fans. We had evened the Series at two games apiece setting the stage for the pivotal fifth game at Yankee Stadium.

—4—

Getting Ready for a Miracle

AFTER THE GAME FOUR YANKEE VICTORY, I stayed around the clubhouse to congratulate Tom Sturdivant for his performance. It was a
great pitching performance and I was very happy for him. I then
headed downtown to meet my friend, sportswriter Arthur Richman.

Artie Richman worked for the *New York Mirror* for over 20
years. He first joined the newspaper as an office boy in 1942.
Richman's popular column in the *Mirror* was called "Arm Chair
Manager." He was one of a colorful breed of sportswriters of the
day, along with Milton Gross and Jimmy Cannon of the *New York
Post*, Arthur Daley of the *New York Times*, and Dick Young and Jim
McCulley, who is credited with labeling Dodger pitcher Sal Maglie,
"The Barber."

I met Arthur and his brother Milton in 1953, during the St.
Louis Browns' training camp. They were friends with Harland Clift,
the third baseman for the team, as well as Buddy Blatner and Dizzy
Dean. Since Arthur was single, we used to go out on the town
together. In fact, I called Arthur, "Night," because he roamed the
streets and nightclubs with me, and Milton, "Day," because he
wouldn't.

I also became close with Arthur's parents. They took me under their wing and I used to visit them often. They were both very
short people, under five feet, so I towered over them at six-four.
They were good people, and I appreciated their friendship and
support.

Arthur Richman has not only been one of my closest friends for over 40 years, but a witness to what I did the night before the Fifth Game of the 1956 Series. That became a point of debate when Mickey Mantle included the following passage in his book, *My Favorite Summer 1956:*

I've heard and read a lot of stories about how Don Larsen was out all night drinking and partying the night before he pitched Game Five of the 1956 World Series. But I'm here to tell you that it's just not true. I know because I spent part of the night with him.

I'm not going to tell you Gooney Bird was a Goody Two-Shoes. He loved to party and he could do it with the best of them. He liked to drink and he was a champion in that league too. But he also was one of the best competitors I have known. He liked his fun, but on the mound he was all business. There might have been times when he stayed up all night, drinking and partying, and pitched the next day, but he never would do that for such an important game as a World Series game. He just wouldn't let his teammates, and himself, down like that. Larsen told me he was going to have dinner with some friends, then go over to Bill Taylor's saloon on West Fifty-seventh Street, across from the Henry Hudson Hotel, where Gooney was living at the time. He asked me to join them there, and I did.

Taylor was a big, left-handed hitter from Alabama who was an outfielder with the New York Giants. He spent a little over three seasons with the Giants, then a season and a half with the Detroit Tigers before retiring. He wasn't much of a major-league player, but he was a good guy, and when he opened this saloon, a lot of players started hanging out there. It was one of Larsen's regular stops.

I caught up with Larsen and his friends about nine o'clock and I stayed there about an hour and a half. In that time, I didn't see Gooney Bird have one drink. He was drinking ginger ale. And he was cold, stone sober.

I left Taylor's about ten-thirty and went back to the St. Moritz. Later, I found out that Larsen left a few minutes after I did. He stopped for a pizza and took it back to his room at the Henry Hudson. One of Don's friends told me later that he saw Gooney go upstairs to his room with his pizza. He was sober at the time and that's how he spent the night, unless he got smashed in his room, which I doubt. But, of course, it makes a better story to say Larsen was out all night the night before he pitched, partying and drinking and falling-down drunk. And because of his reputation, it was easy to believe those stories. It almost seemed that people wanted to believe them, as if that made what he did even more remarkable and dramatic.

Of course, I can't imagine what ol' Mick was talking about regarding my reputation, but that's another matter! While I loved the Mick and will miss him dearly, his recollections of the night before don't coincide with what really happened.

Besides his version, there are three other stories by two men about the night before the fifth game that also circulated at the time. One was told to the press by my friend, the famed restaurateur Toots Shor. He told reporters he and I had drinks in his eatery the night before the fifth game. Toots also said he introduced me to the Chief Justice of the Supreme Court, Earl Warren. Toots says Justice Warren, a Yankee fan, told him that he wasn't going to bother to go to the game the next day because I was "going to be drinking all night with him."

Two separate accounts were offered by Arthur Richman; the first one in a column that included a prediction of a no-hitter:

> The fellow sitting next to us in the taxicab that rolled along the Grand Concourse Sunday night toward his hotel, said: "Don't be surprised if I pitch a no-hitter tomorrow."
>
> "Just pitch a four-hitter," we replied, "and it should be good enough."
>
> Thousand-to-one shots have been called before. But never the zillion-to-one shot that Don Larsen called as we accompanied him home Sunday night on the eve of the most dramatic achievement in baseball history....
>
> Only a relatively few hours earlier—at 9 o'clock Sunday evening—Larsen, a friend of his and this reporter sat down to dinner at Bill Taylor's Restaurant, where a number of players gather.
>
> Don had a steak and a couple of beers before teammate Rip Coleman joined him. Since it was close to 11, we prodded Don to go home and get some rest for the day's assignment ahead of him.
>
> So, after walking a few blocks to 50th St., we hopped a cab and headed for the Bronx. Larsen was completely relaxed as he sprawled his long legs over the seat and lit a cigarette. Although there wasn't much talk about baseball on the ride uptown, we nudged him in the ribs and said: "Fight 'em tomorrow, will ya?"
>
> "Don't worry about it, Meat," he answered in his Hoosier-clipped tone. "And don't be surprised if I pitch a no-hitter." Larsen,

of Lutheran faith, seldom attends church. But as he alighted from the cab when it pulled up to his hotel, he stopped abruptly and said:

"Gee, maybe I should have gone to church tonight. It's too late now. But here, take this money and give it to your synagogue as a donation from me."

As we pocketed the money, we glanced at our watch. It was 12:10 Monday morning. We fidgeted for a moment and said:

"Hope no one sees you coming in after midnight."

"So what," he replied. "I'm going to win, anyway."

Arthur Richman also told author Harvey Frommer a similar version of the story. In *New York City Baseball*, Frommer recalled Richman's words:

The night before Don pitched the perfect game, I went out with him. He wasn't skunk drunk as many would have you believe. About midnight, Don took some money out of his pocket. "I don't go to church," he said, "why don't you give this to your mother and let her give it to her synagogue?" I gave the money to my mother and she gave it to the synagogue the next morning and that day—lightning struck.

I love these stories, especially since they make it sound like I knew I was going to pitch the fifth game, which I didn't. It's also important to remember that we were in the middle of the greatest competition in the history of sport, the World Series. I would never have gotten myself out of top physical or mental condition on the eve of such an important game.

To set the record straight, here's what happened. I met Arthur Richman and we went to Bill Taylor's bar. I had met Bill during my years in the Service. He was a left-handed hitter for the Giants and after his playing days were over, he opened up the bar. It was across from the Henry Hudson Hotel (Mantle was wrong in saying I lived there), where a lot of the players stayed during the season.

Arthur and I had something to eat and a couple of beers, and then we either hit one more place or we parted ways to go home. Before doing so, however, two interesting things occurred. First, we got to talking about the next day's game, and I don't know how it came up, but Arthur is right when he tells people that I told him that *if* I pitched the next day, I might [he says would] throw a no-hitter.

The second interesting thing occurred when I gave Arthur a dollar for the synagogue to bring good luck to me and the Yankees. I don't know why I did that, but looking back, it sure worked!

One thing is for certain. I did return to the Concourse Plaza Hotel before midnight. While that seems late for a ball player in training to many people, I hated to lie around the hotel room with nothing to do. I got more nervous and worked up when I did that, so I tried to get home at a decent hour and then get a good night's sleep.

Coincidentally, I wasn't the only person to make the unlikely carefree prediction that I might pitch a no-hitter the next day. According to Yankee third baseman Andy Carey, his father and mother had gone to Times Square in New York City for dinner.

> While there my dad and mom, Nola, who had become very good friends of Don's, walked into one of those stores where they print up mock headlines on a newspaper front-page format. Dad told me later that he had a premonition about the game the next day. He felt that Don would start the game even though no one, including Casey or Jim Turner, had indicated that he would.

Because of that premonition, Ken Carey had two mock newspapers put together. One said, "Gooney Bird's Pick Larsen To Win Fifth Game," and the other, "Larsen Pitches No-Hitter."

Gooney Bird, of course, referred to a nickname I had been given by my teammates while we were in Japan in the winter of 1955. While there, a couple of players noticed a bunch of large, white gooney birds who were as clumsy as drunken sailors. They would stumble around and try to fly, most times without success. I began to call a bunch of the Yankees gooney birds. As sometimes happens, however, I ended up with the nickname when we got back to the states.

After buying the newspapers with mock headlines, Andy Carey says his dad brought them back to the hotel. He pasted them on my door.

> Later he decided that leaving them there might jinx Don, so he took them down. Mom says dad flushed the one "No-Hitter" headline down the toilet, but the "Gooney Bird" one hangs on the wall in my insurance office in San Diego to this day.

In spite of my nonchalant prediction and the premonition of Mr. Carey, no one in their right mind would have believed I would even pitch the next day. Or even come close to perfection.

In fact, in another part of town, Washington Senators announcer Bob Wolff recently said that he was making another sort of prediction on the evening before the fifth game. He was scheduled to broadcast the fifth game for Mutual Broadcasting. Huddled with Herb Heft, publicity director for the Senators, Wolff was going over his notes in preparation for the game.

"I looked over at Herb and said, 'Wouldn't it be something if Sal Maglie pitched a no-hitter against the Yankees?'" Wolff remembers. "Herb just laughed and replied, 'Nobody pitches no-hitters in the World Series!'"

During the regular season, I stayed at the Concourse Plaza Hotel on 161st and Concord Parkway, which is about a mile from Yankee Stadium. I had a great place there. While some of the other players liked to live downtown, I preferred to live closer to the stadium.

On days when the team was playing at Yankee Stadium, I had a pre-game ritual. I'd awaken late, eat breakfast, and then hang around the room. I always liked to get to the ball park early, but on occasion, I'd stop at one of the ball fields around Yankee Stadium where I could watch the kids play, sometimes right up to game time.

I never ate a big meal before a game, so I'd just get a sandwich at the ball park and sit around and eat, read comic books (still a favorite pastime of mine), or sign autographs and baseballs.

The Yankee clubhouse was sacred ground for all of the Yankees. It was tucked away on the lower level, directly behind home plate. To get to the field, the ball players left the locker room and headed down a passageway where guards were posted. I became friends with many of the security people. One used to bring me sauerkraut and pigs feet. I loved that stuff.

My locker space was beside Bob Turley's. Mickey Mantle's and Yogi Berra's lockers were to the right side of the entry; Casey Stengel had his own office across the way.

Pete Sheehy and Pete Previt were the clubhouse attendants who took care of me and my teammates. Yankee players never wanted for anything.

On days when I was scheduled to pitch, I would get a rubdown from the long-time Yankee trainer Gus Mauch. I never spent too much time in the trainer's room, but it seemed like Mickey Mantle, who had so many injuries, was always in there.

Casey delivered his pre-game speeches like a college cheerleader. He'd stand before us like some kind of a czar. Believe me, Casey wasn't afraid of anything.

Most times, he started off with a lecture or pep talk about baseball, and then he'd veer off to politics or whatever was on his mind at the time. Of course, this was true whether he was talking to us, to the reporters, or to the President of the United States. Casey had an opinion about everything, and he wasn't shy about sharing it.

Once the pre-game Yankee meeting was over, I would go down the ramp to the ball field. Even if I was going to pitch, I'd still bunt and hit with the regulars, and then go warm up in front of the dugout. On days I wasn't the starting pitcher, I'd shag flies or play pepper with the guys. I loved to run, and so I'd take off with the other pitchers and run around the outfield until it was time to start the ball game.

When I woke up on October 8, 1956, which happened to be Thanksgiving Day in Canada, I realized it was a perfect day for baseball. There were sunny skies, 60-degree temperatures, and little wind. I went through my morning ritual and then arrived at the ballpark around 10:30.

Many times Casey and Jim Turner announced the starting pitcher for the next day's game the day or night before. If that was in doubt, Frank Crosetti performed a little-known Yankee ritual.

Frankie, our third base coach, took it upon himself to place the warm-up baseball for that day's game in the starting pitcher's baseball shoe prior to game time. In the '56 Series, the pitchers for the first four games were set, but who would pitch Game Five was anybody's guess. That meant Crosetti would be in action.

In a recent interview, Frank explained the origin of the ritual.

The baseball-in-the-shoe ritual originated when I was forced to take care of the bags of baseballs in the first place. Nobody else would do it because it was a pain in the ass. Bill Dickey didn't want to, and of course Turner wouldn't, so I was left to take care of the damn baseballs. It was then that I started to put the warm-up ball in the shoe before each game.

Although Crow's probably right on point, I have my own theory as to why he was responsible for the balls.

Crosetti was a very quiet and gentle man while he was with the Yankees, and we all understood when he didn't join us for those wild and crazy Yankee pennant and World Series celebration parties. But the reason the Yankees wanted Crosetti to be in charge of the balls was because he had quite a reputation for one simple thing: He was as "tight" with the baseballs as he was with his nickels and dimes.

Whatever the reason, Yankee back-up catcher Charlie Silvera remembers that the Yankees even used the ball-in-the-shoe routine to razz a young pitcher named Bill Miller. This was during the 1953 World Series against Brooklyn.

Silvera still laughs when he recalled the incident.

Miller was a real cocky kid. He always was saying how he wanted to pitch the big games, bragged about it. Well, we worked it out with Crosetti to put the ball in Miller's shoe for the Seventh Game that year. Everybody was in on it. After he saw the ball, we all went up and told him that we were countin' on him, all the money was on him, and so forth. Poor guy, I thought he was going to have a heart attack.

Dodger pitcher Clem Labine told me he almost fainted when he found a ball in his shoe before Game Six of the '56 Series. "That's the last thing I wanted to see," he said. "The last thing in the world."

That was my feeling too when I reached down to pick up my shoes and found a baseball in the left one. I realized I would be the starting pitcher for Game Five.

Later I'd learn that Stengel and Jim Turner apparently had decided they were going to start me the night before. For some reason, they chose not to tell. They were probably concerned I would get nervous, worry too much, and not get a good night's sleep.

Hank Bauer recently said that he and Bill Skowron were standing close to my locker when I saw the ball in the shoe.

"You had a look of shock and disbelief on your face," Hank told me. "And then you took a big gulp. It was like you had an apple stuck in your throat."

I must admit I was shocked. Many thoughts went through my mind as I began to put on my uniform and get ready for my second chance at the Brooklyn Dodgers.

After I put on that treasured New York Yankee uniform with the number 18 on the back, I headed for the ball field. I was ready to go. I knew I had to do better than last time, keep the game close, and somehow give our club a chance to win. Casey was betting on me, and I was determined not to let him down this time.

5

Inning #1

Three and Out

	1	2	3	4	5	6	7	8	9	10	R	H	E
Brooklyn											0	0	0
Yankees											0	0	0

WHEN I FACED THE ARCH-RIVAL BROOKLYN DODGERS in the fifth game of the 1956 World Series, I was a long way from my home town of Michigan City, Indiana.

I was born to James and Charlotte Emma Gimple Larsen on August 7, 1929. Michigan City is a town of nearly 35,000 near the Indiana/Michigan border. It is perhaps best known as the location for the Indiana State Prison.

My parents told me the family doctor was running a little late for my scheduled arrival, so my father assisted a neighbor in helping my mother bring me into the world. My sister, Joyce, was four years old when I weighed in at ten pounds.

I was exposed to sports early in life. My sister and her boyfriend took me to South Bend to Notre Dame football games and to nearby Chicago for Black Hawks hockey games. My first introduction to baseball was watching my father play sandlot ball.

It made quite an impression. I remember bugging him after work to play ball with me. I was only four years old when I got my first bat. It was bigger than me, but I'd still swing it around. Dad and I spent hours together, especially on Sundays, with him throwing the ball as I tried to hit it with that heavy bat.

Finally, my father bought me a new, lighter bat so I would have a better chance hitting the ball. I loved to hit then, but as I got a little older, I told my dad that I wanted to be a pitcher. That's when he and I switched positions. From then on, I pitched to him.

It was nearly 20 years after those early days of playing ball with my dad that I began to warm up in front of the dugout for the Fifth Game of the 1956 World Series. The catcher I threw to that day was Charlie Silvera, who backed up Yogi and Ellie Howard.

Perhaps never in the history of baseball has there ever been a more dedicated ball player than Charlie. When interviewed by writer Roger Kahn for his book *The Era 1947-1957*, Charlie described himself as "a spear carrier among a bunch of emperors and lords. You gotta have spear carriers, and I was a damn good one."

In fact, Silvera was a talented catcher in his own right and he considered it a privilege to be a part of our club. He once told me, "I'd pick up the players' towels after they showered in order to be a Yankee!"

Besides his catching chores, Charlie was the team cheerleader. He ran the bullpen and kept things loose for the relief pitchers while they were getting their suntans and talking to the fans. Charlie nicknamed me "Froggy," because of my love for frog hunting. That was something I did with my dad when I was young. Later on, I saw a frog in Texas so big it ate a rattlesnake.

Charlie Silvera spent eight years with the Yankees before joining the Cubs in 1957. In 227 games, he had 482 at bats, and ended up with a highly respectable .282 lifetime average.

Ironically, the mitt that Silvera warmed me up with before Game Five was a Wilson-Roy Campanella model that Silvera still displays at his home near San Francisco. He's very proud of his playing days as a Yankee and remembers clearly our pitch and catch before the fifth game. "There was nothing unusual," Charlie said in an interview. "Don was sharp. In those days, he always had good stuff. It was just a matter of whether he could get it over the plate."

At a minute or two before 1 p.m., Charlie and I finished our regimen. I then retreated to the dugout. The introduction of the players followed and then the National Anthem. At 1:03, I made my way to the mound to face the Dodgers. A few warm-up pitches later, Yogi Berra put his catcher's mask on, and 61-year-old home plate Umpire Babe Pinelli shouted: "Play Ball."

Television announcer Mel Allen, also known as "The Voice of the Yankees," noted that it was sixty degrees at game time. He also told his viewing audience, "A slight wind is blowing out to left."

I felt confident as I prepared to face the Dodgers. Pitching in Yankee Stadium was the reason. A pitcher always feels more comfortable in his home park. Besides, our club had won eight of the last nine games we'd played there.

The first batter for the Dodgers was their fine second baseman, James William "Junior" Gilliam. Born October 17, 1928, in Nashville, Tennessee, Junior Gilliam gained his nickname from members of the Baltimore Elite Giants of the Negro League for being the youngest player on the team. He started his baseball career with Montreal of the International League in 1951 at the age of 23. That season he hit .287 in 152 games and led the league in runs scored with 117.

The last minor league season for the switch-hitting, 6-foot, 180-pound Gilliam was 1952. When he improved his batting average to .301 and had 112 runs batted in, the Brooklyn Dodgers knew he was ready for the majors.

In fact, not only did Gilliam take over as the Dodgers' regular second baseman, he won Rookie of the Year honors. In addition, he collected eight hits, including three doubles and two home runs, off the Yankee pitching staff in the 1953 World Series.

Gilliam would go on to play in 39 games in seven World Series for the Dodgers. He became as fine a second baseman as there was in the game during that time. Known for his consistent play both in the field and at bat, Gilliam played all of the positions except shortstop and catcher.

During his 12-year major league career (he was a player-coach in 1965-66), Junior Gilliam played in 1,956 games. He drove in better than 550 runs and hit a steady .265.

All of the Yankees had great respect for the Dodgers' players, and Gilliam was no exception. Not one Yankee pitcher ever took Junior Gilliam for granted. Especially me.

Yogi Berra had sized up Gilliam pretty well for me prior to Game Two. He told me that Gilliam had the keenest eye for the strike zone of any of the Dodgers hitters. "He's very selective," Yogi said, "and he'll make you pitch to him. Because of his small stature, he gets a lot of bases on balls."

What made Gilliam doubly tough was that Pee Wee Reese was coming up behind him. With Pee Wee's ability to hit and run or sacrifice, a walk or single usually put Gilliam on second or third. If that happened, our club could be down several runs before the game was more than a few minutes old. That was because Duke Snider, Jackie Robinson, and Gil Hodges and their long-ball capability came next in the Dodger lineup.

My strategy was to pitch Gilliam on the corners. I'd deliver him a mix of sliders and fast balls, both high and low.

The first pitch to the Dodgers' second baseman, who had the worst 1956 Series batting average of any Dodger regular prior to Game Five (1-14, .071 in the first four games), was a fast ball outside. Gilliam fouled off the second pitch, another fast ball. I then threw a slider, which was down and away, to make the count two and one.

I got a called strike from Pinelli on a fast ball that had good movement on it and then threw a sneaky slider low on the inside corner for a called strike three. Gilliam bowed his head and headed for the dugout. I had my first out of the game.

Dodgers' shortstop and captain Pee Wee Reese, playing with a severe cold, now stepped to the plate. He never had a bad World Series. He had seven hits in 1947, 10 in 1952, eight in 1955, and already six by the time he came to the plate in Game Five.

I started Reese out with a called strike fast ball on the outside corner, but then threw him a slider, missing the corner. I got another strike from a fast ball on the corner, making it one ball and two strikes, but then threw two straight balls, one inside and one high, to run the count full. One ball away from a base on balls, Yogi called for a slider, and when Pinelli raised his right hand with a called strike three, I was very relieved. Two batters up, two down, with two strikeouts. Now that was the way a game was supposed to start.

The next batter to test me was the Dodgers' center-fielder Duke Snider. He was 4 for 14 in the first four games of the Series with six strike-outs. Always a threat though, Snider was a powerhouse batter who could hit the ball out of any ball park.

In the television broadcast booth, Mel Allen told his viewers that our fielders were in motion for Snider's at bat. "Mickey Mantle shifts to his left. Slaughter also. Bauer is almost out of sight in right," he told his audience. The future Hall of Fame announcer also noted that Snider was a fast ball hitter. "Larsen will show Snider a change of pace," he suggested, "and that sets up his fast ball."

Mel Allen was right on target. I threw the Duke a fast ball that was outside, another for a called strike, and then a low curve that missed the outside corner. With the count two and one, Snider hit an inside fast ball harmlessly to Hank Bauer in right field. Hank came in a bit to make a knee-high catch.

Any pitcher will tell you that getting through the first inning sometimes is the toughest part of a game. That's especially true with a powerful team like the Dodgers. I hoped the one-two-three first was a good sign.

Patrolling right field for our team in Game Five was barrel-chested Hank Bauer.

Hank Bauer was a pro's pro, a gritty, no-nonsense, in-your-face warrior. He was a throwback to the ball players of yesteryear, and a damn fine example for the ball players of today. He gave his teammates 100% every time out, and Hank's hard-nosed play made us all work just a little harder than we might have otherwise. Why he isn't in the Hall of Fame, I'll never know.

A twice-honored Bronze-star winner for his heroics as a Marine at Guadalcanal, Bauer was born in East St. Louis in 1922. He had a distinguished career as both a player and a manager. He became the Yankees' regular right fielder in 1949. For the next eleven seasons, he was a member of *nine* pennant winners, and *seven* World Championship teams!

The right-handed, rough and tough Bauer began his career in 1941 at Oshkosh, Wisconsin, where he not only played the outfield, but pitched as well. After his heroics in World War II, Hank played for Quincy, Illinois, in 1946, where he hit .323. He then joined Kansas City of the American Association in 1947, and stayed through the early part of 1948. He hit better than .300 both years.

The Yankees finally called up Bauer in the latter part of 1948, and he became a fixture in the outfield. In 1950, he hit a career high .320. The greatest achievement of his career, however, came during the 1956-1958 World Series when Hank hit in 17 consecutive games. That record still stands today.

Hank Bauer also hammered four home runs and knocked in eight runs in the 1958 Series as the Yankees clobbered the Braves for the World Championship. He was traded to Kansas City in the winter months in a deal that brought Roger Maris to the Yankees. Hank then played two years with them before being named manager, succeeding Joe Gordon in the middle of the 1961 season.

The Kansas City team finished ninth that year and the next, and owner Charley Finley fired Bauer for the team's poor performance. Hank bounced back in 1964, when he became the manager of the Baltimore Orioles. He led the club to two third-place finishes before the team went on to become World Champions in 1966, when pitcher Dave McNally beat the Los Angeles Dodgers 1-0 in Game Four to give the Orioles a sweep.

Nineteen sixty-seven saw the Orioles finish a disappointing sixth, and in 1968, while the team was in third place at the All-Star break, Bauer was again fired. He was replaced by the flappable Earl Weaver. Charley Finley brought Hank back to manage Oakland in 1969, but even though Bauer had his team in second place in its division, Finley fired him once again.

Over his 12-year major league career, Hank Bauer amassed an impressive record. He hit better than .275 in more than 1,500 games, was named to the All-Star team three times, and drove in more than 700 runs.

I will always remember Hank Bauer as a winner, both as a player and a manager, and he always encouraged me to never give up. Hank gave it everything he had and more.

He was especially helpful to the younger players on the team. I roomed with Hank in New York, and he would introduce new players like me to the Big Apple when they first came to town. We enjoyed a great relationship on and off the field, and we often slipped into the night life of New York between games. After one escapade, he looked at me, then at himself in the mirror. "How come you've got those pretty blue eyes and mine look like Atlas road maps?" he asked.

Hank was also a battler when it came to salary time. Our G.M. George Weiss was a notorious penny pincher. (One time Skowron hit .300 for three consecutive seasons and never got a raise.) We had no agents so it was us against him. After a good season Hank asked for a raise from $10,000. Weiss said no. Hank said, "Listen, Joe D. (DiMaggio) is makin' $100,000 and he's not ten times better than me." The strategy worked. Weiss gave Hank a raise to $16,000. He was tickled pink.

Hank Bauer was one of those no-nonsense, serious players who set the tone for the team. He used to say, "When you cross the white lines, the fun is over and the business begins." Everybody knew he meant it.

Mickey Mantle, in his book *My Favorite Summer 1956* echoed those thoughts. He called Bauer "one of the toughest guys in baseball ... with a face that somebody once described as looking like a clenched fist." Mantle also said, "Hank was a great competitor and a much better ball player that he was given credit for."

Mickey's right. Hank was a great hitter and a damn good defensive outfielder too. He was steady, ran very well, and had a good arm that came in handy in right. He was also a first-class clutch hitter.

I've played with, against, and for Hank Bauer. He was a respected foe when I faced him as a member of the Browns in 1953. I enjoyed my years as his Yankee teammate, and I considered it a privilege to play for Hank when he managed at Baltimore in 1965.

Hank Bauer said recently that he remembers me most for my mantra, "Man ... oh Manochevitz ... Let the good times roll." We did have some great times on the streets of New York. After the fifth game, Hank told me I was "in outer space from the first inning on." He's a beauty.

In the Yankee half of the first inning, Sal Maglie, making his first appearance ever in Yankee Stadium, put some additional excitement into the game. He was throwing what broadcaster Bob Neal called "varying speeds of a curve ball." Well, the second pitch he threw to Hank ended up behind the Yankee right-fielder's head. Whether it was intentional or not, Maglie innocently looked down at his hands as if to say, "it slipped."

"Bauer, on the other hand," noted Mel Allen, "is standin' there starin' out at Maglie."

After brushing himself off, Hank, who came to bat 5 for 18 in the Series, could not solve the mastery of the Barber. He popped out to Pee Wee Reese behind third base. First baseman Joe Collins, 2 for 12 in the first four games of the Series, then tried to bunt his way on. Jackie Robinson fielded the ball cleanly and threw him out at first.

Mickey Mantle, hitting against the modified "Ted Williams shift" as Mel Allen called it (Dodger shortstop Pee Wee Reese joined

Junior Gilliam and Gil Hodges between first and second base), lofted a soft fly to Sandy Amoros in left. Our club was through.

A one, two, three inning by Maglie matched mine, and the score was 0-0. Sal had looked as tough as he had been in Game One. We knew we had our work cut out for us against the Dodgers' crafty, ageless wonder.

6

Inning #2

Hot Corner Magic

	1	2	3	4	5	6	7	8	9	10	R	H	E
Brooklyn	0										0	0	0
Yankees	0										0	0	0

IN THE TOP OF THE SECOND INNING, I faced who most baseball experts believe to be one of the game's greatest all-around athletes.

Batting clean-up for the Dodgers, 37-year-old Jackie Robinson strode to the plate. Just nine years earlier, in 1947, Robinson had changed baseball forever. He became the first African-American to openly play in the major leagues.

The grandson of a slave, Jack Roosevelt Robinson was born near Cairo, Georgia, on January 31, 1919. He was the youngest of Mollie and Jerry Robinson's five children, but he never knew his father. He had deserted his family when Jackie was only six months old.

Jackie Robinson's athletic prowess surfaced at an early age. Even though he showed great promise, no university was interested enough to offer him financial aid. He ended up at Pasadena Junior College. There, his athletic achievements, especially in track, caught the attention of the athletic officials at UCLA.

It's little wonder they did. Future Dodger great Duke Snider remembers seeing Robinson at Pasadena Junior College. He described those days in his biography, *The Duke of Flatbush:*

> I saw Jackie when he was in Pasadena Junior College and I was in junior high school. Five or six of us kids saw him play a baseball game, leave in the middle of it with his uniform still on to trot

over and compete in the broad jump in a track meet, and then run back and finish the baseball game just as if nothing unusual had happened. That's how great and versatile he was, and how bright the fire of competition burned inside him.

I have another early memory of Jackie Robinson. I was in the eighth grade when he was playing football for Pasadena, the big rival of our own school, Compton Junior College. I was in the stands when he took a kickoff, reversed his field three times, and returned it for a touchdown. It was as dazzling a piece of broken-field running as you could ever hope to see, by the same guy I had seen play a baseball game and compete in a track meet on the same afternoon. No wonder he was my boyhood idol.

Jackie Robinson's early experiences with racial prejudice have been documented, but my awareness of him began when he joined the Dodgers in 1947. That year, he not only broke the color line in the major leagues, but was voted Rookie of the Year. In 1948, Robinson hit .296, hit 12 home runs, and knocked in 85 runs.

While 1948 was a good year for Robinson, 1949 was a breakout one. He was named the league's Most Valuable Player after hitting .342 and driving in 124 runs. Also, over ten seasons with the Dodgers, Robinson hit .311, with 137 home runs and 734 runs batted in. His all-around skills earned him the honor of being the first black player to be inducted into the Hall of Fame in 1962.

I loved to watch Jackie play. By 1956, he was 37-years-old and still electrifying. Roger Kahn said it all about Jackie in his book, *The Boys of Summer*:

> He [Robinson] had intimidating skills, and he burned with a dark fire. He wanted passionately to win ... he bore the burden of a pioneer and the weight made him more strong. If one can be certain of anything in baseball, it is that we shall not look upon his like again.

Jackie Robinson's at-bat in the second inning proved to be a memorable one for me and the millions of baseball fans who were watching the game. Before the game, Yogi Berra had discussed with me the best way to handle the Dodgers' third sacker, who was having a very good World Series.

"We can't throw anything soft to Jackie. Never let up. Anything tight and up is his wheel house, so we gotta be careful to keep the ball away from him," Yogi instructed.

True to Yogi's orders, I started Robinson, who batted with a very closed stance, off with a waist-high fast ball a bit outside that he fouled off.

I then tried to throw a fast ball, but the ball got up and in. Robinson hit a smoker toward third baseman Andy Carey that punctuated the designation of third base as the "hot corner."

Fortunately for me, the ball was hit so hard that it ricocheted off Andy straight to Gil McDougald, who instantly scooped it up and fired the ball toward first base to get Robinson by a step.

Later, McDougald would tell reporters, "I threw that ball so hard [to first] I could feel the muscles pull right down to my toes."

Andy Carey described the play this way:

> I was playing at regular depth. Jackie Robinson hit the shit out of the ball on the ground to my left. I extended myself way out for the ball and it hit off the fingertips of my glove. It glanced toward Gil McDougald and he threw Robinson out.

Andy said there were two unusual things about the play.

> Number one, we would have never gotten Robinson out if the game would have been played two or three years earlier when he still had his speed. Second, that same play had happened twice ... I think against Detroit and Baltimore ... earlier in the year. In fact, I told a reporter after the game, "we practice that play."

Later, I learned that Gil's play warranted one of sportscaster Mel Allen's famous "How About That!" quips. He praised the Yankee shortstop's "tremendous alertness" on "a vicious liner" that was "too hot to handle."

From my vantage point, Jackie's line drive was a bullet, but Andy somehow had gotten his glove on it. I then watched as the ball made a quick right turn toward McDougald, who was moving over to back up the play. He in turn picked the ball up and threw it to first base—boom, boom.

Looking back, this was the first of several crucial plays that day. Robinson's hit was a hard-driving ball that could easily have gone by Carey into left field for a sure hit. The ball also could have careened off Carey into no-man's land, resulting in a hit.

In addition, the batter could have been a faster-than-blazes rookie or a seasoned veteran with lightning speed. He also could have been as Andy Carey says, "a few years' earlier version of Robinson, who ran with the best of them in his prime."

Instead, and perhaps as a sign of later things to come, the ball had hit cleanly off of Carey, and caromed straight to McDougald. He then threw perfectly to first to nip Robinson by half a step.

Over the years, many baseball aficionados have debated whether Phil "Scooter" Rizzuto, McDougald's predecessor at short-stop, could have made the play. In his prime, Rizzuto, who was released on Old Timers Day during the '56 season, was a great fielder, but undoubtedly McDougald's fresh legs and strong arm gave him more range than Rizzuto would have had in that year.

Historians later called this play perhaps the most important defensive one in the game, but for me it was simply out number one in the second inning. At the time, I was just happy that the spectacular play by McDougald kept Robinson off base.

Though the play at first was razor-close (radio announcer Bob Neal called Robinson "out by an eyelash"), neither Robinson, third base coach Billy Herman, first base coach Joe Becker, nor Dodgers Skipper Walt Alston protested. I heaved a sigh of relief and readied myself to face Gil Hodges, the hard-hitting Dodgers first baseman. He had already driven in eight runs in the Series. The record at that time was nine, set by Lou Gehrig.

My first pitch to him was a fast ball outside and high. I then threw a fast ball a bit low, but Gil swung and missed, evening the count at one and one.

One of my best sliders of the game came next. It was a riv-eter right across the outside corner, an unhittable pitch that Hodges watched go by.

Having shown Hodges the fast ball and the slider, Yogi called for another slider. The Dodgers' big first sacker swung at it and missed for out number two.

Up in the booth, sportscaster Mel Allen commented that I seemed to have a "sneaky fast ball ... not like Score's [Herb Score of the Cleveland Indians], but one that jumps on you."

The ability to throw Hodges the hard slider was no accident. I had been working on that pitch since learning it from catcher Les Moss and pitcher Duane Pillette of the Browns during the 1953 season.

After that slider got by Hodges, I thought I might be in for a good day. I was getting my fast ball over, and the slider was first-class. If I could pick the spots for the curve and have it find its mark, then the Dodgers, who entered the game with three regulars hitting over .300, would be facing at least *three* good pitches each time they came to bat.

Putting those pitches where I wanted them was still the key. A pitcher can last forever if he can find good location for the various pitches.

Whitey Ford, Early Wynn of the Indians, and Billy Pierce of the White Sox were probably the best control pitchers I ever saw. Whitey had great concentration and could keep the ball right around the strike zone. I only hoped some of his magic might rub off on me as I sorted through the Dodgers' order.

With two down in the second, the third batter in the inning was 26-year-old Dodgers left-fielder Sandy Amoros, who was 1 for 10 in the first four games of the Series. I knew the number six hitter in the Dodgers' lineup was important since two potential extra-base hitters, Carl Furillo and Roy Campanella, followed.

I followed Berra's orders by throwing a fast ball down and away for a strike on my first pitch to Amoros. A slider followed but Babe Pinelli saw that it missed the outside corner and called ball one. Yogi then called for another slider. This time Amoros fouled it off, making the count one ball, two strikes.

I threw a third straight slider, but it missed low. That evened the count at two and two.

I figured Yogi might go elsewhere, but either he was gaining faith in my slider, or his fingers were stuck together because he signaled for a fourth consecutive slider. Amoros connected and a pop fly danced to the right of second base toward right-fielder Hank Bauer.

Lady luck was with me because Hank probably could have never caught the ball. It was headed for the no-man's land just beyond and to the right of second base and in front of where Hank was playing. I thought it would fall for a bloop single, but suddenly, there was Billy Martin back-pedaling toward the pop. At the last second, while stumbling to the ground, he somehow caught the ball. Quickly, he held the ball up for the umpires to see.

Two innings up, two down. Six batters up, six down, and two great fielding plays had been made behind me. I knew I had control of a good fast ball, a sneaky-fast slider, a decent curve, and best of all, no walks. I couldn't wait to get back on the mound for inning three.

7

Inning #2—Yankees

Yogi at Bat

WHILE I HAVE VIVID MEMORIES of Yogi Berra during our playing days, Roger Kahn in his book, *The Era*, describes Yogi better than I ever could. He wrote:

> Thick body. Baggy knickers. Shirt puffing at the waist. Absolutely the shortest neck in town. Yogi Berra doesn't look like an athlete until he poles buzzing fast balls all the way into the third tier behind right field, the topmost deck of the old Yankee Stadium.

The great Yankee catcher was born May 12, 1925, in St. Louis, Missouri. Legend has it that he got his famed nickname from boyhood pals who lived on "The Hill," a heavily populated Italian section of St. Louis.

Berra, 5-feet 8-inches and 190 pounds, could very well have been a St. Louis Cardinal instead of a New York Yankee. Somehow the Cards underestimated Yogi's enormous potential when he tried out in 1942. When they offered him a measly $250 bonus, he promptly rejected it.

Yogi Berra began his career in 1943 with the Yankees' farm club in Norfolk of the Piedmont League. He spent 1944 and 1945 in the service, and then returned to Newark of the International League in 1946 until he was called up to the major league club.

Roger Kahn in *The Era 1947-1957,* recalled the Yankee catcher's early days:

> Yogi Berra could pound a baseball. In 1946 at Newark he batted .314 and hit 15 home runs in half a season. MacPhail promptly promoted him. When the veteran catcher Aaron Robinson went down with a painful back, Berra became the starter. He was marginal defensively, but he learned fast and he covered up for imperfections with consistently punishing swings.

According to his teammate Andy Carey, Yogi was "the best bad-ball hitter I ever saw." In the 1947 World Series, he became the first player ever to hit a pinch-hit homer.

The '47 Series also served as a prelude of things to come nine years later. Yogi caught the game in which Bill Bevens came within an eyelash of pitching the first no-hitter in a World Series.

Yogi had caught the first two Yankee games in that series, both victories. Sherm Lollar handled those chores in the third, which the Yankees lost 9-8.

In Game Four, even though the Dodgers had a run, due in part to a throwing error by Berra, Bill Bevens had a no-hitter going into the ninth. The pressure was intense.

In his autobiography, *It Ain't Over, Yogi,* he says, "When I went out for the ninth inning [in Bevens's game] I was sweating, and I could feel the back of my neck getting hot."

The Yankees led by one run. With two out and Dodger runners on first and second, Eddie Stanky was the scheduled hitter. Out of the dugout came Cookie Lavagetto to hit for him. Berra described what happened in his book when Cookie finally strode to the plate.

> Cookie dug in. Strike one. The next pitch was a ball. It was a ball for most people, and Cookie was a part-time player and it was a ball for him. He whipped the bat around and creamed that high pitch on a line to right field. Ballplayers call a hit like that a frozen rope. It gave us the shivers. It hit the wall on the fly. Not close to going over, but Tommy Henrich never had a chance. The ball seemed to hit the wall as Tommy moved. It hit a shaving cream sign. By the time I got it back, we had egg on our face, and Bevens lost both his no-hitter and the game.

While Berra proved himself to be a good hitter in his early years, his catching abilities still left something to be desired. In fact, in August of 1948, Yankee manager Bucky Harris moved him to right field. He was hoping that since Berra would not have to worry about catching, he could beef up a batting average that had gone south as well.

In the final seven weeks of the season, Berra proved Harris correct by batting almost .400. The Yankees lost the American League Crown though, and Harris lost his job. No one will ever know if Yogi Berra would have ever caught again if Bucky Harris had remained the manager. Fortunately, we didn't have to find out.

In 1949, Casey Stengel replaced Harris and Yogi Berra was installed as first string catcher for good. Fortunately for him, Stengel brought with him the great former major league catcher Bill Dickey. Dickey took Berra under his tutelage and turned him into the great, versatile catcher of the 1950s.

Although they had their battles from time to time, I saw first-hand that Stengel and Berra were as close as father and son. Casey always told the press that Berra was his "assistant manager." He relied on him for insight as to how to throw to certain hitters and whether a pitcher had had enough for the day and needed to be removed from the game.

During the 1952 season, Stengel told reporters he saw great things ahead for Berra:

> Mister Berra may not be the prettiest man in this here game, but I would say that he is one of three outstanding catchers in the American League because you've got Mickey Cochrane and Bill Dickey, and in the National League Roy Campanella and Gabby Hartnett, which is also great, and I would say that's pretty good company for a young feller.

First and foremost, Yogi Berra was a fierce competitor. It wasn't smart to get him riled. Opponents were the enemy and we pitchers certainly weren't immune. He would chastise all of us on occasion, trying to rev us up when we were pitching poorly.

Nineteen forty-nine ended up being a banner year for Berra when he batted .277 with 20 homers and 91 RBI's. Some felt that Berra got cheated in 1950 when shortstop Phil Rizzuto won the M.V.P. since Yogi hit a cool .322 with 28 homers and 124 RBI's.

In 1951, the sportswriters corrected that wrong when they finally named Yogi Most Valuable Player. He richly deserved it with a .294 average, 27 homers, and 88 RBI's.

Berra ended up with a .273 batting average, 30 homers, and 98 RBI's in 1952. The next year, he went on to bat .296 with 27 dingers and 108 runs batted in as the Yankees won their fifth straight World Championship.

Even though the Yankees' streak of championships would stop in 1954, Yogi Berra continued his fine play by winning a second Most Valuable Player award when he hit .307, with 22 homers and 125 RBI's.

Yogi Berra won the last of his three Most Valuable Player Awards in 1955. When he finished his playing days as a player/coach with the Mets by appearing in four games in 1965, Berra had amassed nearly 20 years in the majors.

Berra's career totals included a career .285 batting average, 358 homers, and more than 1,400 RBI's. His lifetime defensive average was .989, and during one stretch, he handled 950 chances in 148 consecutive games without making an error, the latter being a major league mark.

In his career, Berra would be a playing member of *14* pennant-winning Yankee clubs, and be the key player who led the New York team during its five consecutive World Championships from 1949 to 1953.

In my opinion, Yogi Berra possessed three important traits that set him apart as the greatest catcher I ever saw play ball.

The first one was that he was the most feared hitter in the game with men on bases. Opposing pitchers used to tell me that they would rather face *anybody* but Berra with the game on the line.

As mentioned before, Yogi was also the greatest "bad-ball" hitter I ever saw. One time in St. Louis when I was with the Browns, he hit a home run off of me on a pitch that almost bounced in the dirt.

Second, Berra really knew how to call a game. Contrary to published reports, never *once* in the fifth game did I ever shake him off or change the pitch he asked me to throw. I trusted his judgment too much. Berra's sign was the final word as far as I was concerned. I knew if a pitcher could consistently pitch where Berra told him to, he'd win twenty every year.

Third and foremost, Yogi Berra was a winner. He was finally voted into the Hall of Fame in 1972, along with such great players as Sandy Koufax, Early Wynn, and Lefty Gomez. He would beat you in some way, whether it was with his defense behind the plate, a great throwing arm, or that clutch hitting that every winning ball club must have.

Many have made fun of Berra and his "Berra-isms" over the years, but as a player he was the catalyst every team needs. Somehow he's remembered for his quotes ("It ain't over 'til it's over" is the most famous), but Yogi was a fooler and had impressive career statistics to back up people's feelings that he might be the greatest catcher to ever play the game.

Yogi Berra's sense of humor and playfulness separate him from any other catcher in the history of the game. If Berra had been a mediocre player, sportswriters and broadcasters would have attacked his foolhardiness with vengeance, but Yogi was the best at his position, causing his idiosyncrasies to be looked upon as charming.

Mickey Mantle shared two of the best Yogi Berra stories in *My Favorite Summer 1956.*

"Billy Martin locks his keys in his new Lincoln. Billy tells Yogi he did it and doesn't know what to do. Yogi says 'you gotta get a blacksmith!'"

Mantle also said that Berra told Ted Williams, one of the greatest hitters in the history of baseball, that he should be a switch-hitter. Mantle says Williams just looked at Berra like he was crazy.

To be sure, Yogi Berra was never the scatterbrain many wanted to make him out to be. Perhaps Yankee ball player Jerry Coleman said it best in Yogi's autobiography:

> I think he was the smartest player I ever knew. He was smart enough to know how to play. And even more important, how to learn. He was able to learn from Bill Dickey. Yogi got better, and Ralph Houk and Charlie Silvera just couldn't keep up. Everybody thought they were smarter than Yogi, but they were wrong.

When Berra, who was 5 for 15 in the Series, came to bat leading off the second inning of Game Five, he was coming off a 1956 season where he batted .298, hit 30 home runs, and knocked in 105 runs. Sal Maglie got the best of him this time, however, as the power-hitting Berra popped out to the Dodger's shortstop Pee Wee Reese.

Enos "Country" Slaughter, who was awaiting word from Kansas City about a new arrival in the family, followed Yogi to the plate, but he in turn flied out to Sandy Amoros for the second out. The inning ended when Billy Martin, 4 for 15 in the first four games of the Series, struck out on a dastardly Maglie curve ball and then was tagged out at first when Roy Campanella dropped the third strike.

Two complete innings were now in the book. I left my dugout seat for the mound to face the bottom third of the Dodgers' lineup. The score was tied 0-0. Sal Maglie and I had tossed two perfect innings.

Starting the 3rd, I'd thrown 27 pitches, right on the minimum. Carl Furillo, Roy Campanella and Sal Maglie would come to bat. In a pivotal game like this one, I knew that grabbing the lead was important. If my control stayed with me, I was confident I could keep the Dodgers off the scoreboard.

8

Inning #3

Lots of Goose Eggs

	1	2	3	4	5	6	7	8	9	10	R	H	E
Brooklyn	0	0									0	0	0
Yankees	0	0									0	0	0

CARL FURILLO WAS SET TO LEAD OFF inning number three for the Brooklyn Dodgers. Maybe it was the day-old beard he sported every game that made him look so fearsome, but pound for pound, he was one of the toughest men who ever played baseball.

Armed with a ferocious desire to win, the chisel-boned Furillo, who carried nearly 200 pounds on his six-foot frame, was a mainstay for the Dodgers. He played almost every game and anyone close to baseball knew that Carl always gave one hundred and fifty percent.

Born in Stoney Creek Mills, Pennsylvania, in 1922, Carl Furillo began his professional baseball career in 1940 when he joined Pocomoke City of the Eastern Shore League. Besides playing the outfield, Furillo pitched both there and at Reading of the Inter-State League in 1941.

Batting averages of .319, .367, and .313 in his first three years in the minors brought him to Montreal of the International League in 1942. Furillo spent three years in the military and then joined the major league Dodgers in 1946. Averages at or around the .285 to .320 range sprouted forth in six of the next seven years, and Furillo established himself as a solid, dependable right-fielder for the Brooklyn team.

Known for having a great throwing arm, the right-handed Furillo, nicknamed "The Reading Rifle," wound up with a percentage point short of a .300 batting average during 15 years in the majors. He capped a great year in 1953 when he hit .344 in 132 games to win the National League Batting Title. His former teammate George Shuba told me he marveled at the way Furillo played balls off the right field wall at Ebbets Field. "Other players had trouble with bounces off the wall," he said, "but Carl was a magician."

Carl Furillo never quit hustling from the moment he stepped on the playing field, and he was a great performer on seven World Series Brooklyn clubs. Furillo's hard-nosed style rubbed off on the other Dodgers' players, and they highly respected his hard work and winning attitude.

Center-fielder Duke Snider described Furillo in his book *The Duke of Flatbush*:

> The man I played beside for the next eleven years was in the 1947 training camp in Havana too—Carl Furillo, the one we called "Skoonj" because he led the league in eating his favorite Italian snail dish, scungilli. I always thought he was the most under-rated of all the Dodgers, and Buzzie Bavasi, our general manager in those years, told me not long ago that he agreed. Carl did more things to win games for us than he ever got credit or. He played the tricky right-field wall in Ebbets Field with precision. I'd always been told that Dixie Walker played it well, but I don't see how he could have played it any better than Skoonj. And I know Walker never had the arm that Furillo had. We called him the "Reading Rifle" because of his throwing arm and his home-town. Carl was a private person who never socialized much with the rest of us. But when there was a game to be played, Carl was right there ready to do whatever it took to win.

Author Roger Kahn in *The Boys of Summer* described perfectly the persona of the Dodger right-fielder:

> Drives to right field activated stolid Carl Furillo. A powerful mono-lithic man, Furillo possessed an astonishing throwing arm and a prescient sense of how a ball would carom off the barrier. The grandstands did not extend behind right field. Between the out-field and the sidewalk of Bedford Avenue, a cement wall rose sloping outward. It straightened at about ten feet and then 15 feet higher gave way to a stiff screen of wire-mesh. In straight-away right a scoreboard jutted, offering another surface and de-

scribing new angles. Furillo reigned here with an arm that, in Bugs Baer's phrase, "could have thrown a lamb chop past a wolf."

Yogi Berra's book on how to pitch to Furillo wasn't anything fancy. Every pitcher who faced the Dodgers' right fielder knew too well that he was simply a tough, tough out. He was a smart batter and knew the strike zone very well.

Our Yankee plan was to pitch the Dodgers' spray hitter high and outside and never come inside to his power. The first pitch I threw him was up and away and looked like a ball from where I stood. Babe Pinelli saw it differently though, and gave me a called strike.

Furillo's expression indicated his disapproval, but when the next pitch, a fast ball, came in at about the same spot, Furillo, who was hitting .333 in the Series, swung away. He got under the ball, and sent a high fly to Hank Bauer for out number one.

Dodger catcher Roy Campanella, 4 for 12 in the Series, was batter number eight in the Dodger lineup. I started Roy, who batted with an open stance, with a fast ball, low and outside. I then threw a good fast ball for a called strike to even the count at one and one.

Another fast ball followed on the inside corner and Campy flailed away with no success. Having set him up for an outside delivery, I threw a fast ball just a hair outside, but to Campanella's dismay and my delight, Pinelli closed out Campanella with a called third strike.

My mound opponent was next to bat, and Sal Maglie had a reputation for being a pretty good hitter. In fact, pitchers as a whole were doing pretty well in the Series. Their combined batting average was .375, as compared to the .267 average for the mighty hitters.

Yogi signaled for a fast ball, which I delivered across the plate. Maglie got good wood on it, but sent a harmless fly ball to Mickey Mantle in center for the third out.

I had now gone through the complete Dodger lineup in order. Maglie and I had a real duel going, and I had proven that I might very well be a tough opponent for the Dodgers' hurler.

Between the third and fourth inning I remember thinking that I needed a few runs to give me a cushion. When you've lost twenty-one games only two years earlier as I did, you still remember all the times you didn't get any.

In the Yankee half of the third, Gil McDougald, Andy Carey, and I were the scheduled hitters.

I believe that 28-year-old Gil McDougald, born three days after Billy Martin and a San Francisco native, was as fine a defensive infielder as ever played the game. Nicknamed the "glue man," Gil could play second, short, or third base.

"It was during spring training of the 1951 season that Casey Stengel impressed upon me the need to learn to play as many positions as possible," McDougald told reporters after the 1956 Series. Although he had never played third, McDougald took to the position naturally, and while he played some second base as well (Phil Rizzuto was the "regular" shortstop), McDougald played both positions well enough to be selected the American League Rookie of the Year in 1951.

Gil McDougald was the consummate team player. In the book, *The Bronx Bombers*, he was quoted as saying:

> Today, 50% of every team is brand new. In the 1950s, the Yankees were the same year after year ... You could go to the ballpark any spring and see me or Rizzuto at short, Moose (Skowron) or Joe Collins at first, Richardson at second, Yogi behind the plate, Whitey on the mound, and the Mick in center. The Yankees were a family and we were a familiar family with our own fans   ...
> There was a special bond there that didn't exist anywhere else.

McDougald, a 6-foot, 180-pound, right-handed batter and fielder, who was almost *too* serious at times, was always respected by his teammates. Even though he ended up with just a .276 lifetime batting average, McDougald could be counted on to deliver in the clutch. He was a vital part of *eight* New York Yankee World Series teams.

The self-described pudgy McDougald had a square-jaw and sported a very unusual batting stance by cocking the bat below his shoulder level. Casey Stengel once told a reporter that McDougald was the "lousiest looking ball player he ever saw ... but he gets things done."

Gil McDougald probably never did receive the recognition he deserved, but that was understandable with all of the Yankee superstars grabbing the headlines. One incident the players used to kid him about was the time when President Dwight Eisenhower threw out the first ball to open the 1956 season.

After the special pitch was thrown out, Gil asked Eisenhower to autograph a ball. Wearing a smile as big as the Senator's stadium, he raced back to the dugout to show it off, only to see the inscription "To *Joe* McDougald. Best Wishes, President Eisenhower"!

Gil McDougald was also nicknamed "Smash" and "Old Red Neck" by some of the Yankees since he was known to be a rabble-rouser who tirelessly argued even the silliest point if he believed he was right. He and Hank Bauer were natural friends, and when Gene Woodling tagged along, they made a fearsome threesome.

Most people don't remember who finished second in the American League MVP voting in 1956 next to Mickey Mantle, but it was Gil McDougald. He hit a career high .311. Many believed he was headed for even greater stardom, but Gil wasn't ever the same player after the tragic accident when his vicious liner hit Cleveland Indian's pitcher Herb Score in the face in the early part of the 1957 season.

I watched from a vantage point in the dugout. I'll never forget the thud I heard as the ball smashed into Score's face right between his eyes. He was bleeding profusely and fell to the ground. He never lost consciousness, but I had an empty feeling in the pit of my stomach that lasted for days. For all practical purposes, that pitch ended Score's career.

Two years later, I witnessed a similar situation that reminded me of the day Score was hit. I hit a line drive scorcher in batting practice that hit coach Ralph Houk, who was pitching. It shattered his cheekbone. Later, he told me he felt bone slivers blow through his nose and mouth.

Hank Bauer rushed to Ralph's side. He pulled the tobacco chew out of his mouth so he wouldn't choke. I turned white. Seeing Ralph lying motionless on the ground scared me to death. Luckily, even though he sustained a fracture, Ralph recovered without any scars, but I never will forget that incident.

The only time I remember hitting anyone with a pitch and being frightened was when I decked Billy Gardner of the Orioles in the back. He swallowed his chew, fainted, and then fell to the ground when he couldn't get his breath. He recovered fully and was back in the lineup the next day.

When I came to the Yankees in 1955, McDougald was in the prime of his career. I always hoped the batters would hit a ball his way because 99 percent of the time Gil would make the play. McDougald always just looked confident to me, as if he was saying to the batter, "Hit the ball to me; I can handle it."

In the third inning, McDougald, 2 for 11 in the Series, couldn't solve one of Maglie's "slinker balls" (combination slider and sinker), and grounded out to Jackie Robinson at third. Robinson's counterpart, Andy Carey, just 2 for 12 in the first four games, then fouled out to Roy Campanella.

I batted next. In the broadcast booth, Mel Allen said I was a "better than average hitting pitcher," but I fouled out to Campy too.

Up in the radio booth, Mutual broadcaster Bob Neal talked about Sal Maglie being called "the surveyor." "The lines around the plate are being cut off sharply by The Barber," Neal told his listening audience.

Three innings of scoreless ball were behind the two teams as we headed to the top of the fourth. The pressure to retire the Dodgers was back on me, and the tension mounted since everyone knew that the outcome of the fifth game might very well decide who would walk away with the 1956 World Championship.

9

Inning #4—Dodgers

Dodging Duke's Bullet

	1	2	3	4	5	6	7	8	9	10	R	H	E
Brooklyn	0	0	0								0	0	0
Yankees	0	0	0								0	0	0

WHEN I TOOK THE MOUND in the top of the fourth inning, I faced Junior Gilliam, Pee Wee Reese, and Duke Snider.

Edwin Donald "Duke" Snider was born to Ward and Florence Snider in Los Angeles in 1926. Snider was a left-handed power hitter from day one in the majors. The Duke, who garnered his nickname at age four from his dad, wore that famous #4 on his uniform and compiled an amazing record over his 18-season career, 16 of which he spent with the Dodgers.

Duke Snider, described by legendary sportswriter Roger Kahn in his book *The Era 1947-1957*, as "one of the five or six best center-fielders since the dawn of man," first came to the Dodgers as a rookie in 1947. That year the spotlight was on Jackie Robinson, and Snider watched history unfold from a seat on the bench.

Snider's path to sports stardom was never in doubt, since he had been an outstanding football, basketball, and baseball player. From the time he played softball in the fourth grade at George Washington Elementary School, through his days at Enterprise School, to the college years at Compton Junior College, Snider excelled at every sport.

In his book, *The Duke of Flatbush*, Snider, never known for his modesty, described his early achievements:

I threw a pass 63 yards in the air for a touchdown with 40 seconds left to win a game for the Compton Tarbabes, and we won the school's first championship in 15 years. I pitched a no-hitter in the first high school baseball game I ever played in, struck out 15 batters, and got three hits. I was one of our leading scorers in basketball. I was voted to All-Star teams in every sport, and I won 16 letters in four years of school.

Snider's relationship with the Brooklyn Dodgers began in the early part of the 1940s when his high school coach Bill Schleibaum contacted Dodger executive Branch Rickey. In his biography, Snider says that one scout was quoted as saying, "Snider has steel springs in his legs and dynamite in his bat."

After showing promise in the minors, Duke headed for the Dodgers' training camp in Havana, Cuba, in 1947. There, along with Gil Hodges, Carl Furillo, and Jackie Robinson, he performed well enough to make the big club and head for Brooklyn with the Dodgers.

Snider and his new teammates infused a brand new enthusiasm into a veteran Dodgers ball club, which already had Pee Wee Reese, Dixie Walker, Hugh Casey, and Pete Reiser. Snider made the league minimum, and sat the bench in 1947, just waiting for his opportunity to play.

Three years later, I remember reading about the day the Duke hit three home runs in one game. He also made the All-Star team hit .321, and spanked 31 home runs. In 1951, when the Dodgers were burned by Bobby Thomson's miracle home run, Duke had 29 homers and 101 RBI's to go with a .277 average.

In 1952, Snider posted good numbers again (21 homers, 92 RBI's, .303 batting average) during the regular season, and collected 10 hits, four home runs, and eight RBI's in the World Series loss to the Yankees.

1953, when I first played in the major leagues, saw Snider bat .336 with 42 home runs, second to the Milwaukee Braves' Eddie Mathews's 47. New York spoiled the Duke's chances for a World Series sharing four games to two, but Snider hit .320. In 1954, Duke hit .341, with 40 homers, and 130 runs batted in.

While Snider had played well in his early seasons with the Dodgers, in 1955 he blossomed into the *Sporting News* Player of the Year. That award was richly deserved, since he hit .309, with 42 home runs, and led the majors with 136 runs batted in. Overall, Duke Snider, who garnered the nickname "The Silver Fox," had a lifetime average of .295, with more than 2,000 hits, 407 home runs, and better than 1,300 RBI's. He was one of the few power hitters of all time who could also hit for average; he not only had five seasons where he hit 40 homers or more, but seven seasons where he hit over .300. Twice he hit three home runs in one game, was an All-Star eight times, and played in six World Series.

Based on his stats, it's little wonder Duke Snider was voted into the Hall of Fame in 1980. Besides spring training, my first encounter with him was in the 1955 Series, and I especially remember that the Duke never got cheated on a swing.

Those powerful arms of his scared any pitcher, and I'm one who just hoped that I could keep his hits in the ballpark. Mickey Mantle, Ted Williams, and Willie Mays are the best three ball players I ever saw, but Duke wouldn't be far behind.

The Duke had batted .292 with a league leading 43 home runs and 101 RBI's for the Dodgers in 1956. I still get the shakes when I remember going face to face with him in Game Five.

Of course, Yogi Berra knew of Duke's power as well. We decided to pitch to him differently at Yankee Stadium than we had at Ebbets Field. At the Dodgers' home park, a pitcher could ill-afford to give the Duke anything on the outside of the plate, because he had the strength to muscle a pitch into the short left field stands. In Yankee Stadium however, we knew that with the long distance to the left-field fence, anything Duke hit out there would probably just be a long fly-out.

Every pitcher who pitched against Snider knew for certain that he had to keep the ball away from the inside portion of the plate, because Duke would send those unfortunate offerings into the stratosphere. Yogi and I planned to squeeze the outside corner, and see if we could get Duke to hit one to left field, where Country Slaughter could catch it.

Before Snider came to bat in the fourth, I had disposed of both Junior Gilliam and Pee Wee Reese on one pitch each in their second time at bat against me. The Dodgers' second baseman and lead-off hitter had hit an inside slider to Billy Martin for an easy out. Then Pee Wee Reese did likewise on a low slider, that was for the most part an accidental check swing.

I had recorded outs numbers ten and eleven in the game rather easily, and up came Duke Snider. He always looked imposing standing at the plate, but I tried to focus on throwing where Yogi told me to.

As planned, he set up on the outside of the plate, and I brought the first two fast ball deliveries close to where his mitt was positioned. Duke Snider didn't swing at either outside pitch though, and suddenly I was behind in the count two balls and no strikes.

Now the Duke had me, and we both knew it. Two and zero in a close game meant I had to bring one to him. He backed out, then readied himself, and I delivered the baseball to him like it was a beautiful present on Christmas day.

Duke's eyes looked the size of baseballs when he saw my mediocre fast ball coming in on the inside part of the plate. At just the right time, those powerful shoulders heaved themselves around, and the bat met the ball with a solid crack.

Instantly, I knew I'd made a critical mistake, but I could only watch as the spiraling baseball made its way through the blue afternoon sky. Up, up and away it went, sailing higher and higher toward the right field stands.

Every pitcher knows from the click of bat to ball that he's had a home run hit off of him, and I was no exception. Duke was into his slow home run trot, and I readied myself to continue the game trailing one to nothing.

But suddenly, I noticed that the ball was hooking just a bit, heading more and more toward foul territory.

Could I be saved from my mistake? Could the ball possibly go foul? As I watched the curvature of the ball, I knew this was going to be very close. Finally, the ball landed in the stands, and now my eyes focused in on umpire Ed Runge.

With little hesitation, Runge quickly and boldly signaled the ball foul. Later that year, I ran into Ed, and he informed me that the ball hit foul by *less* than a foot.

As Duke Snider trotted swiftly back to the plate, my heart quit pounding as I tried to take a deep breath. I had dodged a bullet, but I knew Duke would now be even more determined to beat me.

Up in the television broadcast booth, Mel Allen described the foul ball as being "mighty close."

Duke Snider re-entered the batter's box, and Yogi Berra again sat himself on the outside part of the plate. After settling myself, I threw a good low slider, and Pinelli gave me my second strike, evening the count at two and two.

Duke fouled off another low slider and then, praise the Lord, I threw maybe my best fast slider of the day and caught Snider looking. I couldn't believe it. From a sure home run to a strikeout.

Looking back, I now see all of the signs that pointed toward October 8th being a special day for me. By the fourth inning, I had seen a great play by McDougald on Robinson's billiard-like shot, Martin's hustling catch of a pop-up while falling down, and now Snider's miss of a home run by less than a foot. When you're so caught up in a game, all these things don't add up until later. After the fourth, I just felt relieved and unbelievably fortunate that I now had completed four scoreless innings against the Dodgers.

In the Yankee dugout, the players were excited, but for a different reason than my fine pitching. I think Duke had shown them all that I was certainly hittable. In the back of my teammates' minds they knew they better get some hits off Maglie and score some runs to keep us in the ball game.

Even though I had given up no hits through four innings, thoughts of a no-hitter never entered my mind. Also, contrary to reports, I never thought about a perfect game, since I was forced to admit after the game that *I didn't know what one was.*

Of course, no one will ever know what my fate might have been if Snider's powerful clout had been hit 12 inches to the left for a home run. As it was, I had thrown 34 pitches, 22 of them for strikes, and somehow kept the Dodgers off-stride against me.

I did share my teammates' feelings that we needed some runs as soon as possible. Maglie had a history of getting tougher as games went along, and so far he hadn't given us anything.

Sportscaster Bob Neal described my performance through the first four innings. He told his millions of listeners that it was "unbelievable to see the ball the way it is jumpin' around [to the Dodger hitters] ... and that Larsen has made only one bad pitch to the first twelve men he has faced."

10

Inning #4—Yankees

Mantle's Blast

	1	2	3	4	5	6	7	8	9	10	R	H	E
Brooklyn	0	0	0	0							0	0	0
Yankees	0	0	0								0	0	0

HANK BAUER LED OFF THE FOURTH INNING for the Yankees, but Jackie Robinson threw him out on a routine ground ball play. First baseman Joe Collins was then called out on strikes, and Sal Maglie had retired 11 men in a row. Together, he and I had served up 23 consecutive outs to start the game, which is still a World Series record to this day.

Broadcaster Mel Allen discussed Sal Maglie's pitching prowess after Hank Bauer's out. He told his viewers that "Maglie calls himself a curve ball pitcher ... His fast ball is just a waste pitch." He also noted, "Man, we're lookin' at some pitchin'," and that many of the "hitters on both sides are takin' a lot of pitches."

While Sal had been unhittable, his attempt to match me out for out finally came to an end when the great Yankee center-fielder Mickey Mantle came to the plate.

What a sight it was for me to see Mickey bat over my years with the Yankees. I always felt a sense of excitement like none I have ever known. To me, he was flat out the greatest switch-hitter I ever saw in the game.

In 1953, when I was with the Browns, I recall first seeing the Mick. I'd heard about how good a batter he was, but I was more impressed by how fast he was. Hell, he could out-run a deer.

Mickey was a fierce competitor who could not bear to make an out. I saw him break water cooler bottles and hit his elbow against the bench or a wall. He just hated to make an out, and sometimes in the next at bat he seemed determined to hit the ball 5,000 feet just to make it up.

Many people look at Mickey Mantle's great feats and ask what he could have been if severe injuries hadn't hampered those God-given abilities. I've never focused on that, because Mantle's achievements speak for themselves and he should be appreciated for what he accomplished, not for what might have been.

The facts about Mickey Mantle are pure and simple. The good Lord never put a better ballplayer on the face of the earth. He had it all—speed, power, athletic ability, a great instinct for the game, and a way to rise to the occasion when our team needed a super-human play to save us from defeat. Hank Bauer put it best recently: "Mickey could run like a deer and hit balls out of sight." Clem Labine said Mickey Mantle was by far the fastest ballplayer he ever saw.

Mickey Charles Mantle was born on the 20th of October, 1931. From the day when young Mantle took the field in the little league diamond in the tiny town of Spavinaw, Oklahoma, people knew that he had the potential to be a big leaguer.

Elvin C. "Mutt" Mantle, Mickey's father, first bought his son a twenty-two dollar Marty Marion brand baseball glove because young Mick wanted to be a shortstop. Named after catcher Mickey Cochrane, the star catcher for the Philadelphia Athletics and "Mutt" Mantle's idol, Mantle's achievements with the bat and in the field in high school quickly made him the target of professional scouts. It wasn't until 1949 (Mantle was only sixteen), however, when Yankee scout Tom Greenwade signed him for little more than $1,000 bonus plus $400 to play the rest of the season in the minors.

A shy, unobtrusive young man, Mickey Mantle first played at Independence, Kansas, in the Kansas-Oklahoma-Missouri league, where he hit .313. At Joplin, Missouri in the Western Association the next year (1950), the young shortstop hinted of things to come when he banged 26 homers, drove in 136 runs, and led the league in hitting at .383.

In the winter months of 1951, Mantle participated in Casey Stengel's "instruction school" for promising Yankee minor leaguers held in Phoenix. Yankee coach Frank Crosetti remembered Mantle coming to the plate: "I was pitching batting practice when he took his first swings," related Crosetti. "The kid hit the first six balls nearly five hundred feet, over the lights and out of sight."

Casey Stengel, in an interview with *Collier's* magazine in July of 1956, remembers the young Mickey Mantle as well.

I first saw the boy at a school which the Yankees ran in Phoenix in early 1950. We had all kinds of infielders there, like McDougald, who was a second baseman then, and Coleman, who was my second baseman in the World Series, and Martin, who was a short-stop then. This kid is just standing behind 'em all in practice, like a scavenger, being timid and just shagging balls which gets away from others. He kept his head down, like his shoes was gonna fall off or somethin' and blushed when you talked to him.

Being so shy wasn't remarkable, seein' he was only 18, but if he wasn't fielding balls, what could you tell about him? Finally, we have sprint races and Mantle wins all the time, lookin' back over his shoulder to see what was keepin' the others. And also he hits the ball out of sight, right-handed and left-handed, like he does now.

It didn't take the Yankee front office long to notice Mantle's proficiency. They called him up to the major league club late in the 1950 season.

Apparently Mickey Mantle was quite a sight to behold when he showed up as a rookie. Hank Bauer remembered: "He had on rolled-up blue jeans. His shoes had sponge-rubber soles, and he was wearing white socks. Mantle had on a tweed sports coat and he wore a wide tie that featured a big peacock."

After the "instruction school," Mantle then joined the Yankees for spring training in 1951. Manager Casey Stengel promptly converted him to an outfielder.

This change was necessary because the future Hall of Famer Phil "The Scooter" Rizzuto was firmly established as the Yankee shortstop. Since there was uncertainty as to how long Joe DiMaggio would continue to play, Stengel began to teach young Mickey about the trials and tribulations of playing the outfield.

Casey Stengel said in the same *Collier's* article:

The first thing I had to teach Mantle was to run in the outfield, looking back over his shoulder, which DiMaggio was so great at, and not run looking down at the ground. "They have no plowed fields up here boy," I tell him, "and you don't have to run and watch out for furrows at the same time because this is the big leagues and the fields are all level and they have groundskeepers and everything."

Mickey Mantle started the 1951 season with the Yankees; an early season slump caused the club to send him back to K.C. After an emotional pep talk with his ailing father he drove in 50 runs and batted .361 in 40 games. The budding star was brought back up to the majors.

Although many don't ever recall him being anything but a center-fielder, Mantle, then just 19 years old, played in right for the Yankees and led off for the New York Club in the first two games of the World Series.

The pressure that Mickey Mantle felt when he first joined the Yankees overwhelmed him. Much of it was due to Casey Stengel.

In his book, *My Favorite Summer 1956*, Mantle said:

> When I came up, Casey told the writers that I was going to be the next Babe Ruth, Lou Gehrig, and Joe DiMaggio all rolled up in one. Casey kept bragging on me and the newspapers kept writing it, and of course I wasn't what Casey said I was. I don't mind admitting that there was incredible pressure on me because of what Casey was saying, and the fans were expecting so much, which I wasn't able to deliver. I got booed a lot.

The serious knee injury that most believe kept Mickey Mantle from even greater accomplishments occurred in Game Two of the 1951 World Series against the New York Giants, and ironically involved three of the greatest players in the history of the game.

Mickey Mantle, on the dead run, pulled up and tried to step aside so that Joe DiMaggio could catch a fly ball hit by Giants' center-fielder Willie Mays. Unfortunately, Mickey caught his spikes on a rubber top covering an outfield drain and fell to the ground in agonizing pain.

The Yankees' famous #7 had immediate surgery on his torn ligaments, and despite playing with great pain, hit .311, with 23 homers, and 87 RBI's during the 1952 season. He later led the Yankees to the 1952 World Championship by hitting .345 and two homers in the Fall Classic.

A 1974 inductee into the Hall of Fame along with Whitey Ford, Mickey Mantle had great years in 1953, 1954, and 1955, slugging 85 home runs and driving in nearly 300 runs. Being the finest switch-hitter in the majors earned him the nickname "The Switch." In 1956, the right-handed throwing Mantle put everything together.

I remember pitching against Mickey in spring training. He batted left-handed, which I felt gave him an advantage. I tried to mix up speeds with him and had pretty good luck.

On opening day, with me pitching against Washington Senators' hurler Camilo Pascual, Mantle served notice of the great things that were to come that season. In front of President Dwight Eisenhower, the great outfielder hammered two home runs, one a tremendous clout over the center-field fence that Senator's announcer Bob Wolff called one of the longest balls he ever saw sail out of the stadium.

Midway through the 1956 season, when Mickey Mantle was hitting singles and doubles as well as for power, Joe DiMaggio, when asked whether Mantle had a chance to hit .400 or better, told *Collier's* Magazine,

> Mickey has everything going for him. He has the speed to beat out bunts, so they can't play him too deep, and the power to drive it past them if they creep in on him. He bats both ways, so you can't play him in any particular field. And he has Yogi Berra hitting behind him, which means the pitchers can't put him on base without leaving themselves open to two runs instead of one.

In his book, *My Favorite Summer 1956*, Mantle described the 1956 season. "Everything just seemed to go right for me that year. The big thing was I was healthy most of the season and everything else just kind of fell into place."

I guess so. All he did was slam 52 home runs, knock in 130 runs, and lead the league with a .353 average to win the triple crown and the Most Valuable Player award.

Ironically, I pitched the game in Boston the last day of the season when Mickey and Ted Williams were neck and neck for the batting title. I felt badly when Ted hit a home run off me, but Mickey still won the title by eight percentage points.

Mickey Mantle went on to several more great years during his eighteen-year career with the Yankees. He was selected Most Valuable Player again in 1957 and 1962, and battled Roger Maris to the wire in 1961 when Maris broke Babe Ruth's home run record.

Overall, Mantle compiled a near .300 batting average (he had ten seasons at .300), with better than 2,400 hits in his career. He drove in more than 1,500 runs and led the league in homers four times.

Mantle slugged a total of 536 regular season American League home runs and hit an additional 18 in 65 World Series games. Incredibly, on ten occasions, he hit two homers in one game, one from the right side and another from the left, and belted a blast that measured some 565 feet in Washington in 1953.

He was an All-Star sixteen years, from 1952 to 1968, missing the 1963 and 1965 contests due to injury. More importantly, Mantle was on pennant-winning Yankee teams *12* years in his first 14 seasons, and the Yankees finished second and third the other years.

To me, Mick *was* the Yankees, just like the great players of the past like Gehrig, Ruth, and DiMaggio had been in their time. He used every ounce of talent God gave him, and when the pressure was on, we could always count on him.

Besides his wonderful playing ability, I will always remember Mickey as one guy who never bad-mouthed anybody. He was a shy, reserved kid at heart, and if he didn't like someone, he just ignored them and went on his way. I was pleased to call him a good friend, and was devastated when he passed away on August 13, 1995.

Recently, Hank Bauer, Moose Skowron and Bob Grim and I talked about the Mick. "He was a tough ballplayer, but he had a sensitive, generous side," Hank said. "He always picked up the check. I also remember seeing him cry right after he'd see a crippled kid. Mickey was the best."

Mickey Mantle felt he had something to prove in the 1956 World Series, because the Dodgers had held him to a .200 batting average while winning the 1955 Series. He had already homered twice in the first four games of the 1956 Series when he came up with two out in the fourth inning of Game Five.

Clem Labine told me the only way to get Mickey out was to have the ball coming in to him. "You had to keep him from extending," Clem said, "and either throw over his head or down on his shoe tops."

From my vantage point on the bench, I knew Mickey wasn't up at the plate looking for a single. Casey used two expressions, "butcher boy," to signal the batter to hit a line drive or "tra-la-la" to indicate a let-it-go swing for the fences. Mantle's at-bat would definitely be "tra-la-la."

Sal Maglie worked Mantle, whose 5-foot-11, 195-pound frame was perfect for a ball player, very carefully. They battled on every pitch, but then like an explosion, our big slugger blasted a hanging curve just inside the right field foul pole to stake me to a 1-0 lead. Mantle began his famous home run trot and rounded the bases with his head held high. Hitting homers against Brooklyn was the best thing that could happen to a Yankee.

Mel Allen's call of the Mantle home run was short and sweet. "Mantle hits a long fly . . . if it stays fair . . . going . . . going . . . gone! How About That!" Bob Neal commented, "Sal Maglie threw one bad pitch to the first twelve men he faced."

Ironically, Mantle hit the home run with a bat that he borrowed from our reserve infielder Jerry Lumpe, himself World Series ineligible. Normally, Mantle used bats belonging to Hank Bauer, but this time he had decided to try his luck with a different model.

After Mickey Mantle's homer, Yogi Berra hit a ball hard toward center field that appeared to be for extra bases. Out of nowhere sped Duke Snider, who made a spectacular catch that was described by Mel Allen as "one of the most sensational catches you'll ever see."

Mantle's home run pumped up our club. Winning Games Three and Four had given us confidence, but now we had the lead in Game Five. That Yankee bravado was definitely back, and we were gonna be a tough club to beat.

—11—

Gooney Bird

My path to the big leagues was a crooked one. In my day, every boy dreamed of becoming a big league ball player, but I never believed it would be possible. Looking back now, though, I can see that it was meant to be.

I believe my talent to play the game came directly from my dad. Although he never played organized baseball, he was a decent first baseman in American Legion and semi-pro ball. It was fortunate for me that he wanted his son to be a ball player too.

According to my mother, I was lucky to have ever survived childhood to have played sports at all since I was always getting hurt.

Don was only two when he accidentally closed his father's knife on his finger and almost cut it off. At six, some neighborhood kid threw a tin can at Don and cut his head and ear badly. A year later, he almost gave me a heart attack when he fell on some rocks, and it took seven stitches to repair his right arm.

In spite of my early injuries, I was healthy enough to play on the high school basketball team in Michigan City before moving with my family to San Diego in 1944.

My first contact with sports at Point Loma High was with basketball. My former coach, Herb Ward, says he first noticed me when I was "making baskets from all over the court." In a San Diego newspaper article, he described me as "a six-footer with good spring in his legs and exceptional coordination for a sophomore."

I really enjoyed playing basketball. Even though my eligibility ended at mid-term in my senior year, I finished first among all Metro Conference scorers with a 19 point average. I also received a "star of the month" award once during the regular season and was named to the all-conference team.

I had several college basketball scholarship offers, but my heart was more with baseball than basketball. Besides, I was never much with the studies, and I didn't really have an interest in going to college and studying my life away.

During the 1944-45 season, I had tried out for shortstop on the baseball team, but was beaten out by Don Blackman, who became one of my lifelong friends. Blackman told a reporter in 1956 that, "As a sophomore, Don swung the bat a lot better than he fielded, but he didn't begin to find himself in baseball until the summer of 1945, when he turned to pitching for his neighborhood team, the 'Frontier Village.'"

Baseball coach Herb Ward described my high school junior year in baseball for reporters after the fifth game of the 1956 World Series as follows:

> Don suffered from lack of support, and was a victim of several heartbreaking defeats ... He pitched about half of our games, and he had a good fast ball to go with a roundhouse curve. He was no Ted Williams though, as big league prospects go. At the time I thought Larsen was better in basketball, and a better prospect as a hitter than as a pitcher in baseball.

When high school ended in the spring of 1946, I joined the American Legion Post 504 team and helped them to the finals of the Southern California playoffs. "Don Larsen pitched almost every game for us," coach Jack Dawson told reporters, adding:

> He [Larsen] had a better fast ball than any of the other pitchers in the area, but his favorite pitch was his curve. It was a big, sweeping thing, and it fooled most of the hitters.
> Larsen fanned 15 batters in one game, but he didn't have any no-hitters or many low hitters for that matter. Once we were safely ahead, Don would usually let up, and make 'em hit the ball.

My high school teammate and friend, Joe Medina, and I were just two of the more notable baseball players in Southern California. That area was a hotbed for athletes in the early 1940s. "All of us used to work out with the minor league San Diego Padres," Joe Medina recalls. "I was ball boy for them in 1941, when Pepper Martin was the manager. Ted Williams also played there in 1937, before they sent him to the Red Sox."

Medina remembers Williams well, although he and I never played against him. "Williams came right out of Hoover High in San Diego," Joe says. "He was a pretty good pitcher … but a great hitter. You could see right away that he had a wonderful talent."

Both Joe's and my baseball abilities had caught the eye of major league scouts who were roaming the area. "Branch Rickey, Jr. had a school up in Arcadia," Joe remembers. "A high school coach in San Diego who was also a scout for the Dodgers invited us both up there. We had a two-day work-out in front of all kinds of scouts."

Joe says his father prohibited him from becoming a professional player "since he believed the major league made 'slaves' out of young kids by being able to own and trade them."

We both could have gone to St. Mary's where my future teammate Andy Carey played on scholarship, but Joe's dad was against it. Joe says, "I decided to enter City College in San Diego and Don wouldn't go to St. Mary's alone, so that's when he decided to turn professional."

I ended up signing with the St. Louis Browns through their scout, Arthur Schwartz. After the perfect game, Bill DeWitt, the assistant general manager for the Yankees, told broadcaster Bob Neal how that took place. "I was general manager of the Browns. Our west coast scouts told us about this big boy from San Diego who could hit and throw hard, and was a very fast runner," Bill said. "After a few weeks of checking on him, and watching him in some games, we signed him to a contract in the Browns organization."

Arthur Schwartz took my father and me out to dinner, and when he offered us a deal, we signed right then and there. I believe I got $850; $400 or $500 up front, and the rest if I stayed with the team.

I can't remember exactly what I did with the money. That was a lot to me in those days, and I think I used it to buy clothes and get ready to play professionally.

A few weeks later, Ray Mendoza, another young ball player from San Diego who had also signed with the Browns, and I boarded a train in San Diego. In Kansas City, Ray headed for another minor league club, and I switched to a train destined for Aberdeen, South Dakota, where I would begin my career as a professional baseball player.

If a person finds himself standing at the point where State Roads 12 and 281 cross in the east-central section of South Dakota, he'll be smack dab in the middle of Aberdeen.

Apparently no one from the minor league ball club knew I was arriving that night, because nobody met me at the train station. I had no idea where I was supposed to go. I headed for the Sherman Hotel, but there weren't any rooms available, so I stayed in the lobby and spent a sleepless night worrying what the next day would bring.

My first day as a professional ball player was an unusual one. I took all my luggage and headed toward the ball park, which was located some distance from the hotel. There was no one at the ticket gate to pass me through into the Pheasant's scheduled double-header, so I had to pay my way in to my first game as a professional ball player.

As improbable as it may seem, I didn't want to bother anybody, so I watched the first game from a first base line seat with my luggage next to me. During the lull between games, the newest Pheasant player went down and tried to locate the manager Don Heffner, who would later manage the Cincinnati Reds at the start of the 1966 season.

This goofy-looking guy with a crew cut that accentuated my big ears, must have been a sight standing there with my glove and luggage. Heffner was surprised to see me because he had expected me a couple of days earlier.

I was relieved that Heffner seemed happy I had finally gotten there. I did dress for the second game and, even though I was still just a young punk, Don took me under his wing. He and I got along well right from the beginning.

In my first season, I recorded a 4-3 won-loss record in 16 games. I struck out 28 men, walked 31, and had a 3.42 E.R.A. in 72 innings. I didn't feel too bad about my performance and Don seemed pleased with the progress I made. Our club, the Aberdeen Pheasants, won the league that year. We posted an impressive 82-36 record under Heffner.

When my first professional season was over, I rode home with Don. He lived in Arcadia, California, just up the road from the Santa Anita Racetrack.

After working and playing ball in the San Diego park leagues that winter, I was sent back to Class C Aberdeen. This time, the manager was Jim Crandall, the son of Doc Crandall, the relief pitcher for the Giants in the early part of the century.

Our Pheasants placed fourth (64-59) in 1948. We finished behind St. Cloud, Eau Claire, and Grand Forks, who won the regular season title and then the championship by beating our club in the finals in four straight games.

I made new friends at Aberdeen in 1948, and became more comfortable with my role as a professional ball player. We had a pretty good ball club that year, and Crandall and the older, more experienced players taught me a lot about not only pitching, but the whole game of baseball as well.

I ended that second season with a 17-11 record, and a 3.75 E.R.A. I struck out 151 batters in just 211 innings, and walked only 77 men. Control was no problem at that stage of my career.

Nineteen forty-eight saw the passing of the immortal George Herman "Babe" Ruth. The Yankee slugger succumbed to throat cancer at the age of 53, leaving a legacy of super-human feats that grow more incredible as the years pass by.

I never saw the Babe play in the majors, but when I was seven or eight, I saw him put on an awesome hitting exhibition in Michigan City. He swatted several long home runs, and then signed autographs for all the kids.

I began the 1949 season with the Class B Springfield, Illinois Browns of the Three I League. I had a 4-4 record in 18 games when disaster struck. I became perhaps the only professional ball player in history to pick a fight with a pinball machine and lose.

The team was ready for a long road trip when I showed up with my pitching hand swathed in bandages. I had cut the side of my hand on the broken glass top of the pinball machine. The local doctor said that I wouldn't be able to pitch for some time.

I worked out at the Browns' park while the team was on the road, but didn't come back in very good shape. I probably rushed my arm a bit, and that resulted in some soreness that sidelined me again. Another injured pitcher, Bill Pilgram, and I tried to get some "local" help, but we both suffered minor burns when Jim Crandall's wife tried a "hot" home remedy that put us out for another week.

Unfortunately, we didn't have much of a ball club in 1949, and finished dead last with a 53-73 mark under Crandall. My arm trouble and intermittent wild streaks caused management some concern, and I faced a critical point in my career. My hitting at the time continued to be good, and with considerable doubts about my pitching potential, the powers that be seriously thought about scrapping my pitching altogether and making me an outfielder.

With such thoughts in mind, Jim Crandall called me in and told me the team was shipping me off to the Globe-Miami of the Arizona-Texas Class C League. Ironically, Bud Swartz, the son of the Browns' scout who signed me, was a member of that Apaches team.

At Globe-Miami, I played for manager Eddie Dancisak, who had replaced Frank Volpe for the last-place Browns. Fortunately for me, the outfield experiment didn't work out, and I ended up doing some more pitching when my arm started to come around. My final record with Globe-Miami was just 2-4, and I ended the season with a giant-sized 5.27 E.R.A., but the last couple of outings were good ones.

My 1949 season was spent with two last-place clubs, and I almost became an outfielder instead of a pitcher. At 20 years old, I was at the crossroads of my career, teetering on the brink of losing any opportunity to ever play in the big leagues.

In the winter months, I worked hard to prepare for the 1950 season. I kept in good shape and pitched for several San Diego league teams while waiting for a directive from the Browns regarding my spring assignment. In early January, word reached me that I was headed to the Western League.

I became a member of the Class A Wichita Indians in a league where the president was a Senator named T.C. Johnson. Our team would go 77-77.

Two members besides me in the famous 1955 trade between the Orioles and Yankees were also members of that Wichita team. Pitcher Mike Blyzka went 13-6 with a 3.43 ERA and Bob Turley won eleven games while losing fourteen.

While Aberdeen and Springfield had seemed small-time to me, I had different feelings about my new team. Wichita was more big league, even though it was still the minors. I felt like I was moving up the ladder, and there was a chance I could make it to the big leagues.

Unfortunately, I hurt my arm again and ended up only 6-4 in 21 games with a 3.14 E.R.A. I played for Joe Schultz until mid-season and was then sent to Wichita Falls, Texas, of the Big State League, where my arm strength steadily improved.

I only pitched in nine games with the Spudders before I rejoined Wichita. My record was 3-3, but unfortunately my ERA ballooned all the way up to 5.93. The good news was that my arm had come around, but by the end of the 1950 season, I still wasn't certain whether I was on the right track.

When I returned home to San Diego after the 1950 season, I wasn't sure where things stood. In fact, I had thoughts of giving it all up. I was seemingly a ball player who couldn't pitch well enough to be considered a prospect as a potential major leaguer, and a hitter whose power didn't make up for my terrible lack of consistency at the plate.

I wasn't a quitter though, and I just told myself to try harder. Faith is all the good Lord gives us sometimes, and that winter, I just kept telling myself things were going to get better.

During that 1950 season at Wichita, I kept one eye on the ball field and the other on the morning newspaper. The conflict in Korea was escalating, and I knew I would be called into the service. Inevitably, my mother received my draft notice.

After a few days in San Diego, I left for basic training at Fort Ord, California, a military base south of San Francisco, along the Monterey Coast. Within a month, I developed, of all things, an infection on my foot. I couldn't seem to escape injury no matter where I went. After spending time in the base hospital, I was transferred to a special weapons outfit.

The infection proved to be a disguised blessing. While I recovered, my previous unit was shipped off to Korea. I ended up being sent to Hawaii as a Corporal in a Cadre unit. There I helped train troops headed to the fighting front. I expected to receive my combat assignment, but an officer checked my records and discovered I was a professional ball player.

I was immediately transferred to a Special Services outfit at Fort Shafter in Honolulu. There I pitched and played first base for the military team.

Sammy Souza, a local baseball player, and Tom Hopkins, a Honolulu newspaperman, organized a Service All-Star squad, and our squad played several games, including one against Lefty O'Doul's All-Star team, which included great players such as Joe DiMaggio, Pee Wee Reese, Yogi Berra, Robin Roberts, Hank Bauer, and Jackie Jensen. Watching them made my mouth water. I got autographs and dreamed of one day playing with them in the major leagues.

The businessman who accompanied the All-Star team was Frank Scott, who later became my personal business manager. After the Fifth Game of the 1956 Series, Frank told reporters where he first met me:

> I took an All-Star team to Japan and Robin Roberts pitched for this club against a service team with a guy named Larsen doing the throwing.
>
> After the game I saw a big fellow outside the All-Star dressing room talking to Yogi Berra and getting autographs from the major leaguers. That player was Larsen.

I spent all of the 1951 and 1952 seasons in Hawaii. While 1951 was just an average year for the service ball club, 1952's team improved with the addition of second baseman Charlie Kaiser and infielder Frank Malzone, who ended up playing over ten years with most of them as the spirited third baseman for the Boston Red Sox.

I hated the strict rules and regulations, but they treated me fair in the service. In those two years, I was forced to grow up and be responsible for myself and my actions. I realize how fortunate I was to play baseball for the military, especially in Hawaii. The alternative would certainly have been combat.

When I was discharged from the service, I was ready to concentrate full-steam ahead on baseball. With a more mature outlook and a greater love for the game, I was ready to prove I could pitch in the big leagues. I only hoped that I would get the chance.

When I signed with the St. Louis Browns organization in 1947, I never considered the history of the club. I was so damn excited to have the opportunity to sign with anyone that I didn't realize I'd joined one of the great losing organizations in sports history.

I was placed on the San Antonio Browns' Class AAA roster and went to spring training without a contract. I remember that spring well because it snowed in San Bernardino. Even though the weather was bizarre, I enjoyed that time with the Browns. Who wouldn't have? I felt like I'd hit the big time with Satchel Paige, Vic Wertz, Les Moss, and Billy Hunter on the roster.

In spite of the efforts of owner Bill Veeck, the Browns, who had finished dead last or next to last 22 times, were a hopeless team. In fact, one sportswriter wrote that "the Browns are only in the majors because the American League has to have eight teams."

During this time I got an opportunity to get to know Satchel Paige. God only knows how old he was when I was first met him. He lied so much to folks about his age that I think he lost track himself.

Even at his advanced age, ol' Satchel could still throw pretty hard. He had great control, but it's hard to describe his pitching theories because he never was one to share his "secrets" with anyone. I tried to listen to what he had to say, but most times it didn't make too much sense.

Besides his ability as a pitcher, Satchel was a real character and a great storyteller. Whether many of them were true, I don't know. He'd played all over the world, and I enjoyed hearing him talk about exciting places I'd never been. Satch also had some memorable quotes. When asked why he didn't run before a game, he said, "Where I come from we throw the ball across the plate; we don't carry it across."

One of my prized possessions is a baseball signed by the great Satch. I can't recall when I found the courage to ask him for the autograph, but I'll always cherish the ball.

I played some outfield that spring and hit pretty well, but the greatest improvement came with my pitching. Even though I was a long shot to make the big club when training camp opened, I began to believe that I had a chance after several good pitching performances.

Marty Marion, who still played some third base, was managing the Browns' club that year. Harry Brecheen, who still pitched, was also the pitching coach.

Apparently my potential had impressed the Browns' management, especially Bill Veeck. I'll never forget how excited I was when I found out I made the club; it was like Christmas in springtime.

The clubhouse man gave me uniform #27. Celebration late into the night followed.

That Browns' lineup included outfielders Dick Kokos, Johnny Groth, Don Lenhardt, and Vic Wertz. Infielders were Dick Kryhoski, Roy Sievers, Bobby Young, Billy Hunter, Jim Dyck, Bob Elliot, and Vern Stephens. Les Moss and Clint Courtney handled chores behind the plate. Besides me, the pitching staff included Virgil Trucks, Satchel Paige, Marlin Stuart, Dick Littlefield, Duane Pillette, and Bob Turley, who joined our club later in the year.

One of the big highlights my first year in the majors was pitching for the first time in Yankee Stadium. I remember how starstruck I was just stepping onto the field. The knowledge that Ruth, Gehrig, DiMaggio, and Mantle—all the great Yankee stars—had played there completely overwhelmed me.

The game between the Browns and the Yankees was memorable as well. I had the Yankees beaten 3-2 going into the ninth. I had even garnered a couple of hits off of Whitey Ford. One more half inning and I could celebrate.

Unfortunately, Ralph Houk got a base hit. Then Johnny Mize pinch hit and singled. When Irv Noren followed with a single, the score was 3-3. Duane Pillette relieved me, and we ended up losing the game.

Since there were only eight teams in both leagues, we played four times at home and four times away. That meant I got to play in Yankee Stadium three more times that year.

Our 1953 club finished eighth and last, winning 54 games while losing 100. I won 7 games and lost 12, with a 4.15 E.R.A. in 38 games. That's the year I learned how to throw a slider when catcher Les Moss took me under his wing and showed me how to hold the ball.

Bill Veeck loved to take chances and play out his hunches on unknown or discarded ball players. With my erratic minor league record, there was no reason for the Browns to put me on the major league roster. Veeck had a hunch though. He wanted me in the big leagues and that's how I got there. Bill Veeck believed in me, and I'll always be very grateful.

Despite my mediocre pitching record, 1953 was an astounding success. I heard rumors that the Browns might be moving to Baltimore, but I didn't care. I would have followed the team to hell's lowest level as long as they'd let me play major league baseball.

I regret that I wasn't able to save my uniform from the days I spent with the St. Louis Browns. Unfortunately, my friend Bob Haddock sold his car in the winter of 1953 while we were playing semi-pro ball, and the uniform was in the car.

That winter, I readied myself to join the Browns in St. Louis, but they relocated to Baltimore. Owner Bill Veeck sold the club to a syndicate located there, headed up by Mayor Tommy D'Alesandro and attorney Clarence Miles.

Even though I had contract problems, I reported to spring training in Yuma, Arizona. I pitched very well in the Cactus League and easily made the major league roster.

The newly christened Orioles sported a lineup that included players such as Eddie Waitkus and Dick Kryhoski at first, Bobby Young at second, Billy Hunter at short, Vern Stephens and Bob Kennedy at third, Gil Coan and Chuck Diering in center, Cal Abrams in right, and Sam Mele and Jim Fridley in left. Unfortunately, nobody batted over .300 that year (Cal Abrams led the club with .293), and no one hit more than eight home runs the entire season!

The manager of the Orioles (54 wins and 100 losses) team that year was Jimmy Dykes, the former Philadelphia Athletics skipper. With poor offensive support, and sporadic pitching, the team finished seventh, just edging out the last-place A's.

Many sportswriters believe that if Marty Marion had been retained as manager of the Orioles for the 1954 season, my major league career as a pitcher would have been over. That's because Marion was convinced that I had a much better future as an outfielder. He was intent on sending me to the outfield so the weak-hitting club could take advantage of my hitting every time out.

But Dykes wanted me to stay in the rotation. I landed a spot in the rather shaky starting crew that included Bob Turley (14-15), Joe Coleman (13-17), Duane Pillette (10-14), Lou Kretlow (6-11), and Bob Chakales (3-7). A combination of bad pitching on my part and poor play by our team even when I pitched well left me with a disastrous season-ending record of just three wins and 21 losses.

Looking back, it's hard to imagine having that kind of season. A pitcher's dream is to win 20 games, not lose that many, but that's what happened.

Even with all of the disappointing losses, I managed to keep my sanity until the last game of the season. Jimmy Dykes decided to start me. At a time when I wanted to crawl into the woodwork, I was stuck going to the mound in front of thousands of people.

My heart simply wasn't up to the task. It's the only time in my career that I can remember not wanting to play. I'd had such a horrible year, and I hated to go out there again. With that kind of attitude, it's no wonder that I got knocked out in the third inning. I shuffled off to the locker room and got the hell out of town.

When a ball player's in a slump or on a losing streak, he tries everything he can think of to snap out of it. At least that's what I did in 1954. Of course, many times I tried too hard. Then I'd over-throw and things just got worse. About the time I felt like I was back on track with good pitches, the other team would hit them. So then I'd make bad pitches and walk batters. It was like a continual upset stomach. The more I tried, the worse the results.

Living in Baltimore was the only thing that made the season bearable. Chesapeake Bay was great for fishing, and the crab cakes were the best anywhere.

Joe Medina, my close friend from my boyhood days in San Diego, says during my first season in Baltimore that he saw that my lifestyle had changed.

> The first time I really saw a change in Don was when I saw him back east. My wife and I stopped in Baltimore and called the club to see where Don lived. The lady was very nice, but said they couldn't give out that kind of information. I explained who I was . . . that Don had been best man at my wedding and so forth. Finally, the lady says, "I'll give you the name and address of three bars where you can look for him. And . . . by the way . . . if you do find out where he lives, please let us know 'cause we don't know where it is!"

Joe and his wife finally found me in a tavern. I was matching wits with a pinball machine and having a good time. Losing ball games drives a pitcher nuts. Pinball machines, comic books, and the like kept me from losing my mind.

Joe knew how tough it was on me to lose all those games in 1954. He said in a recent interview, "We watched him pitch one night, and he had a one or two-hitter going into the ninth. Then some guy drops a pop fly and somehow he loses 1-0. Don was very disgusted . . . he hated losing."

Joe's right. One time I had a lead in the ninth. I was one out from a victory and a batter hit a fly ball to right fielder Gil Coan. He had a finger missing, and the ball hit that spot in his mitt and fell through for an error. The runner scored and we ended up losing. I almost committed suicide.

When I look at the way things turned out, thank God I won three games that year and two were against the Yankees. In fact, maybe if I hadn't gone 3-21, I wouldn't have been a Yankee at all.

Later I learned that while I had been toughing it out during the gut-wrenching season, their brass was doing some soul searching. With the Yankees' failure to continue their streak of championships in 1954, General Manager George Weiss was looking to improve the club.

Weiss and Casey Stengel started scouring the talent on other major league clubs. They were looking for two pitchers who could strengthen their staff in 1955.

Apparently, the New York braintrust scouted out several different players that year. I was one of them. My Oriole teammate and good friend Duane Pillette deserves credit for my becoming a Yankee, since he suggested to Yankee pitching coach Jim Turner that I had a great deal of potential.

At the same time the Yankees were looking to acquire pitchers, wheeler-dealer Paul Richards took over in Baltimore as both the field manager and general manager. Since our team had finished 57 games behind Cleveland, Richards immediately wanted to put his imprint on the team. He became interested in dealing with the Yankees when George Weiss called and inquired about the availability of the Orioles' strong right-hander Bob Turley.

I understand Richards told Weiss that he in turn liked Gene Woodling, the Yankee outfielder who platooned with Hank Bauer, and Gus Triandos who was biding his time as a back-up catcher. Weiss countered that he was interested in catcher Darrell Johnson of the Orioles. One thing led to another, and finally, on November 18, 1954, the initial announcement was made that a large exchange of players had been made by the New York Yankees and the Baltimore Orioles.

After the second part of the trade had been completed in early December, a total of seventeen players had swapped teams. From the Yankees, pitchers Harry Byrd, Bill Miller, and Jim McDonald, catchers Hal Smith, Don Leppert, and Gus Triandos, infielder Kal Segrist, and veteran outfielders Gene Woodling and Willie Miranda all went to the Orioles. The Yankees, in turn, picked me as one of the pitchers along with Bob Turley and Mike Blyzka. Outfielders Jim Fridley and Ted Del Guercio, catcher Darrell Johnson, and infielders Dick Kryhoski and Billy Hunter were also picked up.

When I first heard about the trade in San Diego, I couldn't believe it. Despite my awful season in Baltimore, I felt I'd learned a lot about pitching. I was really looking forward to the 1955 season with the Orioles.

Being traded is part of a ball player's life. While I hoped to spend my whole career with one club, that's just not realistic. Besides, how could I dwell on any negative parts of the trade when I was now joining a legendary contender like the New York Yankees?

—12—

Yankee Pinstripes

I'LL NEVER FORGET THE FIRST TIME I put on a Yankee uniform. Clubhouse Manager Pete Sheehy issued me number 18. After I tried it on, I stood in front of my locker like a bantam rooster, just as proud as I could be.

Nineteen fifty-five was a very enlightening year for me with the Yankees. I joined the club in spring training in St. Petersburg, and tried my best to perform up to what they thought my capabilities were.

My reception from the Yankees was a good one. Our Baltimore contingent stayed together, but I became great friends with Hank Bauer and many of the other ball players.

Unfortunately, I developed a sore arm at the beginning of spring training. I tried to pitch sooner than I should have. The soreness wouldn't go away, and I was never able to get any velocity on my fast ball or throw a good slider.

To my surprise, the Yankees put me on the major league roster. Somehow Casey must have thought I would come around, and so I headed north with the club.

I remember the thrill the day when I found out I was on the roster. Everybody's dream is to play with the Yankees and I had done that. "Celebrating" doesn't begin to describe what I did that night.

Opening day at Yankee Stadium gave me goose bumps. I was 26 years old and standing in a stadium that was as beautiful as a cathedral. That first game and several others after it were a blur. I just couldn't believe I was a Yankee.

After a few inconsistent starts, the soreness in my arm persisted. I was finally shipped down to Denver of the American Association. Being dropped to the minors wasn't a complete shock, but I can't describe how disappointed I was when I cleaned out my Yankee Stadium locker.

I spent two-and-a-half months at Denver under player/manager Ralph Houk, who would go on to manage the Yankees to world titles in 1961 and 1962. The first time I started for Denver, I wasn't impressive, but after that I settled down, and pitched well.

My won-loss record in 1955 was 9-1 in 13 games. I pitched 100 innings and compiled a 3.69 E.R.A. When I was called up to join the Yankees in mid-season, I hated to go because the Bears were in first place and headed toward a division title. But, when the call came, I didn't waste any time packing my bags.

Ironically, the great Eddie Lopat was waived by the Yankees so I could be brought up. When I re-joined the team in late July, they were in a tight pennant battle with the Chicago White Sox.

The Yankee pitching staff included Whitey Ford, Bob Turley, Bob Grim, Johnny Kucks, and Tom Sturdivant. I figured I would be a spot starter and a reliever. I made my first appearance starting against Kansas City on Sunday, July 31st.

In that game, the first of a double-header, I pitched a four-hitter. It was a complete game victory and I struck out four and walked four. I never knew I was going to start until I arrived at the ballpark, but the short notice didn't bother me because all the Yankee pitchers were prepared to pitch everyday. Casey liked to keep us guessing as to who would start or relieve, so we always had to be ready. Everybody contributed when they were a Yankee.

As we headed down the stretch in 1955, I pitched some of the best baseball of my life. Late in the year I went 13 innings, the longest of my major league career, against the Red Sox and won by the score of 3-2.

I also started what turned out to be the pennant clincher the day before the season ended against the Red Sox. I pitched seven strong innings before Whitey Ford relieved me and completed the win that sent us to the World Series. Imagine that—Whitey relieving me.

Once I was out of that game, I was so nervous that I went in the clubhouse and sat on a stool in the shower area. I turned on the showers to block out any noise, and I sat there until someone came in to tell me we'd won the game. I jumped for joy, and that night I lived up to my reputation as the "night marauder."

When I woke up the next morning, I was afraid I had only dreamed that we were going to the Series. But it was no dream, and I was more excited than any other time in my life.

My next stop was the World Series. It's difficult to imagine how great I felt getting ready to participate as a New York Yankee in the fall classic. The season before I was 3-21 with a last-place team, and now I was getting ready to face the Brooklyn Dodgers in the Series. How quickly things had changed.

Our club took the first two games, 6-5, behind Whitey Ford, and 4-2, a complete game win for Tommy Byrne. Game Three went to Brooklyn, 8-3. Tom Morgan, Johnny Kucks, Tom Sturdivant all got cuffed around. I sat and watched.

I got the starting nod from Casey Stengel in Game Four, but it wasn't an experience I like to remember. Kucks replaced me in the fifth inning, but I was the losing pitcher in an 8-5 loss.

I started against Carl Erskine. I gave up five runs and the Dodgers ended up getting 14 hits in the game including home runs by Gil Hodges, Roy Campanella, and Duke Snider. We also lost Game Five, 5-3, when Roger Craig beat us. Whitey Ford tied up the Series with a 5-1, four-hit win, but then Johnny Podres pitched the masterpiece eight-hit shutout to give Brooklyn its long-awaited World Championship. I was very depressed afterward. We had plenty of chances to win, but we blew it. The fact that I didn't contribute to the team's effort made it worse.

I also hit a foul ball that could have ended my career with the Yankees. It hit Del Webb, the owner, in the head. After I got knocked out of the game, I went to the locker room. There was Webb on the training table looking a bit groggy. I tiptoed out of the room before he saw me.

The poor performance in Game Four of the 1955 World Series was my only one until I pitched again in Game Two of the 1956 Series. All in all though, the '55 season was an incredible one. I had stretched beyond my childhood dreams by pitching for the Yankees and in the World Series. Even though we lost the championship to the Dodgers, I was thankful to have even been there in the first place.

It was during that regular season when I achieved my dubious reputation as a playboy. Mickey Mantle in *My Favorite Sum-*

mer 1956 spelled out his memories of me during that first year
with the Yankees.

> When he came to us, Larsen already had acquired something of a
> reputation as a hard drinker and a hell-raiser, even though he had
> been in the league only two years at the time. I must admit that
> none of it was exaggerated. Larsen was easily the greatest drinker
> I've known, and I've known some pretty good ones in my time.
> But I was also surprised at the kind of guy he was. When you
> have the reputation Don had, people who don't know you think
> you're a difficult person and a guy who doesn't take too many
> things seriously. Nothing could have been further from the truth.
> Larsen was one of the most likable guys you'd ever want to meet.
> And while it's true that he liked his booze and he enjoyed his
> good times, he was all business when he was on the mound; one
> of the best competitors I've ever known.

On the goodwill tour of Hawaii, Wake Island, Guam, the Phil-
ippines, and the Far East, Mantle and Billy Martin gave me and my
teammates a sample of their antics together. I remember the night
when the two played a trick on the whole team.

The two pranksters wanted company to party, and so at three
a.m. one night, Billy called all of the players, coaches, and Casey's
room to let us know that Mickey was in a fight and getting the shit
beat out of him. Once everybody got there, of course, there was no
fight, but after we wiped the sleep from our eyes there was one
hell of a party. But I had the last laugh. Before we left I signed Billy
and Mickey's names to all the bar tabs.

More than anything in 1955, I got my first taste of what it was
like to be a New York Yankee. It's hard to define, but wearing the
pinstripes alters a player somehow. Wherever I went, there seemed
to be a certain aura that surrounded me, and people just treated
me differently.

During the remainder of my career, I played hard and was
loyal to the clubs I played for. But even when I had to leave New
York later on, in my heart I would always be a Yankee.

The regular season in 1956 ended up being a remarkable one
for me, but it certainly didn't start out that way.

Between the end of the 1955 season and the start of spring training in 1956, I returned home to San Diego. My Yankee salary didn't stretch very far, so I took several jobs, including one where I worked as a construction worker with the company that eventually built the San Diego Padres' Jack Murphy Stadium.

I also played in a Sunday choose-up league made up of professional players and kids from semi-pro, college, and high school teams. Sponsors like the Hayne Streamliner Tavern gave the players uniforms. One of my managers that year was future major league umpire Ed Runge. Ed would figure heavily in the outcome of Game Five of the '56 Series.

In March, it was off to St. Petersburg to join the Yankees at spring training. I loved that part of baseball. It was great to see all the guys again. We worked hard, but there was always time to play. Several of us would always do the town, but sometimes previous "acquaintances" caused problems for a ballplayer, especially when he brought a new wife with him.

On one occasion, after I married Corrine, we sauntered into the Sorreno restaurant with Mickey Mantle and Whitey Ford. Out of nowhere came a great-looking woman in jeans and a fur coat. She grabbed me like an old friend, but I managed to quickly introduce her to Corrine. Later, Mick and Yogi found out she had recently married a guy who was a pickle grower. They never let me live down my encounter with the "Pickle King's" wife.

To make certain the ball players kept curfew in those days, Casey devised an interesting scheme. He gave the hotel elevator operator ten bucks and a brand new baseball. His job was to see that all of us signed the baseball on our way up to the rooms. That worked pretty well until Casey realized that some of the players (certainly not yours truly) simply signed the baseball, went toward their room, and then scampered down the back stairs or fire escape to freedom.

The first few nights on the town at St. Petersburg in '56 I managed to have a good time and stay out of trouble. Then I made a mistake that could have cost me not only my ball career, but my life.

I was visiting the local waterholes one night and didn't head home until the wee hours of the morning. Somewhere along the way I fell asleep and ran my brand new charcoal gray Ninety-Eight Olds convertible straight into a telephone pole. I quickly leaped out of the Olds because live wires fell on the car and were making a sizzling sound. Fortunately I was not injured beyond a chipped tooth.

It was almost 5 a.m., but I decided to hitchhike back to the Sorreno Hotel where we stayed. I attracted the attention of a bakery truck driver who picked me up and dropped me near the hotel. I woke up Darrell Johnson to ask for his advice. We decided I'd better notify the police, so he took me to the station, and I told a police officer what had happened.

When I arrived at Miller Huggins Field, I got some of the best advice of my life. Jim Turner was there and I told him what had occurred. I asked him whether I should tell Casey up front what happened before he saw it on a television news report or heard about it from a local news reporter.

Jim told me I better go to Casey and explain myself. I sat around trying to build up my courage because I knew he wouldn't be pleased. While I waited for Casey to come to the ballpark, I kept thinking about what his reaction would be. A thousand thoughts crowded my mind, all of them bad.

Finally, I cornered Casey in the clubhouse. When I finished telling him what happened, I held my breath and waited for his reaction. I'm sure he knew I was extremely nervous, and I was, because Casey was liable to do anything at any time.

At first, the ol' man didn't say anything. He just stood there shaking his head. He did that for thirty seconds or so, and then, to my great surprise, he told me to head toward the batting cages.

While I continued to work out, Casey fended off reporters who had heard about the incident. His comments concerning the accident were beauties. When asked if I had been fined, Stengel told the reporter he didn't know what to do because "Larsen was either out too late or up too early!"

The fact that Casey stuck up for me cemented the personal relationship between us. I was very grateful for his support.

I had a bit of the odd-ball tag put on me through the years and Casey, probably for good reason, did too. Maybe that helped him understand what had happened with the early morning wreck, since ol' Casey had done a few crazy things himself in his time.

The close call made me avoid the nightspots for a while. But only for a while. Over the years, many people told stories about my "party-boy" days. Mickey Mantle said I was always on the go and in *My Favorite Summer 1956* told a great story that summed up my drinking proclivities.

During spring training ... we all went down to see Frank Sinatra at a hotel in Miami Beach. As soon as he [Larsen] sat down, the first thing he did was order a beer. Then a rum and coke. Then a scotch and soda. And he followed that with Canadian Club. I couldn't believe a guy could mix drinks like that.

Mickey forgot to mention that he was matching me drink for drink.

What effect the accident would have on my making the club was very important to me. Although I hadn't been drunk, the incident was embarrassing. I could only hope that Casey and Jim Turner and the Yankee brass would judge me for my on-field performance and not for what I was doing off the field.

As spring training progressed, I felt confident that I was headed for a good year. My arm was healthy, and I seemed to have good control of all my pitches.

I faced most all the clubs in both leagues that spring. Later, I recalled that of all the teams, I had the best success against the Dodgers. I remember sailing through seven innings against them in Miami without a scratch.

My pitching during the 1956 season convinced Casey Stengel that he could count upon me to be consistently inconsistent. From April 17th when I pitched and beat the Washington Senators until I wound up the regular season with a win against the Boston Red Sox, I took a roller coaster ride in my 38 game appearances.

I hit a bad stretch in May when I couldn't get anybody out and became so disgusted that I told a reporter, "The hell with it ... if things don't get better for me soon, I'm going to join the Navy."

That negative thinking stayed with me until close to the end of the season. Then I reeled off four good consecutive outings that resulted in four victories. That success came after I decided to change my pitching delivery.

Prior to that time, I had always taken the full wind-up like most all of the other pitchers. Since I'm tall and lanky, it took a long time for me to go through the full wind-up and then deliver the ball to the plate.

Although many different versions of the story as to how I came to successfully use the no wind-up delivery have been given, this is how it really happened.

During the 1956 season, I struggled with my control from time to time. I had a so-so 7 and 5 record going into the last month of the season. In a ball game against the Red Sox in Boston, late in the season, I noticed that their third base coach, Del Baker, was watching me very closely. Del had a great reputation for being able to somehow steal pitching signs, and relay them to his hitters. After some thought, I came to the conclusion that with my full pitching delivery, he was gaining an advantage for the hitters by honing in on how I held the baseball before I threw it to the plate.

How I or any other major league pitcher held the baseball was important for a hitter to know, because those hitters were always looking for the slightest edge. For instance, my method was to hold the fast ball on the cross-seams if I wanted the ball to rise. So, if Baker or any other coach or player could tell I was gripping the ball that way, they could signal the batter that a particular pitch was coming.

For the life of me, I cannot remember where I got the idea to try the no wind-up delivery. I may have seen it on television or something, although I don't recall seeing any other pitcher using it at that time. All I knew was that if I could somehow deliver the ball more quickly to home plate, it would be harder for the batter to know what pitch was coming.

Besides that, the no wind-up had other advantages. I felt I had better balance, and somehow that seemed to help my control. Also, the fact that I pitched with no wind-up put the hitters a bit off-guard because they had less time to get set and less time to prepare to hit.

Yankee pitcher Bob Turley also experimented with the no wind-up. He told a reporter after the fifth game, "I tried the no wind-up as well and found I could throw just as hard as with the full wind-up. Actually it's just like the motion with a man on base, except that you kick your leg a little harder."

When I decided I wanted to try the no wind-up, I went to pitching coach Jim Turner, who handled all the decisions regarding the pitchers on the team, and asked him if I could try something new. Casey ran the ball club, but Turner had authority over the pitchers, including who would start, and when.

Jim Turner always talked at great length about better concentration on the mound. Despite my reputation as an independent cuss, I was never one to shy away from taking advice, especially from a guy like Jim Turner. He knew pitching inside, outside, and backwards.

It was simple with me and Turner: When he talked, I listened. Most people around baseball believe ol' Jim may have been the best pitching coach of all time, and I wouldn't argue with them.

When I talked to him about using a no wind-up delivery, he agreed to let me try it. Jim's nearly 94 years old now, and he remembered it this way:

> Don Larsen was a fine lookin' athlete. He had a live arm ... lots of natural ability. I first saw him with the Browns, and I told Casey ... he's a fine lookin' athlete ... can run like a deer.
>
> Don got along well with people ... which was really important in those days because if you didn't get along with people ... you didn't stay a Yankee very long. The Yankees were like a family then ... and Don fit in quite well.
>
> Now, as far as the "no-wind-up" delivery goes, Don came to me one day and asked if he could change his delivery. He told me he thought that Baker, the third base coach for the Red Sox, was stealin' his signs by watchin' Don's wrist move one way or the other. Don asked if I minded if he didn't wind-up, and I sort of chuckled and laughed and told him I didn't care.

After the fifth game, Turner told the baseball writers that "it [the no wind-up] wouldn't be good for all pitchers ... you wouldn't want to do away with a natural rhythm like many pitchers have in their motion—it helps them. But in others, the pumping doesn't help."

Red Sox third base coach Del Baker jokingly told reporters following the Series, "You know I'd never steal a sign from anybody, but I noticed Bob Turley of the Yanks also was doing it ... But the way they pitch they sure don't show you anything."

In the weeks that followed the 1956 World Series, writer J. Roy Stockton of the *St. Louis Post Dispatch* wrote about the no wind-up.

> Don James Larsen may well have started a new school of pitching, as a result of his spectacular performance in the World Series.
>
> The school may be known as simplified pitching, or Larsen's no-spectacular school. The results Don James achieved were

spectacular, but the way he did it was about as spectacular as rocking in a rubber-tired rocking chair on a well-padded veran- dah.

Larsen's way of pitching, which was the same employed the following day by Bob Turley when he held the Dodgers to four hits and one run in ten innings, will confound, confuse and shame the average pitching instructor. In recent years especially, young pitchers have been told that they must go through as many ma- neuvers as possible to distract the batter. Herm Wehmeier, for instance, had considerable success with the Cardinals after he had been put through pitching courses by Coach Bill Posedel. Wehmeier, under instructions, learned several ballet dancer kicks, raised his foot into full view of the batter, meantime hiding the ball and his back swing behind the big leg.

Paul Derringer was one of the first of that raise-the-foot school of pitching. Vinegar Bend Mizell spent many hours learning to give the batter a fine view of one big foot, then a glance at his rear bumper department, so that when the ball finally came into the picture, the batter would be surprised.

Much time is devoted too, during instruction of pitchers, to the development of a windmill windup. Dizzy Dean had a great windup and so did Bobo Newsom. Sometimes they gave the batter a double or triple take of the windmill motion and the batter would be so intrigued, trying to guess just when that fel- low out there on the mound was going to untangle himself and let the ball go, that the business of trying to hit the ball would be forgotten.

They tried to teach Don James Larsen some of those tricks, but he wasn't doing too well and finally, near the end of the re- cent season, he decided to do a little experimenting. He just put his right arm back in throwing position and fired the ball to his catcher. No windup, no windmill motion, no kicking of the foot, no hiding his right hand behind him for a few seconds to make the batter guess what it was all about. He just threw the ball ...

Now they are saying it, of course. Larsen is hiding the ball, not behind his back, but against the white of his uniform. A new school of thought. See.

We've been watching baseball and World Series games for a long time. We can recall only one pitcher who threw with the ease and lack of claptrap motion that accompanies Larsen's pitch- ing. Grover Cleveland Alexander threw that way. He just looked, saw where the batter was standing and fired the ball. Larsen's pitching, and Alexander's, might be compared to the swing of a golfer who uses only about one-third of a back swing.

"It was Larsen's own idea," Jim Turner told reporters in the clubhouse after the game. "People have been saying that I got him to pitch that way. I had nothing to do with it. In fact I was ready to ask him why the hell he was doing it, but I was going to wait till he was having trouble. When he got the batters out, I kept my mouth shut."

The first game I really used the no wind-up was in a four-hit, 5-0 shutout against Baltimore on September 3rd. Three more victories followed; a 5-1 over the Tigers on the 14th, a 2-1 victory over Boston on the 22nd, and a 7-2 win over the Red Sox again on the 28th in my last start before the Series. When a sportswriter asked me where I got the idea, I jokingly told him, "The comic-book ghoulies sent me the message to try it."

That comment was triggered by my insatiable appetite for comic books. It began when I was a kid and continues today.

I read everything that was printed: *Superman, Submariner, The Hulk,* and *Crypt.* Some were exciting, others rather eerie. They cost about twenty cents. I kept a supply of them in my locker, and even though other players would kid me, they'd borrow them for days on end.

Yogi Berra read nearly as many as I did. At one time, I started charging five cents each when a player borrowed them. That offset some of my cost.

In all, the 1956 regular season saw me win 11, lose 5, and total 22 no-decisions. In 20 starts and 180 innings pitched, I had 107 strike-outs, 96 walks, and a respectable earned run average of 3.25.

Nineteen fifty-six was Mickey Mantle's premier year, but my regular season performance, especially in September, was important to the Yankees as well. For me, it was a great confidence booster since my 11-5 record proved I could be a winning pitcher in the major leagues. Heading into the World Series, I was brimming with confidence, but my effectiveness depended on whether the "Ghoulies" continued to favor the no wind-up delivery that had made me successful.

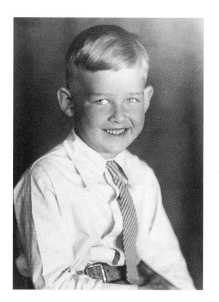

Don Larsen as a boy growing up in Michigan City, Indiana.

Larsen *(back row, third from left)* at his confirmation.

Don Larsen *(back row, fourth from left)*, an outstanding player during his high school days in San Diego, California, was a member of Fort Shafter's military basketball team.

Larsen's first major league team was the St. Louis Browns in 1953. His teammates included the legendary Satchel Paige.

The 1956 World Champion New York Yankees. *(Photo courtesy of New York Yankees)*

Don Larsen poses with brothers Artie *(left)* and Milton Richman and their mother at Yankee Stadium. Artie was with Don the night before the perfect game and has been a lifelong friend.

Don Larsen's official Yankee team photo. He played on two world championship teams for the Bronx Bombers.

At the top of his stretch, Don Larsen readies to deliver a fastball.

The sequence of the "no-wind-up" delivery used by Don Larsen in the perfect game. Larsen told reporters afterwards "the comic book ghoulies told me to use it."

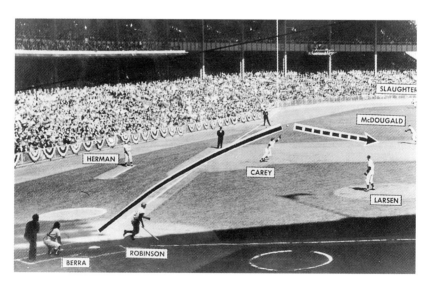

Dodger Jackie Robinson's hot smash careens off Yankee third baseman Andy Carey, then straight into Gil McDougald's glove in the second inning of the perfect game. Several outstanding defensive efforts aided Larsen's performance.

Prior to throwing the perfect game's final pitch to Dale Mitchell, Don Larsen went through his ritual.

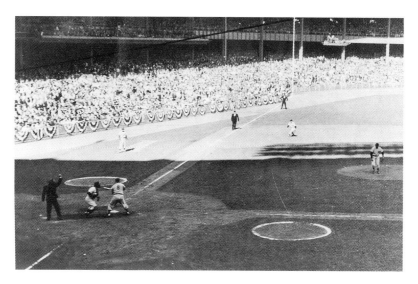

Umpire Babe Pinelli signals strike three as Dodger pinch-hitter Dale Mitchell checks his swing on Don Larsen's final pitch of the perfect game.

Yogi Berra leaps into Don Larsen's arms just seconds after the completion of the perfect game.

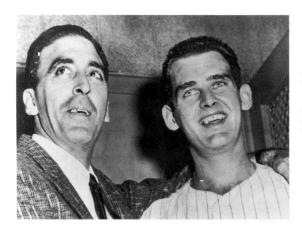

Dodger hurler Sal "The Barber" Maglie congratulates Don Larsen after his gem.

Home plate umpire Babe Pinelli stands between battery mates Don Larsen and Yogi Berra.

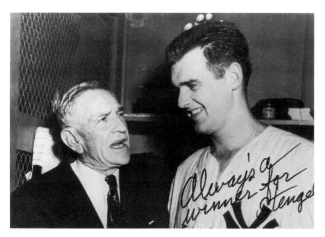

Casey Stengel signed this picture for Don Larsen just days after his perfect game.

Yankee pitching coach Jim Turner *(left)* and manager Casey Stengel *(right)* check out Don Larsen's fastball grip shortly after the perfect game.

Comedian Bob Hope *(right)* hams it up with Larsen during a taping of The Bob Hope Show.

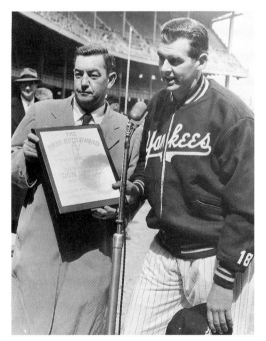

Don Larsen receives the Babe Ruth Award from sportswriter Joe Trimble for being the outstanding player in the 1956 World Series.

—13—

Inning #5

Mantle's Miracle Catch and Pee Wee's Gem

	1	2	3	4	5	6	7	8	9	10	R	H	E
Brooklyn	0	0	0	0							0	0	0
Yankees	0	0	0	1							1	1	0

COMMENTING ON A REPORT THAT GIL HODGES was going to be playing first base with a leg injury, Casey Stengel once remarked, "He [Hodges] fields better on one leg than anybody else I got on two."

Gil was also a great hitter, but before the Dodgers' great first baseman came to bat to face me in the top of the fifth, Jackie Robinson strode to the plate. I knew he'd be looking for a hit to make up for the one that McDougald took away in the top of the first.

I started Jackie with a fast curve too far inside for ball one. He then hit foul a slow curve that might have been ball two if he'd let it go by. Mutual broadcaster Bob Neal told his listeners, "Larsen fed him a big fat curve, and Robinson went fishing for it."

I then got ahead in the count when Robinson swung and missed on a fast curve that tailed away from him. In the broadcast booth, Mel Allen described the pitch as a "beautiful change-up curve. He pulled the string."

With the count now one ball and two strikes, Robinson fouled off a high fast ball and then hit an outside fastball to Hank Bauer for the out.

After Robinson's at bat, Mutual broadcaster Bob Neal explained to his listeners that "[Larsen's] arm comes out of the white uniform. That makes it more difficult to pick up the ball."

Whatever the reason, 13 straight Dodgers had now come and gone, and I readied myself for Gil Hodges.

To everyone who knew him, Gil Hodges, who wore #14 for the Dodgers, was about as nice a man as one could ever meet. The big first baseman always seemed to have a smile on his face and a kind word for just about everybody.

A native of Princeton, Indiana, the right-handed Hodges later gained his greatest fame when he managed the amazing New York Mets to the World Championship in their miracle year of 1969, when they defeated the heavily favored Baltimore Orioles in just five games.

Hodges, a 6-foot 2-inch, 200-pound kindly-faced gentleman, joined the Dodgers in 1943. He quickly made his way to the majors and began to distinguish himself as one of the best defensive first basemen ever to play the game. Three times during his career, he would lead the league in fielding, put-outs, and assists.

Watching Gil Hodges at first was like seeing a gymnast perform. Even though he was tall and stout, Hodges made tough plays at first base look routine.

He went on to be a Gold Glove winner in 1957. I'm sure such acclaim convinced his Dodgers teammates that if they threw the ball anywhere near the big first sacker, Hodges would make the play.

Gil Hodges also sported a .273 lifetime batting average, and once hit four homers in one game in 1950 to become the first National League player to do that in a regulation-length game. He also was a standout with the bases loaded, still holding the major league record with fourteen round-trippers with the sacks full.

Hodges's greatest year was 1954. Along with teammate Duke Snider, who hit 40 home runs, Hodges cranked out 42 while knocking in 130 men and batting .304.

In the book *My Favorite Summer 1956*, Mickey Mantle described Gil Hodges.

> Gil had this real funny batting stance. He kind of held the bat almost parallel to the ground. Later, they changed his stance and got him to hold the bat straight up, but he still looked funny, kind of like a right-handed Stan Musial. But funny stance or not, he could hit.

While Gil Hodges, an ex-Marine who was 32 years old in 1956, was known to be shy and reserved, Duke Snider pointed to a different side of Gil in *The Duke of Flatbush*:

> Gil was a fun guy to be with. He and Don Hoak, our third baseman and another ex-Marine, used to ride each other. Hoak, who later reached stardom with the Pittsburgh Pirates, loved to needle Hodges. They'd race their cars on the way home from Ebbets Field, two Marines trying to beat each other, Hoak in his Packard and Gil in his big white and black Chrysler. One day some of us followed behind them to see who won. Three or four blocks from the ball park we saw Gil run Hoak up over the curb and into Prospect Park. Hoak jumped out of his car and raised his clenched fist, but Gil just tooted his horn and kept right on going, one more victory for the quiet man.

In Snider's book, he also remembered Gil Hodges' terrible slump during the 1952 World Series.

> His strikeouts were almost as many as mine because we were both big swingers. But absolutely the worst slump I ever saw anybody have was the one Gil had in the '52 World Series ... He went 0-for-21. The slump even extended into the 1953 season, and by late spring he was having so much trouble that his pastor at St. Francis Xavier Church in Brooklyn, Father Redmond, said one Sunday morning, "It's too hot for a sermon, so I suggest that you go home, keep the commandments, and say a prayer for Gil Hodges."
>
> The power of prayer is a wonderful thing. Gil caught fire right after that and stayed hot the rest of the year.

Hodges played 15 years with the Dodgers and was an important cog in six pennant winners. Twice he sported a championship ring after the Dodgers won the Series.

Being tall myself, I loved to watch the graceful Hodges play first base. Height is, of course, a great asset in basketball, but it's tough to be tall and pitch or have to stretch down to field low ground balls.

Yogi had pegged Hodges straight-on as a good hitter who really waited to find the pitch *he* wanted to hit. Hodges had a good eye, but early in the 1956 season he became too picky and his average fell into the low .200s.

As with all good hitters, Gil Hodges adjusted, and he ended up hitting around .300 the rest of the season. Since Hodges didn't hit much to right field, Yogi set up both high and low outside.

In centerfield, Mickey Mantle shifted a bit to his right. Mel Allen told his viewing audience, "Mickey doesn't get as good a jump as some outfielders, but he has such speed he sometimes overruns them."

I ended up having to throw more pitches to Hodges (14) than to any other Dodger during the game. My plan was to keep the ball away from the inside of the plate, since that's where I knew Gil could hurt me.

Mel Allen commented that "Larsen is using a variety of speeds on his curve ball. Then he is whipping in the fast ball . . . mixing it up well."

I did not face Hodges in Game Two of the 1956 World Series, but I had pitched to the tall first baseman before in the 1955 Series. This time, I was perfect with my first two pitches, catching Hodges looking on two outside corner fast balls, the first one low, and the second one high.

I thought I had gotten Hodges on the third pitch, a fast ball, but Pinelli called it a ball, high and outside. I followed with another fast ball that was close, but the count evened at two and two when Pinelli said it was outside.

In every game ever pitched, there will be several pitches thrown that are ones that a pitcher would like to somehow get back so he could throw them all over again. "Mistake" pitches are killer pitches, the ones that guys like Mantle or Hodges hit out of the ballpark and out of sight.

Since no pitcher has ever thrown every pitch exactly where he wanted to every time, guys like me just hope and pray that somehow the hitter makes a mistake as well so we don't get hurt on every single mistake pitch. Even when a blazing fast ball intended for the inside corner becomes a mediocre fast ball across the plate, a hitter may not time the pitch correctly, or somehow not be able to swing with enough velocity to hit the ball where he wants to.

Among the 97 pitches I threw in this game, there were only a few that were "mistake" pitches. With the count level at two and two, I threw a mistake slider to Hodges that hung out over the plate.

The ball was flat when it drifted into Gil's hitting area. His brain must have sounded an alarm that this was the pitch that would end up in a home run to tie the score. I'm sure that hung slider must have looked balloon-sized to him.

At the crack of the bat, I watched as Mickey Mantle raced to his right and headed toward the deepest part of left-center field. He was motorin' and with his blazing speed, he raced toward Hodges's hit. The ball would surely have been a home run in most any other park, but it looked to me that while the ball wouldn't go over the wall, it would drop near the base of the fence and Hodges would end up with either a double, triple, or perhaps even an in-side-the-park home run.

Back-pedaling from his starting position, and moving swiftly to his left, the Mick drew a bead on the spiraling ball. Just when it appeared that it would fall to the ground, Mickey stretched full-length toward ground level and snagged the ball into his glove.

Mel Allen's account was as exciting as the play. "Ball to left-field ... Mantle digging hard ... still going ... How About That Catch! ... a World Series play!" Radio broadcaster Bob Wolff said, "Mantle ran a country mile to get that one." He also called the catch, "sure robbery."

In the book *My Favorite Summer 1956*, Mantle described the catch:

> Because Hodges was so strong and such a pull hitter, I backed up a few steps and moved over a bit toward left field. It was a good thing I did. The count went 2-2 and Hodges grabbed hold of a fast ball and drove it on a line into left center. It would have been in the seats in Ebbets Field, but there was plenty of room to run in Yankee Stadium and I ran like hell. I just put my head down and took off as fast as I could. I caught up with the ball as it was dropping, more than 400 feet from home plate. I had to reach across my body to make the catch and luckily the ball just plopped into my glove. If I'd started a split second later, or been a step slower, or if I hadn't shaded over on Hodges, the ball would have dropped for at least a double. It was the best catch I ever made. Some people might question that, but there's certainly no question that it was the most important catch I ever made.

In the radio announcers' booth, Bob Neal called the catch "sure robbery." I must admit that I don't know whether any other center fielder of that era could have caught Hodges's sharp hit. Mantle was great at getting a good jump on a ball, but I still can't believe he caught Hodges's shot.

With the 14th Dodger hitter out of the way, I tried to gather myself and prepare for Sandy Amoros. Getting away with a mistake to Hodges was one thing, but now I had to calm my nerves down and focus on Sandy Amoros.

Left-fielder Edmundo Isasi (Sandy) Amoros was born and raised in Mantanzas, Cuba. The 5-foot 7-inch, 170-pound, left-handed pan-faced Amoros began his professional baseball career in 1952 with St. Paul of the American Association where he hit .337. He went to the Dodgers in 1953, spending that year and part of 1954 with the Montreal farm club where his batting average hovered near .350.

Nineteen fifty-five was the greatest year of Sandy Amoros's career. He played left field for the Dodgers and was known as a good hit/great field performer.

Later on I'd find out that Sandy Amoros might not have been in left field for the Dodgers in 1955 if the club had been successful in hiding a young outfielder with power-hitting potential who was playing at their farm club in Montreal. The Dodgers had signed the Puerto Rican right-handed prospect for $10,000. To discourage other teams from drafting him, they only played him against right-handers since he absolutely killed left-handed pitching.

When the Dodgers left him unprotected, the eagle eye of Branch Rickey at Pittsburgh took note, and the Pirates drafted future Hall of Famer Roberto Clemente. If not for the bungle by the Dodgers, the great Clemente would have stood alongside Carl Furillo and Duke Snider in the outfield.

Despite Clemente's potential, the Dodgers were very high on Amoros's prospects. According to Roger Kahn in *The Era*, Al Campanis of the Dodgers expounded on Amoros's natural gifts during the regular season. Kahn says Campanis told reporters, "Wait 'till you see this kid hit . . . his wrists are so quick, he hits the ball right out of the catcher's glove."

Amoros's .247 season batting average in 1955 didn't back up Campanis' prediction, but in Game Seven of the Series, all was forgiven by Dodger fans when Amoros made a play in the outfield that made him world famous.

In that 1955 Series, the Yankees and Dodgers had split the first six games. In the sixth inning of the deciding seventh game, the Dodgers led 2-0.

Dodgers hurler Johnny Podres walked Billy Martin and then Gil McDougald bunted safely to give the Dodgers men on first and second.

To the plate headed our most dangerous RBI man, Yogi Berra. With one swing, he could put us in the lead. Sandy Amoros was playing toward left-center with the left-handed Berra at the plate, and when Yogi sliced a ball just inside the foul line, he took off at full speed toward the line.

I can still see Amoros as he headed across the field. Both Martin and McDougald took off as fast as they could from second and first, and I was convinced we were about to easily tie the score. Somehow though, Amoros raced like a blur toward the ball, and miraculously reached out with his glove hand to catch the ball. After catching it, he then fired a strike to Reese who threw to Hodges, doubling up the surprised McDougald.

When Amoros (who caught the ball in the glove on his left hand) was questioned following the game by reporters about whether he thought he could make the catch, he told them: "I dunno. I just ran like hell."

Debate among sportswriters after the game centered on whether a right-handed Junior Gilliam who could have been in left would have made the play. Most believed he wouldn't have, and that only the fact that Amoros was left-handed made the catch possible.

Sandy Amoros's play saved the game and the Dodgers went on to win the World Championship. To be sure, Dwight Clark of the San Francisco 49ers may have made what was called "*the* catch" in the 1981 NFC Championship Game, but in the long history of baseball, it will be Sandy Amoros who will be remembered for what many believe was the most spectacular defensive play of all time.

While Amoros did have some power, he was a smart hitter who liked to hit the ball when it was up in the strike zone. He had a good eye and would try to lay off the change-up or any curve balls.

Yogi suggested I give him hard stuff down and stay away from anything up. Similar to Hodges, Amoros would be watching for an unintentional pitch that he could drive to the outfield gaps.

My first two pitches were beauties, one a fast ball, the other a slider. Pinelli called a ball on the first one, saying it was outside, and a strike on the second, even though it seemed a bit high.

With the count one and one, I threw another pitch that almost cost me. The pitch was a fast ball, but I got it up a bit, and Amoros swatted it toward right field.

There was never any question that the ball had the legs to get out of the park. The loud crack of the bat told me it had home run possibilities. I just stood on the mound and watched it head toward the right-field stands.

As I said before, the umpire stationed along the right field foul/fair line was Ed Runge, umpiring his very first World Series.

As the ball sailed over his head, he jerked around to get a good look as to whether it would land inside the foul pole for a home run or outside and become just strike two on Amoros.

As was the case with the ball that Snider hit foul by less than two feet in the fourth inning, this one would be close too. Runge's decision was a quick one, and he raised his hands to point toward foul territory as the crowd collectively uttered a loud "ooooh."

After the game, the *San Francisco Chronicle* captured the drama of Runge's call under the byline "Extra Ump Saved Don."

> While talking over the game in the umpire's dressing room, Plate Umpire Babe Pinelli asked Ed Runge, the arbiter on the right field foul line, how far foul Sandy Amoros' hooking drive into the right field seats had gone in the fifth. "That much," said Runge, and he spread his thumb and index about four inches apart.
>
> "That shows how valuable it is to have a man down the line in these games," said Pinelli. "If I gotta call that one from the plate, I go the other way."
>
> That means "Babe" would have called it a home run.
>
> In regular season contests only four umpires work, none on the foul lines.

As Amoros discontinued his home-run jaunt toward first base, I heaved my second sigh of relief in less than four minutes.

If Hodges's ball had dropped and Amoros's towering fly had been hit three inches to the left, I would be trailing in the game 2-1 instead of sporting a 1-0 lead. The good Lord had somehow decided to clear the path for me once again. All I could do was try to regain my composure and go after Amoros, who stood ready at the plate.

The next pitch was a fast ball that I thought was strike three. I took a stutter step toward third base, thinking the inning was over. Sandy Amoros laid off the pitch, and Babe Pinelli called it a ball to even the count at two and two. I stepped back on the mound and awaited Yogi's sign. He called for a slider on the inside corner.

Just as a pitcher remembers the "mistake" pitches he throws, he also remembers those seemingly perfect pitches that he comes up with at critical times in a game. Such was the next pitch I threw to Amoros; it was a good sharp slider that was just a bit inside.

The pitch was a tough one for the Dodgers left fielder to ignore, because with two strikes he couldn't afford to take a close pitch that would end up being a called strike three. Sandy had no real choice and he had to hit *my pitch* instead of one that he wanted.

Sliders were not a favorite of Amoros's, and he never got around on this one. When this ground ball ended up in Billy Martin's glove, and he in turn threw to Collins, I had retired Amoros for the fifteenth consecutive out.

Pitchers are always aware of exactly where they stand throughout the game. Many say they don't keep track, but I can't believe that, because if you are really concentrating on what you're supposed to be doing, then you know every pitch you've thrown, the number of hits you've given up, everything.

On that particular day, however, I don't remember thinking as much about where I stood in terms of hits and so forth for two reasons. One, I had just gotten through a real tough inning where hits by either Hodges or Amoros or both could have cost us the 1-0 lead. Second, the score was still *1-0*, and in a close game all you're hoping for is that your teammates go out and score forty zillion runs so you have a cushion to work with.

While it was still only the fifth inning, tension was starting to build in the Yankee dugout. Mickey Mantle described my actions in the bottom of the fifth (I remember it as the seventh) in his book *My Favorite Summer 1956*:

> I came back to the dugout after the Dodgers batted and I was down by the water cooler getting a drink. And here comes Gooney Bird over to me.
>
> "Hey, Slick," he said. "Wouldn't it be funny if I pitched a no-hitter?"
>
> "Get the hell out of here," I told him.
>
> I walked away from him to the other end of the dugout. It's one of baseball's oldest superstitions that you're not supposed to talk about a no-hitter. If you do, the superstition goes, you'll jinx the pitcher. But here was the pitcher talking about it himself. That's how loose he was. Some of the other guys told me he was up and down the bench all day talking about pitching a no-hitter and they all chased him away, or walked away from him, because they didn't want to be the one to jinx him, even if he didn't worry about jinxing himself.

Mickey's account is pretty close. I did try to get someone to talk to me, but everyone treated me like I had the plague.

Looking back, I believe I acted the way I did because I wasn't really taking the no-hit possibility that seriously. I'd never pitched one and I doubted that it would come in the fifth game of the World Series. I was just trying to give Casey as many good innings as I could. Miracles were for other people.

Over five innings, I had thrown 56 pitches, just 11 over the minimum. Thirty-eight of them had been strikes, 18 balls. Fifteen Dodgers had come and gone. In spite of that performance, our club clung to just a 1-0 lead.

I could only hope my teammates would score some more runs. The first batter in the fifth inning with a chance to lead the charge was left-fielder Enos (Country) Slaughter.

Slaughter, with seven hits in 16 at bats in the Series, led off the inning for the Yanks at the ripe old age of 40. The 5-foot 9-inch, 190-pound, personable Yankees left fielder was a colorful character who was winning his own private battle with Father Time.

A native of Roxboro, North Carolina, the crusty, hard-driving .300 lifetime hitter played 24 years in the major leagues. Slaughter was first spotted by Billy Southworth playing the 1935 season with the St. Louis Cardinal Farm Club in the Class D Bi-State League.

Southworth apparently liked what he saw of young Enos, but he quickly noticed that the 19 year old lacked foot speed. He took Slaughter under his wing and Enos did the rest. He ran and ran until he turned himself into a player who could run with the best of them.

In 1937, Enos Slaughter moved on to Columbus of the American Association where he hit an astounding .382 with 26 home runs and 122 runs batted in. There, the sandy-haired gentleman then garnered his life-long nickname when Manager Burt Shotton began calling him "Country."

Slaughter began his twenty-one year major league career with the Cardinals in 1938, and then played with the Yankees, Kansas City A's, and the Milwaukee Braves.

Enos Slaughter, a 1985 inductee into the Hall of Fame, could just flat out hit. While he never busted many home runs, he always seemed to be among the league leaders in doubles and triples. A ten-time All-Star, he helped the National League win the 1953 game with a diving catch of Harvey Kuenn's fly ball.

Slaughter played in the big leagues until 1959. When the Cardinals traded their favorite son to the Yankees in 1954, only Stan Musial with 2,223 hits had more than the 2,064 attributed to Slaughter.

Slaughter, who batted left-handed and threw right, was traded to Kansas City in 1955, but at the age of 39, he still hit .315. In 1956, he had played in 91 games and hit .278 when the Yankees sent Bob Cerv to Kansas City to get "Country" back in time for the Series. He ended up batting .350 including a game-winning homer in Game Three.

Of the players today, Baltimore's Cal Ripken and the Minnesota Twins' Kirby Puckett remind me most of Enos Slaughter. With him behind me, I always knew that I had a left fielder who gave me everything he had, and then some.

I had first seen Enos in the Service in 1952, when he was a member of Lefty O'Doul's All-Star team, and we played against them in Hawaii. In 1953, I watched Slaughter again when our St. Louis Browns team competed in a cross-town series of games against the Cardinals.

A great hustler, Slaughter always ran out ground balls, fly balls, and pop-ups. He was also a great clutch hitter who helped influence the young players on the Yankee squad.

For whatever reason, Slaughter was never a real popular player with Yankee teammates. Some felt that although he played hard for the team, he was a National League St. Louis Cardinal at heart. Others envied his hustling ways as well, believing he was some sort of show-off.

The one man who counted loved him, and that was Casey Stengel. Casey's roots were with the National League as well, and he solicited Slaughter's advice and counsel and even had him sit next to him on the bench.

I liked Slaughter, and I felt he was a good influence on the younger players. He rode some of them pretty hard, but Enos had the track record to back up his stinging remarks.

During this time at bat, radio broadcaster Bob Wolff pointed out that the 40-year-old Slaughter was up against the 39-year-old Maglie. "Two true blue veterans," he called them.

Slaughter was patient and worked Maglie, who had given up only one hit, for a walk. Billy Martin, 4 for 16 in the Series, bunted to sacrifice him to second, but Maglie came charging off the mound, turned, and threw to second forcing Slaughter.

With one out, and Martin on first, Gil McDougald, described by sportscaster Bob Neal as "cradling the bat," hit a blue streaker that looked like it was headed into left field. Just as it zoomed over the shortstop area, Pee Wee Reese leaped in the air, got a glove on the ball, deflected it, and then caught it in his glove.

Broadcaster Vin Scully described Pee Wee Reese's play for the millions of television viewers: "The ball deflected off his glove and then he caught it," Scully exclaimed. "It was like Pee Wee Reese was playing catch with himself."

It was a great play, and when Reese calmly threw to first to double up Martin, who was off at the crack of the bat, any chance to score was squelched and the inning was suddenly over.

Five innings now were in the books in what broadcaster Bob Wolff labeled a "tense duel between Maglie and Larsen."

To be sure, the two of us had given up just one hit. And McDougald, Mantle, and now Reese had electrified the crowd with their spectacular defense play. Enough excitement had occurred for a whole game, and yet the two heavyweight teams still had four innings to play.

—14—

The Perfect Game Club

THERE IS AN ELITE GROUP OF MEN whose perfect games permit them to be a member of a special group unique in the history of sports.

Ironically, the first two perfect games in baseball were pitched within five days of each other in 1880, five years after the National League was first established. At that time, the pitching rubber was only 45 feet from home plate—imagine what a Nolan Ryan fast ball would have looked like to a batter from that short distance!

On June 12, 1880, Worcester played Cleveland before seven hundred fans. Ace left-handed pitcher John Lee Richman took the mound. In one hour and 26 minutes, Richman, who later practiced medicine and became a high school principal, retired 27 straight batters. Fourteen of the outs came through plays at first base, and Worcester won the game, 1-0.

Little else is known about the very first perfect game because news reports of the game only stated that, "the Worcesters played without an error, for all nine innings, and retired their opponents in order, not a man getting a base hit or reaching first base." The report also informed the reader that there were "double plays and fly balls, and that the game was stopped due to rain for eight minutes in the eighth inning."

Less than one week later, John Montgomery Ward pitched the second perfect game in the history of baseball when he took the hill for Providence in a morning game against Buffalo. Ward's teammates backed him up with 13 hits and 5 runs as Ward mowed down the Buffalo lineup in order, winning the game 5-0.

Like Richman, Ward pitched underhanded. In 1878, he had gone 22-13 for the third-place Providence Grays and then won an astounding 47 games in 1889 when Providence won the pennant.

Approximately 1,800 fans witnessed his perfect game, and the *Providence Daily Journal* gave a modest account of the game:

> Not one of the players of the visiting team were able to secure a safe hit off of Ward's delivery, and not even allowing, in the whole nine innings, a man to reach the first bag without being put out.

Monte Ward later experienced arm trouble, but went on to become one of the better shortstops in the league. When he retired, Ward managed both the Dodgers and the Giants. Also an attorney by trade, Ward was known as one of the first "clubhouse lawyers." He was instrumental in founding both the Player's Brotherhood, an early union, and the ill-fated Player's League of 1890, in which the players were to share in league profits.

Whether these performances should actually be placed alongside the no-hitters or perfect games that would be pitched in later years is subject to debate, because the rules of the game were so different prior to 1883. For instance, before 1883, most fielders didn't use gloves, the pitchers threw underhanded, and the number of pitches it took to cause a walk went from nine in 1879, to five in 1887, and then to four in 1889.

The three strikes and you're out rule was not implemented until 1888. Incredibly, before 1887, a walk was considered to be a hit, and a batter could request a low or high pitch to hit.

In *Baseball and Mr. Spalding*, author Arthur Bartlett detailed the "called-pitch" rules:

> The batter could call either for a high ball (above the waist but below the shoulder), a low ball (below the waist but at least a foot off the ground), or a fan ball (below the shoulder but at least a foot off the ground). Any ball not at the specified height or not over the plate, was a ball but the umpire called a ball only on every third "unfair" delivery; and it took three called balls—in other words nine unfair balls—to entitle the batter to a walk.

I wish they'd had that rule when I pitched. And Tommy Byrne would have been right at home with the "called-pitch rule."

Twenty-four years after Ward's performance on May 5, 1904, the great Cy Young of the Boston Red Sox faced off against Philadelphia and future Hall of Fame pitcher Rube Waddell in an American League game. By this time, the pitching rubber was at the present distance of 60 feet, six inches. Young, who also pitched two other no-hitters and ended up winning 510 games in his illustrious career, faced a lineup of Philadelphia heavy hitters, including home-run champion Harry Davis, Socks Seybold, Danny Murphy, and Lave Cross.

Before 10,267 fans, the 6-foot-2, 220-pound Young was flawless against the Athletics that day, and he pitched the perfect game against his arch rival, Rube Waddell, winning by the score of 3 to 0. Ironically, it was Waddell himself who made the last out as Manager Connie Mack surprisingly let him hit instead of sending up a pinch-hitter.

Young later said of his feat:

> Of all the eight hundred and seventy-nine games I pitched in the big leagues ... this was my greatest day. I was real fast in those days, but what very few batters knew was that I had two curves. One of them sailed in there as hard as my fast ball and broke in reverse, and the other had a wide break.

In fact, the *Cleveland Leader and Herald* described Cy Young's delivery as follows: "Mr. Young seems to know almost as much about curves as an engineer on a railroad in West Virginia."

No wonder Cy Young was later elected to the Hall of Fame, and of course, he had the prestigious pitching award named after him.

While Young's perfect game was pitched against a team known for its hitting prowess, Addie Joss's perfect game on October 2, 1908, was thrown against a team that had just the opposite reputation. In fact, the 1908 version of the Chicago White Sox were known as the "hitless wonders." This was due not only to their season's .225 batting average, but more incredibly to the fact that they only hit *three* home runs the whole season. I wish I'd faced a team like that in the '54 season. I might have won 21 instead of losing them.

In spite of their weak hitting, the White Sox had somehow managed to stay in the pennant race with the Indians and Tigers, and so the game between Joss's Indians and the great White Sox spitballer, Ed Walsh, was of great importance.

Addie Joss was prepared for the task at hand. The previous year he had won 27 games, lost 11, and had an E.R.A. of 1.83.

In fact, 1907 was a year when no less than seven future Hall of Fame pitchers showed off their wares. Besides Joss, Walter Johnson, Eddie Plank, Cy Young, Chief Bender, Jack Chesbro, and Rube Waddell all performed well, but Joss was as tough as any of them.

Like Joss, Big Ed Walsh was having an incredible year in 1907. Through both starting and relieving, he played in 66 games, and won 40, leading the league in every category imaginable.

On October 2nd, before almost 11,000 fans, the two great pitchers matched pitch for pitch, with Walsh masterfully holding the Indians to only four hits while striking out a total of 15 batters.

Walsh's great performance was not enough, though, as Joss retired all 27 batters, with 16 put-outs at first base. The Indians won the game, 1 to 0, with the only run coming on a passed ball by White Sox second string catcher, Ossee Schreckengost.

There were three striking similarities between Joss' perfect game and mine 48 years later. First, he was locked up in a tight contest with Ed Walsh and only led by a slim margin going into the ninth. Second, he would face a very dangerous pinch-hitter for his final out, and third, a close call on a drive down the foul line went in his favor.

With two outs in the bottom of the ninth, big John Anderson, a lifetime .290 hitter, came to bat for Walsh. Joss worked him carefully, but Anderson belted his sidearm sinker on a line toward left field. All thoughts turned toward the break-up of the no-hitter and perfect game, but at the last instant, the ball went foul. Anderson returned to the plate and then hit a hard grounder to third sacker Bill Bradley for the final out.

In spite of Joss's great feat, the Indians lost the pennant to Detroit on the last day of the season. Physical ailments restricted Joss's performances over the next few seasons, and the Indians pitcher died in 1911 at the early age of 31.

Of all the perfect games pitched to date, Ernie Shore's is the most controversial. Pitched in the first game of a double-header against Washington on June 23, 1917, Shore's gem is not even considered a perfect game by many baseball purists, because Shore was *not* the starting pitcher in the game.

The 1917 Boston Red Sox pitching staff included Shore, Hubert (Dutch) Leonard, George Foster, and the immortal Babe Ruth. Both Shore and Ruth were originally with the Orioles, but owner Jack Dunn dealt both of them to the Red Sox in 1914. While

Ruth at first proved a bust as a pitcher, Shore went 10-4 in 1914 to help Boston end up in second place.

In 1915, Eddie Shore won 19 and lost eight, and led Boston into the World Series. Grover Cleveland Alexander bested Shore in the opener even though the Boston right-hander gave up only five hits.

Babe Ruth had been outstanding through the first few months of the 1917 season, winning 10 of the first 11 games he pitched. Unfortunately for Ruth, he had gained a reputation for challenging umpires, and on June 23, 1917, he met his match with home umpire Brick Owens.

Ruth was manager Jack Barry's starter, and the first batter he faced against the Washington Senators at Fenway Park was their second baseman Ray Morgan. The Babe's first pitch was a ball, and Ruth instantly criticized Owens's failure to call it a strike.

When the next two pitches, both borderline, were also called balls, Ruth was fuming. According to reports, he ranted and raved around the mound before finally yelling at umpire Owens.

Although there are several accounts of the incident, Robert Creamer provided the following account in the book *Babe*.

> "Open your eyes!" Ruth yelled. "Open your eyes!"
> "It's too early for you to kick," the umpire yelled back. "Get in there and pitch!"
> Ruth stomped around the mound angrily, wound up and threw again.
> "Ball four!" Owens snapped.
> Ruth ran in toward the plate. "Why don't you open your goddamned eyes?" he screamed.
> "Get back in there and pitch," Owens shouted, "or I'll run you out of the game."
> Owens stepped across the plate and waved his arm. "Get the hell out of here!" he cried. "You're through."

An incensed Babe Ruth charged off the mound and confronted Owens. Catcher Chester Thomas tried to get between the men, but Ruth was relentless and swung wildly at Owens, landing a glancing blow on Owens's cheek.

Ruth was suspended for ten days, and over 15,000 fans lost the chance to watch the famous Ruth pitch that game. Little did they know that a much greater experience awaited them.

Ruth's quick departure not only disappointed all of the fans in the ballpark who had come to see him play, but left manager Jack Barry with no pitcher ready to take on Washington. Forced to make a quick selection, Barry chose Shore, the tall Red Sox righthander, who had been an earlier World Series hero.

After a short warm-up time for Shore, Ray Morgan of Washington was immediately thrown out for stealing by new catcher Sammy Agnew. Manager Jack Barry said later he only expected Ernie Shore to try to settle things down and get the team out of the inning. When Eddie Foster and Clyde Milan were retired, Shore had done his job, and Barry was ready to bring in another pitcher.

But Jack Barry stayed with Ernie Shore, who dominated the game as he mowed down the next 24 batters. In fact, newspaper reports emphasized that only one ball was hit very hard as the Senators' batters were completely baffled by Shore's variety of pitches.

Not only did manager Jack Barry choose Shore to pitch that fateful game, but he saved the perfect game in the ninth when Mike Menosky's drag bunt was a half-step shy of Barry's throw to first.

The sixth perfect game in baseball history was pitched by Charlie Robertson in a 4-0 victory for the Chicago White Sox on April 30, 1922. Little more than a rookie, Robertson faced the Detroit Tigers with merely the remnants of the great 1919 White Sox team that was disbanded due to the World Series betting scandal which left eight prominent players, including the great Joe Jackson, banned from baseball for life.

In addition, Robertson faced a great Tiger team that had a team batting average of .305, and featured not only future Hall of Famer Ty Cobb, who hit .401 that year, but sluggers Harry Heilmann, Bobby Veach, and Lu Blue. Robertson's opponent on that day was Herman Pillette, whose son Duane would not only pitch for the Phillies, but became a good friend of mine when both of us were with the Baltimore Orioles in 1954.

Early in the game, the Tigers protested the game, saying that Robertson was throwing spitballs, which had been banned in 1920 when Cleveland player Ray Chapman died after being hit in the head with a pitch. When the umpires found no evidence of wrongdoing, Robertson went on to completely stymie the Tigers, falling behind only two hitters all day.

In the final inning, Cobb, who was also the manager, tried desperately to break up the perfect game by sending up his first string catcher, Johnny Bassler. According to sportswriters of the time, Robertson stepped off the mound and told his shortstop Ed Mulligan, "Do you realize that fat little man up there is the only thing between me and a perfect game?"

Supremely confident, Robertson wasn't to be denied. He got the .323 regular season hitter to fly to left-fielder Johnny Mostil for the final out.

Unfortunately for Robertson, his incredible feat was not a sign of greater things to come and, while many predicted future stardom, he became a mediocre pitcher for the remainder of his major league career. In fact, many years after his achievement, Robertson told reporters that he wished he had never played baseball, despite pitching the perfect game.

Three years after my performance in 1956, Harvey Haddix of the Pittsburgh Pirates pitched perfect ball against Milwaukee for 12 straight innings, only to lose the game in the 13th.

Arguably the finest game ever pitched but lost, Haddix turned his trick on May 25, 1959. Nicknamed the "kitten," the thin left-handed, curve-ball artist Harvey Haddix was known for one outstanding trait: He had great control.

Just as I had a premonition before the fifth game in October of 1956, Harvey Haddix also recalled years later to a reporter that there was discussion in the clubhouse before the game that he might pitch a no-hitter. "I remember telling my teammates that I would pitch this way to one batter, and that way to another, and Don Hoak came over and told me that if I pitched as well as I was talking about, I would pitch a no-hitter."

The Milwaukee lineup that Haddix faced that rainy night at Milwaukee's County Stadium was every bit as formidable as the Dodgers' batting order I had encountered in 1956.

First baseman Joe Adcock was tough enough with his .292 batting average and 25 homers, but he was only one-third of the Braves' powerful attack. Hammerin' Hank Aaron hit .355 that year, and walloped 39 homers, and drove in 123, while third baseman Eddie Mathews hit a major-league leading 46 dingers, and pounded home 114 runs.

Consistent hitters like Johnny Logan, Wes Covington, and Del Crandall were also tough outs for the Braves, who ultimately lost to the Dodgers in a playoff for the National League pennant. Besides them, the Braves had a fine pitcher going for them against Haddix, fireballing Lew Burdette.

Even though Burdette gave up eight hits in nine innings, the Pirates still hadn't scored as the game headed into the ninth. Haddix on the other hand, had handcuffed the Braves by pitching eight perfect innings.

In the ninth, Haddix was again equal to the task, and when he struck out his pitching counterpart Lew Burdette, he had pitched a perfect nine-inning game.

That wasn't enough however because the game was still scoreless. Nine more straight outs from Haddix meant 36 down as the teams entered the 13th inning.

In the bottom of that inning, Haddix's dream ended through a throwing error by his third baseman, Don Hoak, the same man who had predicted Harvey's potential feat. Joe Adcock later hit a Haddix offering over the fence, and the unlucky hurler had not only lost his no-hitter and perfect game, but the game itself, 1-0.

Having lost close games myself, I knew what that was like, but Harvey must have been devastated. In spite of the loss, that's one of the great pitching performances of all time.

The next perfect game took place five years later, on Father's Day, June 21, 1964, when Philadelphia Phillies right-hander Jim Bunning, who later became a United States Congressman, tossed a perfect game against the New York Mets and won 6-0. Bunning was no stranger to the no-hitter, having pitched his first one on July 20, 1958, while a member of the Detroit Tigers.

By 1964, Bunning was a member of the Phillies, and he hooked up with the New York Mets in the first game of a double-header in New York.

Throwing only 90 pitches, 69 of them strikes, Bunning was in control from the start as he struck out ten and only went to a three-ball count with two batters. In the ninth, after two were out, Bunning faced John Stephenson, who was ironically a pinch-hitter for the third Met pitcher, my former Yankee teammate and 1956 World Series hero, Tom Sturdivant.

Working carefully, Bunning got two quick strikes, then a ball, and then finally threw a curve at the pinch-hitter's knees. Stephenson didn't have a chance, and Bunning had his perfect game, winning 6-0.

On September 9, 1965, over a year later, Sandy Koufax, arguably the greatest left-hander to ever pitch in the game, took the mound against the Chicago Cubs in Los Angeles. To understand what Koufax accomplished that night, one must remember that Sandy had already pitched *three* no-hitters in his career.

Nineteen sixty-five was going to be a difficult year for Koufax, as his dazzling array of pitches had taken their toll on his left elbow. Nevertheless, in spite of chronic arthritic pain, Sandy won 26 games that year and lost only eight.

Koufax faced a Cub team that included sluggers Ernie Banks, Ron Santo, and Billy Williams. Before a crowd of nearly 30,000, Koufax and the Chicago pitcher Bob Hendley traded no-hit inning after no-hit inning. It wasn't until the seventh that the Dodgers finally broke through for their only hit when Lou Johnson got a double down the left field line.

In the ninth, as would be the case when I faced the dangerous pinch-hitter Dale Mitchell, Koufax's effort at perfection were blocked by a great veteran ball player, Harvey Kuenn. A career .303 hitter, the American League batting champion in 1959, and a very tough man to strike out, Kuenn did his best to hit Koufax, but the wily lefty struck him out on three pitches.

Koufax's one-hour and 43-minute performance included 14 strikeouts, and he finished strong by striking out seven of the final nine men he faced. Elected to the Hall of Fame in 1971, Koufax won only 165 games in his short career. But he won 97 of those games in four successive seasons, which included three seasons where he struck out more than 300 batters.

On May 8, 1968, Jim "Catfish" Hunter readied himself to face the Minnesota Twins in Oakland's Alameda County Coliseum before a sparse, chilly night crowd of just 6,298 fans. Assisted by the early six o'clock start of the game which made it difficult for batters to pick up the ball in the early evening shadows, Hunter was in command all the way as he kept the vaunted Minnesota hitters (Cesar Tovar, Rod Carew, Tony Oliva, Harmon Killebrew, and Bob Allison) off stride with his assortment of pitches.

In fact, the only bad pitch Hunter threw was a hanger to hard-hitting Harmon Killebrew that somehow got by him. Hunter went to a three-ball count only three times, although he did come back from a three and nothing count to strike out Tony Oliva in the second inning. Hunter helped himself out with the bat by driving in three of the four runs the A's scored.

As in most potential no-hit or perfect games, the last batter to face "Catfish" was a pinch-hitter. In this game, it was Rich Reese, only a .154 hitter for the year, but a .317 pinch-hitter the previous year. Determined to break up the perfect game, Reese worked hard at the plate and got ahead in the count at two balls and one strike. He then tantalized the crowd by fouling off four straight pitches.

With the count two and two, Hunter threw a fast ball that was just a hair high and the count went full. Reese readied himself again, but the great "Catfish" was just too much for him. He swung and missed a fast ball as it blazed by on the inside corner.

Catcher Jim Pagliaroni applauded Hunter for his control after the perfect game, saying that while Hunter had a great slider, it was the control that came through for him in the clutch. Hunter and Pagliaroni both were rewarded after the game by owner Charley Finley. Hunter, who was elected to the Hall of Fame in 1987, received $5,000 and the catcher $1,000.

A baseball game at Cleveland's Municipal Stadium in the spring is a weatherman's crap-shoot. Frosty Lake Erie winds can send hot-dog wrappers scattering across the field, and the springtime temperatures can drop unpredictably into the low forties and below.

I never pitched too well in Cleveland for some reason. Our St. Louis Browns club actually got snowed out one year.

Such was the scene on May 5, 1981, when Len Barker of the Cleveland Indians made baseball history. Less than 8,000 fans showed up to see the Indians battle the Toronto Blue Jays, but it was a game they would never forget.

The 6-foot-5 Barker had compiled a 19-12 record in 1980, pitching 246 innings for the Indians. Early in the season he had a 2-1 record and was ready to face the Blue Jays and their hurler, Luis Leal.

Pitching coach Dave Duncan, who fathered several Championship pitching staffs with the Oakland A's, told the *Cleveland Press* that, "He [Barker] started out slow, but as he went along, his curve ball got better and better. It became awesome. It wasn't breaking much, but the rotation was so tight, it was almost the perfect curve."

Toronto fielded a weak hitting team (.226) during the strike-shortened 1981 season, but their roster included Lloyd Moseby, George Bell, and John Mayberry. Leal was tough as well, giving up only one earned run in the eight innings he pitched.

But this was Barker's night. His curve ball was dazzling, and after Danny Ainge (later of professional basketball fame), and John Mayberry struck out, a reporter wrote in the *Cleveland Press*:

Both batters chased curves that swept across the plate so abruptly it looked as if Barker had turned loose something mystical and magical, something an entire population had never witnessed, let alone something a band of Blue Jays could hit.

In the top of the ninth, with 24 men having come and gone, Rick Bosetti fouled out to third baseman Toby Harrah for the first out. Barker then struck out left-handed pinch-hitter Al Woods, and now only pinch-hitter Ernie Whitt, who would go on to be a great clutch-hitter for the Jays, stood between him and perfection.

Ernie Whitt said later that he really thought he could break up the no-hitter, but Barker worked the count to 1-2 before the catcher hit a fly ball to Rick Manning for the final out.

Tim Rogers, sportswriter for the *Cleveland Press,* put me in good company in a nice tribute he wrote the next day. "Barker was awesome. And he was devastating. And he was brutal. He was Cy Young and Don Larsen and Jim Bunning and Sandy Koufax and Catfish Hunter all rolled into one."

On September 30, 1984, three-and-a-half years later, 24-year-old Mike Witt took to the mound for the California Angels. With a 90 m.p.h. fast ball and a curve that was described by teammate Reggie Jackson in *Sports Illustrated* as "top of the line—a Mercedes," Witt was ready to take his place as one of the top two or three pitchers in the American League.

In his Rookie year, Witt had gone 8-9, with a 3.28 ERA and then followed with a 8-6 record in 1982. Witt dipped to an unexplainable 7-14 in 1983, prompting pitching coach Tom Morgan to exclaim in frustration to *Sports Illustrated,* "Witt doesn't retain anything I teach him."

The breakthrough year for Witt was 1984. He would go 15-11 with improved concentration that helped him cut down his strikeout-to-walk ratio.

Kansas City won the league championship that year, but Witt would take the mound on the last day of the season for his Angels against Texas. Whether the Rangers' minds were in the meaningless game or not is pure conjecture, but from the time designated hitter Mickey Rivers struck out in the first, Mike Witt was in control.

Ageless knuckle-baller Charlie Hough was Witt's opponent though, and he would permit seven hits and one run in nine innings. Before 8,375 fans, the two pitchers threw a one hour and 49 minute game that hung in the balance until the final out. Designated hitter Reggie Jackson drove in the Angels' only run in the seventh, knocking in Doug DeCinces with a fielder's choice.

Tommy Dunbar was a strikeout victim for Witt as he started the ninth. Second baseman Rob Wilfong handed Bobby Jones' grounder for out number two, and then safely played Marv Foley's grounder for the third out as well.

Catcher Bob Boone summed up Witt's performance for the *Fort Worth Star-Telegram*:

> Today he just made great pitches. He was throwing everything for strikes. He put it on the corners. I asked him to make some perfect pitches and he did it every time. It was a classic.

Just eight short years ago, left-hander Tom Browning took the mound for his club in Cincinnati. The date was September 16, 1988, and the 1985 Rookie of the Year (Browning won 20 and lost 9) faced the Los Angeles Dodgers and pitcher Tim Belcher, who became a teammate of Browning's at Cincinnati in the early 1990s.

Managed by Pete Rose, the 1988 Reds were 8½ games behind the Bums as they began a three-game series at Riverfront Stadium in Cincinnati. The action was delayed for over two hours by rain that day, as 16,591 fans waited for the game to begin.

Browning and Belcher hooked up for a great pitching duel and at the end of five complete innings, neither had given up a hit. In fact, Belcher didn't give up a hit until the bottom of the sixth when the Reds got the only run of the game when Chris Sabo's high hopper scored Barry Larkin who had doubled with two out.

Browning told reporters that he first thought about the no-hitter in the eighth inning. In the top of the ninth, veteran Dodger catcher Rick Dempsey led off and flied to right-fielder Paul O'Neill. Shortstop Barry Larkin then stopped second baseman Steve Sax cold by scooping up his grounder behind second and throwing to first for the second out.

With the count 1-2 on pinch-hitter Tracy Woodson, Browning threw a high fast ball that Woodson swung at and missed. Tom Browning had one for the record books.

On July 4, 1989, Tom Browning became the only pitcher in the history of baseball to come within *three* outs of pitching *two* perfect games. Unfortunately, Dickie Thon of the Philadelphia Phillies broke up the no-hitter with a double, but Browning nevertheless had thrown 17 perfect innings.

It was July 28, 1991, when precision pitcher Dennis Martinez threw his 2-0 perfect game for the Montreal Expos against the Los Angeles Dodgers. Only two nights before, the Expos' Mark Gardner threw a nine-inning no-hitter against the Dodgers, but lost the game in the tenth.

When Dennis Martinez woke up on that fateful morning, he decided to attend mass even though it could have made him late for his scheduled start. Besides the other challenges associated with pitching professional baseball, Dennis was a recovering alcoholic who had nearly ruined his life and baseball career.

Martinez had been a standout pitcher from Nicaragua who had been a strong hurler for the Baltimore Orioles from 1977 through 1985. His best years had been 16-game victory seasons in 1978 and 1982, but he was traded to the Montreal team in 1986. Three brilliant years from 1987 to 1989 with the Expos made him one of the best pitchers in the game.

In the fourth inning of Martinez' game, his left foot slipped while making a pitch, and he felt a twinge of pain. Trainers rushed out to see if he was all right, but Martinez wasn't about to leave. In the later innings, Eddie Murray and Kal Daniels were each able to work the count to three and two, but Murray ended up grounding out, and Daniels swung at an outside curve ball and missed.

The closest thing to a hit came in the fourth inning when Juan Samuel hit a vicious grounder to Tim Wallach that the Expos' third baseman fielded on the lip of the infield grass. In the ninth, Mike Scioscia hit a fly ball to medium left field, pinch-hitter Stan Javier struck out, and then pinch-hitter Chris Gwynn flied out to center-fielder Marquis Grissom for the final out.

On Thursday, July 28, 1994, left-hander Kenny Rogers of the Texas Rangers recorded a perfect game when he blanked the California Angels, 4-0. Rogers struck out eight, four swinging and four on called third strikes. He went to the ball three count seven times on batters, including four straight times beginning with two out in the sixth, but got them all out.

Designated hitter Jose Canseco provided Rogers with all of the offense he needed by blasting two home runs. Juan Gonzalez also homered for the Rangers to give Rogers his 11th win against 6 losses.

Rogers used but 98 pitches to achieve perfection. He was aided by rookie center-fielder Rusty Greer, who saved the perfect game with a diving—just above the turf—spectacular catch on a hard-hit ball in short right field by the Angels Rex Hudler.

Besides the regular season perfect games, there have been a number of pitchers who have bid for a no-hitter or perfect game in the World Series. In 1906, Chicago Cubs right-hander Ed Reulbach threw a one-hitter against the cross-town rival White Sox, who lived up to that "hitless wonder" reputation by only garnering one hit by Jiggs Donohue.

Shortly after the end of World War II, when the major league teams were still short on quality players, Claude Passeau of the Cubs flirted with baseball immortality when he one-hit the Tigers in the 1945 Series. Only Rudy York's second-inning single prevented the no-hit game the Cubs won 3-0.

Four Yankee pitchers also bid to pitch the magic World Series no-hitter. The first was Herb Pennock, the great left-hander for both the 1927 and 1928 Yankees. Pennock had been absolutely unhittable for the first seven innings, retiring the first 22 hitters. But in the eighth, the great Pittsburgh Pirate Hall of Famer Pie Traynor stroked a clean single to break up the no-hitter and the perfect game.

Monte Pearson was the next Yankee to approach perfection. In 1939, he pitched $7^2/_3$ innings of hitless ball before giving up a hit to the Cincinnati Reds, who were beaten 4-0.

Three years later, in 1942, Charley Ruffing of the Yankees had not given up a hit for $7^2/_3$ innings when Terry Moore of the St. Louis Cardinals shattered Ruffing's dream. The Cardinals roughed him up with four runs in the ninth and almost cost Ruffing the game, but the Yankees finally prevailed 7-4 when Stan Musial grounded out with the bases loaded.

In 1947, Floyd "Bill" Bevens came within an eyelash of a no-hitter. Although he walked ten Dodgers, two intentionally, he nursed a 2-1 lead going into the ninth. With one away, Dodgers' right-fielder Carl Furillo drew a walk. Johnny Jorgensen then fouled out, and Bevens was one out from a no-hitter. In a daring move, Dodgers' manager Burt Shotton safely sent pinch-runner Al Gionfriddo to second on a steal, and so there were still two out with a man in scoring position.

Hard-hitting "Pistol" Pete Reiser, who had not started the game due to a bad knee, was sent up to bat for pitcher Hugh Casey. Yankee manager Bucky Harris surprised the fans by intentionally walking Reiser, which put the winning run on base. Reiser then came out of the game when Eddie Miksis ran for him.

Lead-off hitter Eddie Stanky was to be the next batter, but Shotton replaced him with Cookie Lavagetto, a dead pull hitter who had not had a hit to right field all season. Against the odds, however, Lavagetto then uncorked his famous double off the right field wall, scoring Gionfriddo and Miksis with the tying and winning runs. Lavagetto's hit cost Bevens his no-hitter, and the outcome of the game.

Ironically, the pitch to Lavagetto was the last one Bevens threw in the major leagues. Since it was Lavagetto's last season and he was held hitless in his remaining plate appearances, his last hit as well.

The mot recent brush with a no-hitter in World Series play came in 1964. Pitcher Jim Lonborg gave up ony one hit, a two-out double in the eighth inning by the St. Louis Cardinals' Julian Javier.

When I take time to think about it, I realize that the perfect game in baseball is unique among all sports achievements. Except in bowling, which has the 300 game, baseball has a finite number of outs that must be achieved for a victory. In a regular nine-inning game, that number is 27, and if a pitcher can retire the required number of batters in order, he has pitched the perfect game.

Because of the absolute standard by which the winning or losing of a game is measured, the baseball pitcher knows firsthand the goal for which to strive. Before a game, pitchers, whether it be in little league, pony league, Babe Ruth league, semi-pro, the minors, or in the major leagues, realize that they have a chance for perfection if they can retire in order 27 straight batters.

At the end of five innings in Game Five, the odds of that happening to me or Sal Maglie were astronomical. No one had ever pitched a no-hitter, let alone a perfect game in the World Series.

Facing respective powerful lineups loaded with great hitters in such a pressure-packed game made the potential for such a feat virtually impossible. Coupled with my poor performance in Game Two, no one could have predicted what the next few innings would bring.

—15—

Inning #6—Dodgers

Campy and the Barber

	1	2	3	4	5	6	7	8	9	10	R	H	E
Brooklyn	0	0	0	0	0						0	0	0
Yankees	0	0	0	1	0						1	1	0

THE BROOKLYN DODGERS PITCHER-CATCHER COMBINATION that I faced in the fifth game was indeed a classic one. Behind the plate was the highly respected Roy Campanella who was the second batter for Brooklyn in the sixth inning. On the mound stood the ageless wonder Sal Maglie.

Roy Campanella enjoyed one of the finest reputations of any ball player who ever played the game. Restrained to a wheelchair since his tragic auto accident in 1958, Campanella was a highly-respected executive with the Los Angeles Dodgers until he passed away in 1993.

In his prime, Roy was the Dodgers' answer to our Yogi Berra. Besides being a great hitter, nobody ever handled the catcher's position any better than Campanella did in his ten seasons with the Dodgers.

In 1955, a *Time Magazine* reporter described Campanella, who was 5-feet-9 and weighed just over 200 pounds, as follows:

> On the bench, ruminating over a cud of tobacco, the Brooklyn Dodgers' catcher Roy Campanella is the picture of tranquillity. He never makes an unnecessary move. Take away the uniform, and he would look for all the world like a displaced Buddha in calm contemplation. But the fans sit up when he waddles to his

place behind the plate. A remarkable transformation takes place: The somnolent bulk becomes a quick and agile athlete. After he has strapped on the "tools of ignorance" [a description of catcher's gear attributed to "Muddy" Ruel of the Washington Senators], hunkered down in the close confines of the modern catcher's box, he is the heart of the team.

Roy Campanella was born in a neighborhood known as Nicetown in North Philadelphia. His work ethic was established early when he delivered milk at 2:00 a.m. with a horse and wagon while he was in junior high school.

He first started playing ball as a professional at age 15. He began with the semi-pro Nicetown Giants before catching the attention of the Bacharach Giants, an all Negro semi-pro team, who told his mom they'd pay 35 dollars for two games for Roy's services. Since that was more than Roy's dad made in a whole week on his vegetable truck, Roy's mom allowed him to play.

Roy Campanella's stellar play with those teams led him to the Baltimore Elite Giants and to barnstorming with various teams in the Negro League. For the next few years, Campanella played in the Negro National League in the spring and summer. In the off-months, he headed for such places as Venezuela, Cuba, and Puerto Rico and played there.

Few people remember that Roy Campanella followed close on the heels of Jackie Robinson as one of the first black players to crack a major league roster. Only John Wright and Don Newcombe preceded him when he signed the Dodgers' contract and reported to their farm club at Nashua, New Hampshire, in 1946.

Campanella hit .290 that first season, then moved to Montreal in 1947 and hit .273 in 135 games. Even though he was ready to join the major league club, Branch Rickey sent Campanella to St. Paul in 1948, where he broke the color line in the American Association.

He stayed at St. Paul, where he also played some outfield, until mid-June when the Dodgers called him up. In 1949, his first full year, Campanella became an All-Star when he compiled an impressive .287 batting average along with 22 home runs and 82 RBI's.

Roy Campanella went on to play in five World Series with the Dodgers, and held the major league records by a catcher for home runs (41) and RBI's (142) until they were broken by Johnny Bench in 1970. He was voted the Most Valuable Player in 1951 (33 home runs, 108 RBI's), 1953 (.312 batting average, 41 home runs, 142

RBI's), and 1955 (32 home runs and 107 RBI's), and then into the Baseball Hall of Fame in 1969.

To appreciate Campanella's popularity and the respect of his peers, one only has to remember that 93,103 people, the largest crowd in the history of baseball, turned out for a benefit game to honor the paralyzed catcher for his contributions to the game. Before his automobile accident, many people thought Roy Campanella might very well have become baseball's first black manager.

In that same 1955 *Time Magazine* article, Campanella was quoted as saying:

> Baseball doesn't owe me anything, but I owe it plenty. Everything it's done for me has been good, and nothin's been bad. The day they take that uniform off me, they'll have to rip it off. And when they do . . . they can bury me.

Roy Campanella also said, "Baseball is a man's game, but you have to have a lot of little boy in you to play it."

In the book, *New York City Baseball 1947-1957*, author Harvey Frommer described Sal Maglie:

> In his prime, he was sallow with sunken cheeks, black hair, black eyebrows . . . He looked like an undertaker coming in to pitch. He threw right under the batter's chin . . . Maglie was real intimidating. He took the fire right out of the hitter.

Campanella's battery-mate and my mound opponent in the important fifth game was Salvatore Anthony "The Barber" Maglie, still a great pitcher at age 39. Also known as the "Renaissance Assassin" and "Sinister Sal" (and other nicknames not printable), Maglie was nicknamed "The Barber" by Jim McCully, a sportswriter for *The New York Daily News*. McCully felt the name was appropriate due to Maglie's propensity to throw as close to a batter's neck as possible if the circumstances called for such a pitch.

Milton Shapiro, who wrote the Sal Maglie biography in 1957, aptly describes why he decided to write about Sal "The Barber" Maglie.

Why did I choose to write about Sal Maglie? As a personality his courage and integrity transgress the world of sports. Youngsters can learn much from such a man, things that have to do with living, not pitching. He is above all honest with himself and his abilities. He thinks out a course, makes his decisions and sticks to them. He doesn't know what quit means. While everyone in baseball thought his playing days were over, Maglie knew that given the chance he'd prove them wrong—and he stuck with the conviction. Players respect him for his honesty and forthrightness, as well as his pitching ability.

Born the son of a grocer in Niagara Falls, New York, in 1917, the 21-year-old, 180-pound, sad-eyed, right-hander began his baseball career in 1938.

After an up-and-down career and even being banned from baseball once, Sal Maglie had great years with the New York Giants in 1950, 1951, and 1952 when he won 18 games (2.71 E.R.A.), 23 (tied with teammate Larry Jansen for league lead), and 18 games, respectively. His magic disappeared for a time, and he went 8-9, 14-6, and 9-5 for the Giants in 1953, 1954, and 1955, respectively.

Longtime Brooklyn and Los Angeles Hall of Fame broadcaster Vin Scully remembered Sal Maglie as "the #1 Brooklyn villain."

In the early 1950s, Charley Dressen managed the Dodgers, and Leo Durocher the Giants. The rivalry was feverish, lots of knockdowns . . . lots of retaliations, including a sequence where Sheldon Jones and Reuben Gomez both beamed Carl Furillo, and then Durocher challenged Furillo, who broke his hand in the brawl.

Sal Maglie was at the center of all this. He looked like a villain . . . had a five o'clock beard . . . hat pulled down . . . looked mean and rough.

Scully also remembered that Maglie gave the Dodger hitters fits. "He'd zip the ball inside . . . then out . . . then back in," Scully recalled.

Another view of Maglie came from sportswriter Marshall Smith, who once described the imposing Maglie as follows:

When Maglie is on the mound, the enemy batter and fans see the most menacing face in baseball, with its famous blue-black 5 o'clock shadow, hawk nose, down-turned mouth, and hooded eyes. Maglie also possesses an encyclopedia knowledge of batters' weaknesses and the skill to exploit those weaknesses. He can throw the ball exactly where he wants to, and hitters complain after facing him four times in one afternoon that they never saw the same pitch twice.

Maglie's ability to place the ball where he wanted it was also described by Marshall:

Maglie's cardinal rule is to never put a ball in the strike zone unless it is low, and with his phenomenal control he can achieve this. When he throws high, it is intended as a waste pitch, or is armed coolly and deliberately to brush the batter away from the plate, and keep him apprehensive and off-balance. When Maglie "throws at their ear" he lets fly as if he is genuinely interested in finding out whether a baseball can penetrate a human skull.

Another ball player told the *Boston Globe*: "Maglie could look a pitch through you. He was so mean he'd get you with sliders. You'd lean forward and think you were safe, and the thing would break right off your neck."

Even his future catcher with the Dodgers, Roy Campanella, used to say: "Maglie's pitching tomorrow; bring your football helmets."

In an interview before the fifth game, Sal Maglie told a reporter: "When I'm pitching, I figure the plate is mine . . . and I don't like anybody getting too close to it." His opponents obviously didn't agree, because they knew Sal's inside deliveries were no accident, as he had a great reputation for pinpoint control.

The 1956 season saw Maglie win 13, while losing just five. His victories included a no-hitter against the Phillies in September during the peak of the pennant race.

Maglie was runner-up to Don Newcombe in the League MVP and Cy Young Award voting. He also had won the opening game of the '56 Series by beating the Yankees 6-3.

Dodger roommate Dale Mitchell attributed Maglie's newfound success to his ability to study opposing hitters. "You don't want to bother Sal when the other team's batting because he's studying all the time. . . . Even if he's never pitched to a man, Sal will know his weaknesses."

Sal Maglie was known as a "money" pitcher. Any club that Sal was on knew damn well that when the chips were on the line, they could expect to receive an outstanding performance from him. With that wicked curve ball of his, and his reputation for having a nasty disposition, batters never got all that comfortable at the plate against him.

Over his career, Maglie ended up with 119 victories and just 62 defeats. Ironically he joined me on the Yankee pitching staff when the Yanks bought his contract in late 1957.

Sal Maglie was the third batter of the inning following Campanella. Leading off, Carl Furillo fouled off a high outside fast ball, and then hit a low outside curve to Martin for a pop-out to become the sixteenth straight Dodger out in the game.

Before Roy Campanella, 4 of 13 in the Series, strode to the plate broadcaster Vin Scully observed "Don Larsen's spinning quite a web today,... retiring 16 in a row."

Yogi Berra's strategy on Campanella was to try to either pitch him low and away, or in on the hands where he couldn't get much of a swing. Berra told me I had to be careful though, because an inside pitch that was too high would end up in the bleacher seats for a home run.

I had fooled Campanella with a good waist-high fast ball in the third, but this time I stopped him with a low outside curve that the Dodger catcher popped to Billy Martin. Campanella was the seventeenth straight batter to go down in order. I had now thrown a total of 55 pitches in the game.

Sal Maglie became the obstacle that stood between me and six no-hit, perfect innings. Yogi gave me the sign for a fast ball, and I threw a good, hard one that became strike one when Maglie swung through it. The count became no balls, two strikes when Sal swung at another fast ball and missed.

I threw a fast ball on the outside corner that I hoped the "Barber" would chase, but Maglie laid off, and the count was one and two. Maglie then fouled off two straight pitches, and let a slider go by that was high and outside.

With the count two and two, I threw a good, popping fast ball for a swinging strike three, and the Yankee stadium crowd gave me a huge ovation.

Vin Scully brought my performance to life for radio listeners with his words of praise. He said, "Mr. Don Larsen has been brilliant ...18 men in a row."

The good news as I returned to the dugout was that I had recorded 18 consecutive outs. The bad news was that I still only had a 1-0 lead.

Inning #6—Yankees

A Risky Bunt

	1	2	3	4	5	6	7	8	9	10	R	H	E
Brooklyn	0	0	0	0	0	0					0	0	0
Yankees	0	0	0	1	0						1	1	0

PLAYING THE CORNERS FOR THE YANKEES in Game Five were Andy Carey and Joe Collins, two first-rate defensive infielders.

The son of a judge, 35-year-old Andrew Arthur Carey was a 6-foot, 200-pounder. He and I shared one extremely important characteristic. We both loved to eat and eat big! While I may have garnered a legendary reputation for having a large appetite, it was Carey who was the king of that sport.

It wasn't unusual to see Andy polish off a few sides of beef, all the side trimmings, and a quart or two of milk without batting an eyelash. He was the only guy I can recall who I couldn't keep up with.

Andy Carey was born in Oakland, California, in 1931, where he starred as a ball player in his early years. In his senior year in high school, Andy hit .350 as a first baseman to make first team all-county. He also pitched well enough to make the second team, a feat never accomplished before.

Andy could very well have been a teammate of mine at St. Mary's College if I had opted to accept a scholarship there. I didn't, but Carey did attend and played well both in his freshman year and later as a third baseman in a summer league in Weeser, Idaho, where he hit .400.

Carey signed with the Yankees in 1951 for a bonus of $60,000. The right-handed ball player joined the Yankee major league club in 1952, after spending two years in the minors with the Kansas City Blues, managed by "Old Twinkletoes," George Selkirk, the man who replaced Babe Ruth. In 1953, at the age of 22, Andy Carey played in 51 games at short, third, and second, and hit a respectable .321.

With Gil McDougald who wore #12 playing mostly second in 1954, Carey more or less became the regular third baseman for the Yankees, and hit .302 while driving in 65 runs for the second-place Yankee club. A .257 average followed in 1955 when Andy played in 135 games while Billy Hunter and Phil Rizzuto manned shortstop and McDougald again played mostly second base.

After the 1955 season, and during a trip to the Far East, Andy secured his post as third baseman when McDougald cemented his claim to Phil Rizzuto's shortstop position. Andy was rarin' to go when the 1956 season came. He had a great defensive year even if his .237 batting average fell short of both his and Casey's expectations.

Apparently Stengel first envisioned Andy as Phil Rizzuto's heir apparent at shortstop when he came up to the Yankees. While it's hard to believe, Carey had the guts to say no to the "old man" when Stengel brought up the shortstop idea.

"I was a bull-headed, strong-willed kid," Carey said, "and I made it clear to not only Casey, but the others that I was a third baseman."

According to Carey, he and Stengel didn't see eye to eye on a number of things. Carey's refusal to play anything but third base didn't endear him to Stengel. They also argued about whether Carey should be a "pull" or "spray" hitter.

Andy recalls:

> The old man and I never did get along too well. I was not one of his favorites, and he would make me mad to get me to play better. One way was to make me try to be a spray hitter when I'd always been a pull hitter.
>   For some reason, after I'd hit .321 [1953], they wanted me to become a spray hitter. I had been a pull hitter all my life ... I tried to adjust and hit .257 and then .237 in 1956.

With some bitterness, Carey said, "If they would have left me alone ... no telling what I could have done."

Andy Carey was someone who knew what he wanted and went after it with determination and confidence. In fact, at the beginning of spring training in 1956, he drew a line between third and short and told all our infielders in no uncertain terms that third base was his and his alone.

I had had two brushes with no-hit fame during my career, and Andy Carey was involved in both of them. The first one came in 1953, when as a member of the St. Louis Browns, I pitched seven no-hit innings only to lose my bid when his pop fly fell in front of Jimmy Dyck's feet. Carey then broke up my second attempt in 1954 when he singled after the ball hit the plate and bounced high in the air toward the mound in the eighth inning.

Across the diamond from Andy Carey was Scranton, Pennsylvania-born, 33-year-old, former coal miner Joe Collins, who struggled through 13 years in the minors before spending nine seasons with the Yankees. "Lefty," as he was known, played little in his first few years with the club, but finally appeared in 125 games in 1951, batting .286 with 48 runs batted in.

Joe Collins, who batted and threw left-handed, became the Yankees regular first baseman in 1952. He hit a solid .280 with 18 home runs that year. Seventeen more homers followed in 1953. In 1954, the Yankee stalwart, who wore #15, hit 12 more.

Collins, who also played the outfield, and "Moose" Skowron divided up the first-base duties in 1955. Joe hit .234 with 13 home runs. Skowron played many more games at first base than Joe did in his final year with the Yankees in 1956, when his batting average dwindled to .225.

Andy Carey led off the bottom of the sixth inning by singling sharply on Sal Maglie's first pitch. I came to the plate next, and everyone on the planet knew that I was going to bunt. Hitting is something that I always loved to do, and I'm proud that I still hold the major league record for consecutive hits by a pitcher with 7 in 1953.

I ended up with a lifetime batting average of .242, hit a total of 14 home runs while knocking in 72. My .371 slugging percentage is one of the highest in major league history for a pitcher.

On August 22nd of 1956, I hit a grand slam home run off Frank Sullivan of the Red Sox. Five days earlier I'd hit a pinch-hit home run against Ike Delock of that club. He was really upset. Pitchers aren't pleased when another pitcher hits a round tripper off them.

When I'd hit a dinger, the boys in the dugout would give me the silent treatment. That was tradition. Nobody acknowledged the at-bat. Pitchers enjoyed these moments, though, and could name the opposing pitcher they hit the homer off of years after it happened. Recently, Bob Grim, the 1954 A.L. Rookie of the Year, kidded Hank Bauer and Moose Skowron, who between them had hit .390. "I hit four in my whole career," he said. "But one year I hit one home run in seven at-bats. Bet my percentage was better than yours."

Being a good hitter made me more valuable to the club and I was known to be a threat at the plate. In fact, one sportswriter described me for his readers after the game:

> Probably the best description of Don Larsen as a major league pitcher...can be gleaned from a line under his name in baseball's registry, which reads: "Outstanding achievement—established major league record for most consecutive hits by a pitcher [7] July 31 and August 5, 1953". This sums up Larsen's rating among major league pitchers. He was a better hitter than a pitcher.

While I might take issue with that statement, I did know that a good bunt was what the Yankees needed in the 6th inning. Stunned by a thunderous ovation when I came to the plate, I was unable to produce on the first two pitches and ended up with two strikes. Good sound baseball strategy dictated that I give up any idea of a bunt. That's apparently what the Dodgers figured, so Jackie Robinson moved back to the edge of the grass behind and to the right of third base.

Most managers would probably have had me hit away in that situation, but Casey gave me the green light to bunt. I came through with a good one out in front of the plate to sacrifice Carey to second.

Casey's unorthodox strategy worked when Hank Bauer, 5 for 20 in the Series, smacked a clean single between third and short. When Andy Carey crossed the plate, I had a 2 to 0 lead. Joe Collins kept the potential for a big inning alive when he moved Bauer to third with a single of his own.

At that point, I felt we had Sal Maglie on the ropes. With everything having gone so well all day, I expected Mickey to blast one to kingdom come.

Dodger manager Walter Alston came out to talk to Sal Maglie. In those days, the rules permitted only the pitcher, the catcher, the manager, and one infielder to gather at the mound. The conference broke up rather quickly, but then Alston walked back to talk to Maglie just before he crossed the first base fair/foul line.

I don't know whether Alston ever considered taking Maglie out. His decision to leave him in went against the book, since Mantle had homered earlier.

Maglie didn't let Alston down, but he was fortunate that Mickey hit the ball right at someone. His screaming grounder bolted into Hodges' mitt for an easy out. The opportunity to bury Maglie was gone when Bauer got hung up between third and home and was tagged out by Jackie Robinson for the third out. The official scoreboard read 3-2-5-2-5.

There are a lot of ups and downs during a game, and Mantle's out was a real disappointment. I've often wondered what would have happened if Mick had hit a home run. That would have made the score 5-0, and I'm sure I would have relaxed a bit. Maybe too much, like in Game Two when I blew the big lead.

Mickey's out made me grit my teeth and head for the mound. Six innings of shut-out ball wouldn't mean a thing if I couldn't stop the Dodgers in the seventh.

─17─

The Men in Blue

As the game progressed, I wasn't the only one in Yankee Stadium who was nervous. Sitting up in the press box were the official scorers for the game, Lyall Smith of Detroit, and his two assistants, Gus Steiger and Jerry Mitchell, both from New York. Any close calls regarding hits or errors would be closely scrutinized in the years to come if a controversial decision had to be made by one of the three men. Through six innings, there had been no need for much decision making on their part, but the potential still existed.

Besides the official scorers, six umpires stood ready in the field, all realizing that I had been perfect for six innings. Being chosen to umpire the World Series was an honor, but each knew they might be involved in a close play that could change the destiny of the game.

Forty-two-year-old Hank Soar was the first base umpire who had made the close "out" call on the Andy Carey/Gil McDougald play of Jackie Robinson's ground ball in the second inning. He would serve the American League as a well-respected umpire for 22 years, but Soar was equally well-known for his great prowess as a collegiate and professional football player.

Soar first starred at Providence and then went on to play ten years for the New York football Giants in the 1930s and 1940s. He made national headlines in 1938 when he caught the winning touchdown pass from Ed Dankowski to win the National Football League Championship game against the Green Bay Packers.

Hank Soar also was an umpire in a no-hit game pitched by Nolan Ryan. He also made headlines in 1971 when the volatile Frank Lane of the Milwaukee Brewers lambasted him for calling a game on account of rain with four-and-a-half innings in the book and the Brewers leading Kansas City 4-1. Lane's comment that there were "only three sound umpires in the league" irritated Soar, who retorted by calling Lane a "showboat."

National League veteran Lynton R. (Dusty) Boggess was stationed at second base. A native of Terrell, Texas, Dusty always told friends the nickname came from someone who coined the phrase from his habit of picking up a pile of dust and rubbing it through his reddish brown hair before he went to bat in the minors.

Boggess was a short, squat man with a great sense of humor. He started his career in baseball after being a star player in different sports at Waco Texas High School. Dusty then played professional ball in the minor leagues with several St. Louis Cardinal farm clubs in the 1920s.

Dusty Boggess also gained notoriety at the time by playing every position in a game three times. He was a .275 lifetime hitter and had his best year in 1925 when he hit .317 with 38 runs batted in. In 1932, the future great National League umpire turned baseball executive by purchasing the Muskogee team of the Western League and becoming owner, manager, player, groundskeeper, concessions manager, and business manager of the club.

Dusty Boggess began his umpiring career with the Western League in 1939. He showed his desire to umpire by hitch-hiking 1,700 miles to Mitchell, South Dakota, to begin his duties when he had no money for bus fare. Work in the Western League, and then the Texas and International League spurred a call from the National League, which he joined in 1944.

Dusty Boggess worked four World Series, five All-Star games, and was present for 14 no-hitters. He caused quite a controversy the year of his retirement in 1963, when he accused the 1962 Los Angeles Dodgers of blowing the pennant because they were all obsessed with Maury Wills's attempts to break the all-time stolen base record.

Boggess, who would end up calling Wills safe on his record-breaking stolen base attempt, told reporters at the time that the hoopla about Wills caused the Dodgers, especially second-place hitter Jim Gilliam, to lose their concentration with their own play. Several Dodgers players reacted strongly to Boggess's comments, but Boggess held his ground.

In his 19 years as a major league umpire, Dusty Boggess told a Dallas newspaper just after his retirement that Game Five was the biggest of his career.

> I was on second base—the best spot in the whole stadium next to the pitcher's mound. There has never been anything like it, especially those last three innings.
>
> The stands were packed, but I couldn't hear a sound—not even a vendor selling hot dogs. Billy Martin had been hollering like a canary for seven innings, but even he was quiet toward the last.

Thirty-seven-year-old American League umpire Larry Napp patrolled third base. A former catcher who advanced as high as Triple-A, Napp had a look-see with the New York Giants in 1948 before deciding to become a major league umpire.

Pug-faced Larry Napp was a tough cookie who had called two no-hitters. He had been a boxer as a kid, and only gave it up after doctors advised him to quit when his nose was broken several times. Using his expertise, he trained several Golden Gloves boxing champions while with the Navy between 1942 and 1947.

Napp went on to umpire in three World Series (1954, 1963, and 1969) in addition to the 1956 Series, and in four All-Star games (1952, 1957, 1961, and 1968). He joined the American League as the assistant supervisor of officials.

Larry Napp was known as a take-charge guy who didn't take guff from anyone. Upon his death in 1993, a friend said that "Larry didn't let anybody run over him. I guess that came from being a boxer."

That type of demeanor came in handy when Napp had several run-ins with Billy Martin when he was manager of the Detroit Tigers. Those differences of opinion with Napp resulted in Martin accusing the umpire and his crew of "costing the Tigers ten or eleven games." Napp was even held out of two Detroit series after death threats were made against him by outraged Tiger fans.

Twenty-five year National League veteran umpire Tom Gorman toed the left-field line during the fifth game. From the Fordham Road section of the Bronx, Gorman was one of the most respected umpires ever to wear the blue uniform, as evidenced by his being awarded the prestigious Bill Slocum Award in 1970 for "long and distinguished service to baseball."

In a newspaper article describing the presentation of the award, Arthur Daley of the *New York Times* described Gorman as follows:

> Tom is a big and hearty man with the majestic look of an umpire and he commands respect because he administers decisions with even-handed justice and even-tempered finality. One advantage he has is his bubbling Irish sense of humor that can lighten tense moments before they get out of hand.

In his childhood days, Tom Gorman had been a great athlete at Power Memorial High School in New York. When the great Lew Alcindor went on those scoring rampages at Power 25 years later, the basketball records he broke belonged to Gorman.

Tom Gorman later became a left-handed pitcher with the New York Giants in 1939 and 1940, but five years of interruption in the military ended his chances for success. When a friend suggested he might make a great umpire, Gorman resisted, but finally he decided to give the career a shot.

In 1970, Tom Gorman told Arthur Daley:

> The first baseball game I ever umpired . . . had Don Newcombe pitching and Roy Campanella catching. I thought it was easy. Three days later I changed my mind. I called out the winning run at home plate and angry fans ripped my uniform off me.

During his career, Gorman was involved in many memorable games, including Warren Spahn's and Lew Burdette's no-hitters and the day that Bob Gibson broke Carl Erskine's record for strikeouts

in the World Series with 17. He umpired in five World Series and
five All-Star games.

Later, Gorman co-authored the book, *Three and Two,* with
famed sportswriter Jerome Holtzman, and described the umpire's
creed: "An umpire . . . should never ask for mercy or ask to be
forgiven. A ball field isn't a church. Look at it this way . . . the ball
players miss a lot more plays than we do."

Forty-year old American League umpire Ed Runge was assigned the right field line chores for Game Five. It was Ed's first
World Series and he had been a major league umpire for only three
years.

Runge was a native of New York, having been raised in Buf-
falo. He was a "mediocre" first baseman in a semi-pro league in
Canada, according to him, but did some managing in the St.
Catherine League where he handled a young pitcher named Sal
Maglie. He recalled "The Barber":

> Maglie was a hard thrower even back then, with a "mean, never
> afraid to pitch well inside to hitters' streak to him. He was out-
> standing, won nine or ten for us and lost but one . . we went to
> the finals that year, and Sal lost a close one for us in the last game
> he pitched for us.

Ed Runge started his career in the Big State League in 1947
down in Texas umpiring games for $300 a month. He moved up
the ladder very quickly though, spending the 1949 season in the
Pacific Coast League where he watched a 17-year-old kid named
Billy Martin play infield for the Oakland Oaks. In 1954, Runge was
finally called up to the American League.

The fact that Ed Runge was selected with such little experience is testimony to the respect with which he was held by his
peers. Many believe he was the best "balls and strikes" umpire to
have ever been in the game, and he certainly deserves the reputation as one of the great gentlemen to have been involved in baseball.

Ed Runge used to tell everyone that it was never the .300
hitters who complained, but the .220 ones. He also told sports-

writer Jack Murphy, whom the San Diego Padre baseball stadium is named for, that "Ted Williams was the best judge of the strike zone he ever saw, and Mickey Mantle was the worst."

He went on to say, "I respected the ball player's right to complain so long as he didn't swear at me." The respect he earned from players, managers, and umpires alike resulted in Ed working three World Series and five All-Star games while in the major leagues.

Ed Runge was present on the night when Roger Maris had a chance to hit his 60th home run in 154 games, tying Babe Ruth's great record. When Baltimore Orioles manager Lum Harris brought famed knuckle ball pitcher Hoyt Wilhelm in to pitch to him in the ninth, home plate umpire Runge recalled for Jack Murphy the fact that Maris was cool as could be, asking him, "Listen, Ed, what does this guy throw?"

Behind the plate for Game Five was 61-year-old Ralph A."Babe" Pinelli. The '56 Series would be his last in baseball; he was retiring as a National League Umpire.

A former professional player with 22 umpiring seasons under his belt, Pinelli was the man on the spot in the ninth inning. He would decide the critical calls of balls and strikes in the ninth.

Babe Pinelli later told reporters that he broke down and cried after the game, but not out of happiness or sorrow. It was because neither I nor my Yankee teammates had come up to him after the game and congratulated *him*. Pinelli said:

> Hell, there was a lot of pressure on Larsen, but look at the pressure there was on *me* . . . I had to call the balls and strikes! Just look back . . . neither of the teams put up an argument over my calls at any time during the game . . . Umpires never get the credit they deserve.

Babe was right to give me hell. I made a mistake by not thanking Babe and the other umpires. I just got caught up in all the hoopla and forgot. That was a mistake, because they called a great game.

My understanding was that Babe Pinelli the player was never a terror in the field or at bat, but he did have his moments. On July

4, 1929, he sat out the first game of the double-header for San Francisco. Slugger Smead Jolley hit two homers to lead the Seals to victory over Seattle in the Pacific Coast League.

In Game Two, Pinelli, who normally batted second, was listed as the clean-up hitter. Responding to the challenge, Pinelli cracked out six hits, including three home runs, two of them grand slams, and knocked in 12 runs.

To show how phenomenal the day was for Pinelli, in 167 games that season he hit only five homers and batted in 65 runs.

In 1934, when Pinelli was being called up to the majors to umpire, a reporter of unknown identity described his background and demeanor:

> Pinelli's rise is an example of what an ambitious athlete can do, if he sets his mind to succeeding in some chosen role. Even as long ago as when he was playing a peppery third base for the Cincinnati Reds, Babe was looking forward to becoming an umpire after his active days were over. He kept the idea in mind through the years. Frequently, before a game, the Italian would go to the umpires' dressing room and ask them questions about their work, their duties and their experiences. He watched them closely on the field, picked out the best features of the work of each man and was prepared to step out in his new field of endeavor when the call came.
>
> Notwithstanding his interest and desire to call balls and strikes, Pinelli never received much encouragement from his associates. He is a genial, likable fellow, with innumerable friends, but always was a hot-tempered cocky young fella whose Latin blood boiled over easily. Babe never exactly looked for trouble, but neither did he sidestep it when it came his way. He would take on challengers, regardless of age, weight, or previous experience—the bigger they came, the harder they fell, was Babe's creed.

To illustrate Babe Pinelli's zest for the game, that same reporter also described Pinelli's determination to find any way to win:

> Babe's specialty in the good old days when he was playing, was the hidden ball trick. He would have the ball under his right armpit and engage the runner in conversation until the latter strayed off the bag and Pinelli would suddenly pounce on him like a puma. He got a bigger kick out of pulling that stunt that some fellows got from making a home run.

Even though Babe Pinelli, who called six no-hitters in his career, had never missed an assignment during his tenure as an umpire that stretched more than 3,400 games, he almost never answered the call for the most important game of his life. In Game Four, Gil McDougald sliced a vicious line drive that curved right along with Pinelli as he tried to get out of the way. The ball hit the umpire in the pit of the stomach and knocked him back to the ground. He sported a black and blue bruise that he jokingly called, "a badge of honor."

The day before, broadcaster Mel Allen told his viewers that "Pinelli has by his solar plexus a black and blue mark. Since he's a National League Umpire, he remarked that it was the first time he had Will Harridge's [American League President] autograph."

After a good night's rest Pinelli felt better, and so the tireless umpire made his way to home plate to meet with the other umpires for the pre-game conference.

That day, joining Pinelli and the other umpires at the plate were Casey and Walt Alston. Pinelli remembers no unusual discussion among them, but recalls nearly every pitch on that fateful day.

In an interview with a New York reporter, he described his umpiring of the game:

In the fifth game, the first batter was Jim Gilliam of the Dodgers. The Yankee pitcher—a rawboned youngster named Don Larsen, with a fair season record of 11 wins, 5 losses, threw Gilliam five pitches. On a two and two count, Larsen bent a fast curve over the low inside corner. Gilliam was caught flatfooted. "Out," I shouted. Then I thought, "ooh-oh, Larsen's got it today."

From then on, I was in the concentrating "trance" of a good plate man. Judging balls and strikes accurately is a matter of fine timing and rhythm, of bobbing and weaving so that the catcher never blocks your view of the ball. Everything else is blotted from your mind. At 90 mph, a baseball is over the plate in 1/75th of a second—you don't even dare blink. So it wasn't until the sixth inning that I realized something startling was under way. Glancing at the scoreboard, I saw all of those goose-eggs.

It hit me harder than McDougald's liner that I might be about to umpire the first no-hit, no-run game in World Series history.

What a spot to be on. By the eighth inning, with Larsen showing a perfect shutout, 50,000,000 fans were pulling heart and soul for him. A base on balls called by me now would go down as the Crime of the Century. To bat came big Gil Hodges. "I'll get to this guy," I heard him mutter.

Until then, Larsen's control had been uncanny. But then I had to do it. Two of his first four pitches to Hodges I called balls. Both were only inches off the plate. But to an umpire—no matter what the stakes—a slight miss is as much as a mile. Hodges let me breathe again by lining out to third base.

Dodger pitcher Clem Labine, who was in the bullpen for the Fifth Game, says he knew the Dodgers were in for a long day when he saw I was getting my curve ball over. "The Dodgers were a team that hit mistakes," he said, "and Larsen wasn't making any. The off-speed curve ball was being thrown for strikes and I could tell we were in trouble because very few of our batters were great curveball hitters."

Clem has also reluctantly admitted to me that in the late innings he began to subconsciously root for me. "As the game went along, I thought to myself that this one could be one I'd tell my grandchildren about. I truly believe it's the first time I ever rooted for the opposition. And certainly for a Yankee. In fact, I wanted to be out there in Larsen's shoes."

The cigarette I sucked on between innings was lit with a shaking left hand. At the time, I'd gladly have traded Clem spots, but instead I was headed out to face the Dodgers in the seventh.

—18—

Inning #7—Dodgers

21 in a Row

	1	2	3	4	5	6	7	8	9	10	R	H	E
Brooklyn	0	0	0	0	0	0					0	0	0
Yankees	0	0	0	1	0	1					2	4	0

EVERY CHAMPIONSHIP TEAM MUST HAVE a power-packed player who excites fellow teammates with his leadership and strong performance, both at bat and on the field.

The seventh inning of Game Five featured two of the best who ever played the game, shortstop Pee Wee Reese of the Dodgers and second baseman Billy Martin for the Yankees.

In 1940, future Hall of Famer Harold "Pee Wee" Reese, born July 23, 1918, in Ekron, Kentucky, was purchased by the Dodgers from the Boston Red Sox where he couldn't crack the lineup due to the presence of the great Joe Cronin. That was the same year that Lou Boudreau first made his mark at Cleveland and a year before Phil Rizzuto came into his own as shortstop for the Yankees.

Manager Leo "The Lip" Durocher says he knew he had a winner the first time he laid eyes on Reese, who acquired his nickname due to his interest in shooting marbles (a pee wee is the small marble aimed at by the shooter) as a boy.

Durocher, as quoted by Roger Kahn in *The Era*, told reporters, "What I got in this young feller is the Babe Ruth of marbles . . . On our ball club, he's a rookie. In the world of marbles, he's an old man."

A ten-time All-Star, the right-handed "Little Colonel's" best year was 1954 when he hit .309. He ended up with a career average of .269 in 16 seasons with the Dodgers and more than 2,100 hits over his major league career.

A 1984 inductee into the Hall of Fame along with Luis Aparicio, Harmon Killebrew, and Don Drysdale, Pee Wee Reese was one of those take-charge, smart players who challenged everybody around him to play better.

Teammate Jackie Robinson once said, "No one realizes what he [Reese] has meant to the Brooklyn club. No one, that is, but his teammates."

Duke Snider, in his book, *The Duke of Flatbush*, was even stronger in his description of Reese.

> Knowing Pee Wee Reese and playing on the same team with him have been two of the blessings in my life. Reese was our captain, and to this day, 40 years after those magical times began, we still address him by that title. He was our unquestioned leader. He led by his example, making so many big plays and getting so many big hits over his 16 years in the majors, all of them with the Dodgers. Without Pee Wee, we wouldn't have won as many pennants as we did. And when we finally won our first World Series, beating the Yankees in 1955, it was only right that the last out of the Series, a ground ball by Elston Howard, was hit to Pee Wee.

Along with second-baseman Junior Gilliam and center-fielder Snider, Pee Wee Reese provided the Dodgers, who won seven pennants during his tenure, with great defense up the middle. He was a reliable hitter who could manipulate his bat in the number two spot and do all the little things that help win a game.

New York Giants pitcher Hal Schumacher once paid Reese, who had a gentleness that hid a fiery desire to compete, the ultimate compliment by saying: "Take Pee Wee Reese and any eight men, and you've got a team."

Former teammate George Shuba said Reese, the captain of the Dodgers, enjoyed great respect from the players. Shuba also loved his sense of humor. "One day Reese and I were talking about fly balls coming my way. 'Open your mouth, George,' he said, 'then you'll have two chances to catch a ball.'"

Pee Wee Reese, who was hardly a "Pee Wee" at 5-feet-9 and 175 pounds, was also known to have been the first player on the Dodgers team to befriend Jackie Robinson when Jackie broke the color line in the major leagues. Unlike some of his teammates, Reese, who wore #1 on the back of his uniform, respected

Robinson's ability as a ball player and helped the troubled Robinson through the tough times he encountered from teammates and fans alike.

Ironically, when Reese first came up, the Dodgers also had a shortstop/manager by the name of Leo Durocher, but Durocher was ready to hand the job over to someone else, and welcomed Reese with open arms. It proved to be a perfect fit as the two combative Dodgers solidified a strong relationship that became the heart and soul of the Brooklyn teams for years to come.

With Reese at the controls, the Dodgers took the pennant in 1941 for the first time in 21 years. They proceeded to add six more in the decade that followed.

Pee Wee endeared himself to the Dodgers' fans with his hustle and durability and he averaged nearly 140 games played a year during his career. In the 1952 Series, Reese was tough as nails, tying Mickey Mantle for the Series lead with ten hits and a .345 average.

In the seventh inning of Game Five, Pee Wee Reese, 6 for 20 in the Series, followed Junior Gilliam, who had been called out on strikes in the first and had bounced to second in the fourth. This time, I started the Dodgers' second sacker out with a fast ball on the inside corner that Gilliam thought was too low.

Babe Pinelli called it a strike, and with the count 0-1, I threw another fast ball, but it missed the outside corner evening the count at 1-1. Gilliam then fouled off a nasty slider, and I had him in the hole one ball and two strikes.

The fourth pitch to Gilliam could easily have been a hit, because I didn't fool him at all with a slider that didn't have a lot of zip to it. Fortunately for me, it was way outside.

The sportswriters and ballplayers had a lot to say about my curveball after the game, but I really didn't have a good curve ball. Those were mainly sliders I threw.

This one was hit by Gilliam to shortstop. Ever the defensive specialist, Gil McDougald made a tough play easy when he scooped up the liner out of the dirt and threw to Collins at first for the first out in the seventh.

Even though I was moving along without giving up a hit, I tried to focus on the task at hand. Others were starting to take what was happening quite seriously.

"From the seventh on, broadcasters start to take the potential for a no-hitter seriously," Dodger announcer Vin Scully said.

"Until then we don't get too excited, but when a pitcher continues a no-hitter into the seventh, I start to think about it."

Nineteen straight batters had been retired as Pee Wee Reese stepped to the plate. Ordinarily, Pee Wee and the other Dodgers might be taking a pitch here and there to see how my control was, but that was tough to do, because I had established over the first six-plus innings that I was going to be around the plate.

No matter how good your "stuff" is, if the control isn't there, then the batter can stand at the plate and wait for his pitch. Getting behind hitters is bad in the majors, and a lot of pitchers ended up in the minors or out of baseball because they couldn't get the ball over the plate.

Walking batters is a nightmare for managers because there is no defense against the base on balls. Good defensive players make no difference if the ball isn't put into play, and walks almost always end up as runs that put a team behind the eight ball.

To the ordinary fan, it might seem that any major league pitcher should be able to throw the ball across the plate from 60 feet, 6 inches and put it squarely within the dimensions of the strike zone. That probably is true, but there's more to it than being able to throw it across the strike zone. That ball had better be going at least 85-90 mph, be on the "paint," either on the inside or outside corner, or be curving, dipping, or knuckling so the batter can't hit it into another time zone.

Lack of control is usually a result of overthrowing the ball or throwing pitches that you're not capable of. That's why a catcher's input is critically important, because a pitcher needs to stay within his ability to be successful.

Why I had such incredible pinpoint control on October 8, 1956, is still a puzzle to me. It was the best it ever was. Just two games earlier, I had trouble finding the plate, but that day my rhythm with the no wind-up was excellent, and I delivered the ball where I wanted to.

As I mentioned, I threw the fast ball with my fingers across the seams so it would rise, and with the seams so it would dip down and into the right-handed batter, and away from the lefty.

The slider was thrown with my second finger hugging the seam, and my thumb curled under the ball. I threw a hard slider, and my ability to throw it for strikes is responsible for most of my success in the perfect game.

I never had a great curve ball. I tried to get my fingernail on the middle finger in the seam of the ball and kind of snap my wrist to get a rotating spin that would keep the pitch down. Having a great curve ball helped make the fast ball seem even faster. I threw a slow curve decently well, but I never used it too much.

Being able to put the ball in a particular spot was a tremendous advantage for me as I continued to face the Dodger lineup for the third time. Since the hitters had gained a feel for my speed and different pitches, location was of paramount importance.

As with every Dodger hitter, Yogi Berra and I had discussed Pee Wee Reese before the game. We both knew that he had a Jekyll-and-Hyde personality when it came to his hitting strategy. If he was playing at Ebbets Field, Pee Wee had the reputation of taking a pitch or two before he got serious about hitting the ball. I never heard why Pee Wee handled his at-bats that way, but a lot of the time he came up with Junior Gilliam on base. I'm sure he wanted to give Gilliam a chance to steal a base.

Pee Wee had a lot of success taking pitches for a while, but after a time all pitchers knew that they could get away with one and maybe two pitches right down the alley. When that happened, I got the advantage, and tried to get Reese to hit a bad pitch out of the strike zone. All the Yankee pitchers knew about Reese. If Gilliam was on, he'd take a pitch. If not, he was much more aggressive.

"I knew Larsen's control had been great all day," Pee Wee Reese told reporters after the game. "When I came up in the seventh, I was looking to punch one into the outfield on the first pitch."

Luckily for me, I threw Reese one of my best sliders, low and away, and Pee Wee fouled it off for strike one.

On the second pitch, Yogi Berra called for a fast ball. I threw one out over the plate but Reese got under it. He hit the ball to Mickey Mantle in center field for the second out of the inning.

Keeping Reese off base three times was a clear victory for me, not only because of his leadership of the Dodgers, but also because Casey probably was trying to gauge how long I could continue to pitch. If Pee Wee had gotten on base in the seventh, Casey would have started thinking about a relief pitcher, because I'd already gone further than he'd ever expected.

Twenty batters had made 20 consecutive outs, and center-fielder Duke Snider, now 4 for 16 in the Series, came to bat with the bases empty.

Snider had flied to Bauer in the first, and taken a nasty slider for a called third strike in the fourth after the near miss foul-ball home run. I knew Duke would be looking to cut the Dodgers' deficit in half with a long home run. My only hope was to get him out with outside high or low fast balls.

Again Yogi Berra's sage wisdom surfaced. After throwing a slider for ball one too far outside, I threw an outside and low fast ball and got Snider to lift a fly to Enos Slaughter in left.

Seven no-hit, perfect innings. 74 pitches (11 over the minimum), 52 strikes, 22 balls. Twenty-one up and 21 down. Never in my high school, service, semi-pro, or professional career had I ever done such a thing. Never had I even dreamed of it.

While my blood pressure had gone to the tower, television broadcaster Vin Scully played down the achievement, telling his audience "Don Larsen has now retired 21 men in a row."

Sitting in our dugout between innings was now like being in a morgue. The usual chatter and banter between the players was replaced by dead silence. I felt like I didn't have a friend in the world.

The tension of the moment made everyone very superstitious. To even *think* of a no-hitter would be enough to jinx my chances, so nobody wanted to say anything or do anything to rock the boat. When Mantle casually deposited himself in a seat that Billy Hunter formally had, Hunter very politely asked him to move, and Mickey quickly shifted to another spot.

Pitcher Tom Morgan told me later he had to go to the bathroom, but was afraid to even leave the bullpen, so he just held it for the rest of the game. There are several versions of what I said to Mickey and what he said back to me about the chances for a no-hitter.

Mickey Mantle's account of that conversation during the ball game notwithstanding, I came back to the dugout after the Dodger seventh and said to Mickey Mantle, "Look at the scoreboard! Wouldn't it be something? . . . two more innings to go." Mantle never said a word, but headed for the other end of the dugout. It was like a big, black shadow surrounded me and kept me apart from everyone else. To be honest, the silence was awful, unlike the usual dugout buzz where everybody is kiddin' around. It was like I was the uninvited guest. Nobody wanted anything to do with me.

—19—

Inning #7—Yankees

Looking for Insurance

	1	2	3	4	5	6	7	8	9	10	R	H	E
Brooklyn	0	0	0	0	0	0	0				0	0	0
Yankees	0	0	0	1	0	1					2	4	0

AUTHOR HARVEY FROMMER, in his book *New York City Baseball 1947-1957*, recalled his thoughts as Game Five stretched into the late innings:

> The haze and the shadows of the stadium in autumn, the railing along the first and third base lines adorned with World Series buntings, Larsen almost nonchalantly pitching to Yogi Berra from a no-stretch windup, the scoreboard stretching out the zeroes— the images forever remain in the mind's eye.

Similar images must have been present for those in the raucous crowd who enjoyed a seventh-inning stretch under conditions never experienced before. Twenty-one Dodger batters had come and gone, and now we came to bat to try to pad my 2-0 lead.

Sal Maglie refused to bend though, getting Yogi Berra, now 5 for 17 in the Series, and Enos Slaughter, 7 for 16, on routine fly outs.

With two down and no one on, that brought fiery, leather-faced, second baseman Billy Martin to the plate.

Fans either loved Billy Martin, who stood 5-feet-11 and weighed 170 dripping wet, or hated him. I will not deny that Martin had a hair-trigger temper, but he wanted to win so badly, he couldn't stand to lose. Players told me Billy and his mom had terrible arguments when Billy was only *five*, so I guess he just grew up being resistant to authority.

An indication of Billy Martin's tendency to be controversial came from the title of a *Saturday Evening Post* article written by Al Stump before the 1956 season. It read:

> Billy Martin—He's Never Out of Trouble—An Unusually Candid Picture of Billy Martin of the Yankees—Probably the Most Unhappy Young Man in the Major Leagues.

Described in the same article by Casey Stengel as a "fresh kid who's always sassing everybody and getting away with it," the right-handed batting and throwing, lean and mean Martin was the product of the tough streets of Oakland, California, where he developed a reputation as a street fighter who wasn't afraid to mix it up.

When Martin hit .410 and .450 in two of his high school seasons, the scouts came courting. After graduation from Berkeley High in 1946, neighborhood friend Augie Golan introduced Martin to Oakland Oaks trainer Red Adams.

Adams, in turn, introduced the young infielder to Casey Stengel, who was managing the Oaks. Later, Stengel described for UPI his first look at Martin:

> I had this college shortstop I was looking at in a workout. He was neat as a pin. Did everything according to the book. Wore his pants just so, put his cap on straight and looked like something out of Spalding's Guide . . . Red Adams came along and said I was signing the wrong guy . . . Well, he brings this kid out. You never saw such a sight in your life. It was Martin and you oughta see him. Uniform all dirty, one pants leg rolled up, and the other falling down. Never saw anything like it in my whole life.

Soon after, the Oaks signed Martin for $200 a month. He was shipped off to Idaho Falls of the Class D Pioneer League where he hit .254, but made 16 errors while playing third base. Martin then went to Phoenix of the Class C Arizona-Texas League in 1947, under player/manager Arky Biggs, who also played Martin at third base.

Ironically, that team took on Martin's fiery personality and became known as the "Junior Gas House Gang" with the war cry "knock 'em down" according to the same *Post* article. In that season, Martin was named MVP in the league when he led the Arizona-

Texas League with a .392 average (while knocking in an incredible 173 runs). This gained him a promotion to the Oaks of the Pacific Coast League for the last month of the season.

At Oakland in 1948, Billy Martin played ball for Stengel who immediately took a shine to his aggressive play. In fact, most people believe the wide-eyed story that Casey actually paid Billy $25 to get hit by a pitch so the winning run was forced in.

David Falkner, in his book *The Last Yankee*, pointed out that while the easy-going Stengel and the brash Martin were different personality types, Casey Stengel loved Martin for "his appetite for the game."

Falkner wrote:

> What also touched the old man, what may even have reminded him of himself as a younger player, was a certain sense that Billy had of himself that allowed him to speak and act on impulse, as though he could simply not help himself . . . He was an original, like Stengel—someone who moved to his own drummer, but whose dancing feet contained almost perfect baseball sense. Stengel, childless himself, did not find it hard to adopt Billy as both a professional project and a prodigal son.

In 1948, Billy Martin hit .277 and became a solid defensive infielder. He was Stengel's leader on the team and a vocal one who never hesitated to speak his mind. The club won the first pennant for Oakland in 20 years, and Martin was given a new Chevrolet by the Oaks as a bonus for his efforts.

Chuck Dressen took over the Oaks the next season after Martin and Stengel's relationship broke up when Stengel was named manager of the Yankees in 1949. Martin and Dressen didn't get along at first, but Dressen soon realized the fiery ball player in Martin, and the two developed a good relationship as the season went on.

Billy Martin ended up hitting .286 in the 1949 season while knocking in 92 runs. In early September, Martin's season with the Oaks was over when his old partner Stengel had the Yankees purchase his contract.

Billy Martin, whose real name was Alfred Manuel Martin, Jr., first linked up with the Yankees in early January of 1950, when Casey Stengel brought together several of the Yankee prospects for the "instruction camp." There Stengel and several of his coaches worked with the young players on fundamentals.

Billy Martin became the regular Yankee second baseman in 1952, when Uncle Sam inducted Jerry Coleman into the Army. Whitey Ford, Bobby Brown, and reliever Tom Morgan were also called up, but Coleman's exit was Martin's entrance into the big leagues.

Together with shortstop Phil Rizzuto, Martin held his own at second base as the Yankees won not only the league crown but also the World Championship behind Mickey Mantle. He hit .267 that year, and played an important part in the Series with a game-saving catch in the seventh inning of Game Seven.

More than that, as David Falkner described in *The Last Yankee*, Martin rewarded Stengel's faith in him:

> Billy just inevitably became the spark plug that Stengel craved for in this machine of his. He was outstanding at nothing, but good at everything. He could bunt, hit, and run, occasionally hit for power; he could fearlessly turn the double play; he knew how to position himself well enough to more than make up for the step that he might have lacked in the field; he was quick, not fast; he was smart in everything . . . He continued to be a shadow at Stengel's side as well as an occasional thorn in it. He was, said all the players who knew him then, a kind of second manager.

In 1953, Martin drove in 75 runs and hit .257. In the World Series, Martin continued to step up his game a notch and was named MVP when he hit .500 with a record tying 12 hits.

The military grabbed Martin in 1954, and kept him for nearly 18 months. He returned to New York in August of 1955, and hit over .300 for the rest of the season. When the Yankees lost to the Dodgers, Martin cried openly, not only for the disappointment he felt, but for the hurt he knew Stengel was suffering.

Billy Martin went on to play seven seasons with the Yankees. He was then traded to the Kansas City A's for Ryne Duren in 1957 after losing his regular position to Bobby Richardson. After a season with the A's, he was traded to Detroit where the club attempted unsuccessfully to play him at shortstop.

One year to the day after he was traded to Detroit, Martin was traded to Cleveland along with Eddie Cicotte for Don Mossi, Ray Narleski, and Ossie Alvarez. Finally, during spring training in 1962, after stints with Cincinnati, Milwaukee, and Minnesota, he hung up his cleats and went on to a successful, roller-coaster ride as a manager with the Twins, the Tigers, the Rangers, the Yankees, and the A's.

There are perhaps more stories about Billy Martin than any other ball player I was ever around. He was a loud, violent, hard-drinking man who couldn't control himself. At the same time, he was kind-hearted and gentle, a man who simply wanted to be the best.

Mickey Mantle, Martin's long-time pal and confidante, sums up Billy Martin best in *The Last Yankee*:

> Billy was the only player ... who was able to raise the level of his game through fury. Other players lose it when they get mad. Billy had this knack of becoming better, he would get angry in clutch situations, and anger seemed to make him that much better.

Much has been said about Billy Martin, and I'm sure the controversy surrounding him will go on. That's because Billy just flat-out played to win and fought anyone who stood in his way.

Andy Carey echoes those thoughts. "Martin was gutsy ... always the antagonist ... do anything to beat you like Pee Wee or Eddie Stanky." Announcer Bob Neal of Mutual Broadcasting told the listening audience for the Fifth Game that he was "a throwback to the days of [Alvin] Dark and [Eddie] Stanky."

Billy Martin worked harder than anybody I knew to make himself a better player. I don't think he had that much natural ability, but he just practiced and played hard until he became an all-star player.

Billy Martin, who had turned 28 in May of 1956, continued his fine hitting in the 1956 Series. With two out and no one on in the seventh inning, he promptly smacked a ground single to left for the Yankee's fifth hit. When Gil McDougald walked, we suddenly had two men on. Unfortunately, Andy Carey hit a sharp grounder to Pee Wee Reese, who threw to Junior Gilliam, and the inning was over.

Keeping the tradition of not mentioning the perfect game, broadcaster Bob Wolff said, "The scoreboard shows four hits and the Yankees have them all."

With seven complete innings now in the books, I headed back to the mound with a 2-0 lead. Six outs stood between me and my first World Series victory.

—20—

Inning #8—Dodgers

Hodges Gets Robbed

DAYS AFTER GAME FIVE, I learned that television broadcaster Vin Scully welcomed back the international viewing audience at the start of the eighth inning with the words, "All eyes are on Don Larsen as he goes to work in the eighth inning."

If I had thought about having 64,519 pairs of eyes on me, I probably would have thrown the ball six feet over Yogi's head. A no-hitter is all any pitcher hopes to achieve, and there I was, just six outs away.

I tried to remain calm as I threw six warm-up pitches to Yogi. "Concentrate," I told myself. "Concentrate and throw strikes." That had been the key to seven no-hit, shut-out innings. Now, I wanted to stay in the same rhythm, trust Yogi with the calls, and just throw strikes.

I tried not to look into the stands, or get caught up in the thunderous roar that made Yankee Stadium sound more like there was a rock concert going on instead of a ball game. The noise was deafening. When I glanced over at Andy Carey, I saw the anticipation on his face. He slapped his glove and gave me a wink. It was time to go to work.

Umpire Babe Pinelli took his spot behind Yogi, and Jackie Robinson stepped into the batter's box. After him would come Gil Hodges and Sandy Amoros.

All three scheduled Dodger batters were tough enough on any day, but now they came to bat knowing each owed me one. Robinson, now 5 for 16 in the Series, had been retired on a fluke play in the first when his sizzling shot careened off Carey to McDougald; Hodges, 7 for 16, had been robbed by Mantle's great catch in the fifth, and Sandy Amoros, now a dismal 1 for 12, had missed a home run in the same inning by inches.

Although my thoughts at the time were how to pitch Robinson, I heard later that manager Walt Alston had talked to him before he came to bat. Various accounts of their conversation surfaced, but suffice it to say that Alston wanted Robinson to somehow shake up my rhythm.

Of course, the crux of their conversation was the furthest thing from my mind as I glared down at Jackie Robinson. I took my position on the side of the rubber, and I tried to remember back to what Yogi had told me about Jackie. "Keep the ball on the inside part of the plate and jam him as much as possible," were the words I remembered.

Sitting on the bench before I took the hill, I realized that the first pitch of the eighth inning would be a very important one, because it would set the stage for my battle with the Dodger hitters. If I threw a ball, they would suspect that I was running out of gas. Throw a strike and set the tone that I was still rough and ready.

A true veteran like Robinson realized I was nervous as hell out there. I knew he was looking to get the best of me and be the man who broke up the perfect game. I'm sure he thought one base hit would destroy my confidence and then his teammates could help send me to the showers.

To counteract his intentions, I had to show him and the rest of the Dodgers that I was still in the "zone." Fortunately, I was able to do that by throwing a good, hard-moving fast ball across the inside part of the plate that Robinson let go for a called strike. Later I'd learn that Vin Scully remarked: "Larsen consistently has been able to get ahead of the hitters. Once again the count is his way." He and I were thinking alike.

When Yogi threw the ball back to me, I caught it and gave myself a silent pat on the back. Throwing that first strike to Robinson really peaked my confidence. My motion had been smooth, and I hadn't overthrown. Just a good, solid, difficult-to-hit strike. Robinson's letting it pass made me feel good. He wanted to see if I

Don Larsen's
grandparents
(seated) gathered
to read about their
grandson's epic
achievement.

Yankee third
baseman Andy
Carey *(left)* and
Larsen celebrate
the perfect game
in the locker
room.

World Series MVP Don Larsen was awarded a new Chevrolet Corvette by *Sport Magazine*. *(Photo courtesy of Sport Magazine)*

Don Larsen and his parents.

Mickey Mantle *(left)* and Don Larsen pose with their awards.
Mantle called his catch of Gil Hodges' fly ball in the perfect game
"my greatest catch ever."

Teammates Tony Kubek *(left)* and Mickey Mantle *(right)* flank "The Perfect Yankee" after Don's World Series victory versus the Milwaukee Braves in 1957.

Corrine and Don Larsen with their four-year-old son, Scott.

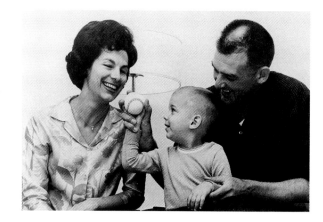

Casey Stengel watches Larsen deliver a kiss to Don's new wife Corrine.

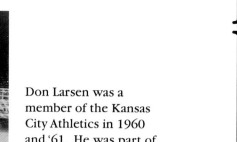

Don Larsen was a member of the Kansas City Athletics in 1960 and '61. He was part of the trade that brought Roger Maris to the Yankees.

Don Larsen went 8-2 with Kansas City and the Chicago White Sox in 1961.

Don Larsen with Houston Colt 45's teammates Ken Johnson and
Don Nottebart.

Manager Hank Bauer *(left)* welcomed his former Yankee teammate
to the Baltimore Orioles in 1965. *(Photo courtesy of Associated
Press)*

All-time Yankee great Joe DiMaggio *(left)* called Larsen's
performance "the best pitched game I've ever seen."

Baseball immortal
Ted Williams and
Larsen share a
laugh during the
San Diego Hall of
Champions dinner.

Don and Corrine
Larsen *(seated)*
pictured with son,
Scott, daughter-in-law
Nancy, and grandson,
Justin *(age 4 ½ yrs.)*.
*(Photo taken by
Quicksilver Studios,
Coeur d'Alene, ID)*

Don and Corrine enjoy retirement on their boat at
Hayden Lake, Idaho.

still had it. I let him know that he better be hitting away because I was still able to throw around the plate.

I didn't take much time to savor the moment, but just as I came "set" to throw the next pitch, Jackie Robinson threw up his right hand and called time. He backed out of the box and I took my foot off the rubber.

Jackie then walked back to the on-deck circle and talked to Gil Hodges for a moment. He also picked up a bat and swung it before returning to the plate.

Robinson's delay tactic was greeted with boos from the partisan Yankee crowd. Later Robinson said he had something in his eye. Questions to Walt Alston as to whether he ordered Robinson to step out went unanswered.

If Robinson was trying to shake me up, it didn't work. To be sure, I was nervous, but that first strike calmed me down. If he had stepped out before I threw it, then maybe his move would have had more of an effect. As it was, I just waited on him to get settled once again in the batter's box.

I must say that the crowd booing was a comforting feeling. Having all of those fans behind me was something I'll never forget. I've gone through enough booing of my own to know what it feels like. I'll take the cheers anytime.

After Robinson resumed his batting position, I threw Jackie a sneaky slider on the inside corner. He just barely got a piece of it and fouled it off to bring the count to 0-2.

Ahead two balls and no strikes put me in control. I had a pitch or two to waste. Jackie had to swing at anything around the plate. If I threw a pitch just outside the strike zone, Jackie might bite and I'd have out number one.

Yogi signaled for a slider. When it left my hand, I thought it might be too good a pitch, but it tailed off low and outside. Despite the fact that it was well outside the strike zone, Robinson took no chances. He swung away, but his bat came over on top of the ball and he hit a harmless grounder back to the mound.

I merely extended my glove a few inches to the left and the ball cradled in my mitt. I had all the time in the world to throw to Joe Collins at first base. I swung around, pivoted off my left foot, and heaved a soft throw to Joe. I saw Umpire Hank Soar's right hand go up with the out call. I had out number 22!

Later I learned that with Robinson's out, I had equaled the major league record for consecutive outs held by Herb Pennock and Detroit's Schoolboy Rowe. The next consecutive out would be a new World Series record.

The crowd roared as I watched Jackie Robinson trot back to the Dodger dugout. I knew retiring him was pivotal, because he was trying to set the table for the other Dodger hitters. Regardless of the situation with perfect games and no-hitters, if I could keep a Dodger hitter off the base, then one swing of the bat by their powerhouse hitters wouldn't even the count on our two-to-nothing lead.

Striding to plate now was Dodger first baseman Gil Hodges. Images from that magical day still are fresh in my mind, and I remember distinctly that Gil Hodges looked like he stood seven feet tall and weighed at least 300 pounds when he walked to the plate.

Usually a fun-loving guy, there was no smile on Gil's face when he came to bat. I knew he and his teammates wanted nothing of any no-hitter, and Gil had the sweet swing to break up my perfection on any pitch.

Yogi's instructions regarding Hodges had been simple. "Keep the ball away," he told me. "Concentrate on throwing good fast balls either high or low outside."

I never thought Gil Hodges would take the first pitch. He was an aggressive hitter and a student of the art of getting the bat on the ball. I took the fast ball sign from Yogi and watched as he set his mitt outside and low.

From the no wind-up position, I unloaded a moving fast ball that hugged the outside corner of the plate. To my surprise, Hodges never swung, but he should have. Umpire Babe Pinelli had been giving me that pitch all day and he did so again.

Yogi zinged the ball back to me after giving me a quick wangle of his glove to let me know, "nice pitch." Yogi was really inspirational back there, and he was always trying to pump up his pitcher. It was a true "we" thing with him. He's a pitcher's dream.

I threw another fast ball. It wasn't far from the location of the first one, but Pinelli called ball one and the count was even.

I knew the next pitch to Hodges was another important one. If I threw a strike, I was in control. If it was a ball, then Hodges would sit on the fast ball.

Yogi called for a slider. I held the ball with my second finger, hugging the seam and my thumb curled under the ball, and buzzed it toward the plate. It was one of the best I threw all day. It really had a lot of bite on it and ended up just on the inside corner. That was close to no-no land for Hodges's powerhouse swing, but he undercut the ball and missed for strike two.

As I stood on the mound and peered down at Yogi, I wondered whether he would call for a fast ball or slider. The signals popped by and I saw the one finger signal the fast ball. I overthrew it just a bit and it landed in Yogi's mitt too far outside and low. That made the count two and two. I quickly resumed my position on the mound and looked in at Yogi. I saw Andy Carey shift just a step to the left. All the infielders were fidgeting more than normal. They were just as nervous as I was.

Most of the first few pitches I threw in the eighth were on the mark, but my next one had disaster written all over it. I'd gotten away with the previous pitch being just a tad too close to Hodges' wheelhouse, but this one was even closer. It was a fast ball, and half way to the plate I knew Gil was going to try to make mincemeat of it.

Unlike the previous fast ball, this one was mediocre at best. The velocity wasn't bad, probably in the high eighties, but it had no movement at all. It was a dying quail ready for the kill, and Gil's eyes widened as it approached his power zone.

Even today I can remember Hodges's swing; his powerful shoulders coming around and that bat hitting the ball with a sickening thud. I flinched at the sound but, luckily, his bat must have caught the ball just a bit on top of the cover because even though it was hit hard, it never got much height.

The ball headed like a frozen rope straight at third baseman Andy Carey and banged straight in his glove just above ground level. The play happened so fast that no one could tell if he caught it for a line drive out or not. He wisely completed the play by throwing the ball to Joe Collins at first base.

In his television broadcast booth, Vin Scully summarized the play in just three poetic words: "Hodges was robbed."

In an interview last year, Andy Carey recalled the play this way:

> When Hodges hit that low-line drive off to my left . . . a difficult play since it was so low, I just reacted. I knew I'd caught it off the ground . . . but I threw the ball to first anyway. Afterwards, I got to thinking . . . oh, you son-of-a-bitch what if you had thrown the ball away!

From my vantage point, I knew Gil Hodges couldn't believe Carey caught his hard-hit ball. He stopped in his tracks midway to first, gave me a passing glance, and then headed for the Dodgers' dugout with his head down. I saw several Dodgers shake their heads. They couldn't believe, didn't want to believe what was going on.

As the ball whipped around the horn, I took a deep breath. Maybe the Good Lord or one of his angels is perched on my shoulders today, I thought to myself. It's the only explanation I could think of.

Due to Andy's fine play, Gil Hodges had become the twenty-third out on pitch number 83. I now held the World Series record for consecutive outs, a record that still stands today. Baseball writer Ted Smits considered Carey's catch one of the seven pivotal plays of the game.

The next day, Smits told his readers that:

> The nice thing about Don Larsen's pitching performance ... was that there were no rhubarbs, no arguments, no disputed decisions ... There were at least seven occasions when the perfection could have been marred, and instead of an incredible no-hit, no run, no-man-reach-first game it would have been merely a wonderful close game.

The seven occasions Smits mentions in the article are:

1)   In the second, Jackie Robinson led off with a hard grounder at Andy Carey, the hard-luck Yankee third baseman. Carey got his glove on it, but the ball caromed off his hand and Gil McDougald picked it up, rifling a throw to first that caught Robinson by inches.

2)   In the third, Sal Maglie, the unfortunate losing pitcher, hit a low, hard liner to center field that was caught by Mickey Mantle, but could have spelled trouble if it had been a few yards to the left or right.

3)   In the third, Duke Snider smacked a long drive into the right field stands that was foul by only a few feet.

4)   In the fifth, Gil Hodges lashed a drive to left center on which Mickey Mantle made a running, back-handed catch, the most sparkling play of the game on the Yankee side.

5)   In the same inning, Sandy Amoros hit into the right field stands, and this time it was foul by less than a foot.

6)   To start the seventh, Gil McDougald made a great back-handed stop on Jim Gilliam's grounder and threw him out.

7)   Then in the eighth, Hodges sent a soft liner to Carey who caught the ball inches off the ground.

Smits is right on all accounts, except I wouldn't characterize Hodges's ball a "soft-liner." I heard someone say one time that he was lucky and also made his luck. That's how I was that miracle day in October. My pitching was good enough to get me by and lady luck was right beside me on every pitch.

Once the shock of Hodges's turn at bat was over, I readied myself to take on Sandy Amoros, who had almost gotten to me for that home run in the fifth. Yogi Berra's sign reminded me that we wanted to pitch the Dodgers' right-fielder low and lower. I therefore set up to throw a fast ball right below the knees.

It was a bit higher than I wanted, but Amoros let it go by just as Robinson and Hodges had done on the first pitch when they were at bat.

When umpire Babe Pinelli signaled strike one, I was ahead on the count for the third straight batter. Yogi motioned low to the ground. He too knew that I had positioned the pitch just a bit too high.

Yogi's sign indicated curve, one of several excellent calls he made that day. I had been relying on fast balls and sliders, and it was time to mix up things.

I positioned the ball in my fingers and let go. Amoros seemed dumbfounded by the pitch. It was not what he expected. It broke down and away. He swung, but the sound of bat to ball let me know it wasn't hit well. I craned my neck and turned around to see it floating out toward center field. Mickey Mantle was positioned perfectly. He lumbered in and settled under the ball. It fell safely into his glove and he began that trot of his toward the dugout.

Joe Collins patted my butt as I ran to the dugout. I saw thousands of fans waving and cheering me as I crossed the fair/foul line. I had recorded 24 outs. Consecutive outs. No hits, no runs, no walks; not even an error or a wild pitch to mar the day. I had been perfect for eight full innings. And not just in some game during the year. Or in the playoffs. Or in the first four games of the World Series. No, all this was happening in the pivotal fifth game. It was too much to comprehend.

Up in the television booth, I'd later learn that Vin Scully had told his viewers, "Thus far we've seen the greatest pitching performance I've ever seen. Don Larsen has retired 24 consecutive batters."

Veteran broadcaster Bob Wolff put it another way when he talked to reporters after the game. "The crowd was no longer rooting for a game," he said. "They were rooting for themselves. I have always believed people root for no-hitters almost as much for their own part in it as witnesses as for the pitcher's part." Another announcer who commentated between innings on radio said, "games like this make old men out of very young baseball announcers."

As I took my seat in the dugout, my mind went blank. It was all too much. Of course, *nobody* approached me. Not even Casey, or any of the ballplayers. I didn't know what to think. It all seemed so unreal.

I sat there and watched as the Dodgers took the field. Where were my parents? Were they watching the game? And my friends in San Diego. And in Indiana. Was this all really happening?

Perhaps Vin Scully was reading my mind. He told his viewers, "Two cities are coming to a standstill. Michigan City [Indiana] and San Diego . . . Imagine when the ninth inning comes. The nation will stand still."

Inning #8—Yankees

A Glorious Strike Out

	1	2	3	4	5	6	7	8	9	10	R	H	E
Brooklyn	0	0	0	0	0	0	0	0			0	0	0
Yankees	0	0	0	1	0	1	0				2	5	0

THE YANKEE HALF OF THE EIGHTH INNING is nothing more than a blur in my memory. Sitting on the bench, I attempted to collect myself and prepare to pitch to the Dodgers in the ninth.

I was perspiring heavily and wiped a towel across my brow several times. I gazed out on the field, oblivious to what was transpiring before me. "Was this really happening? Was I really three outs from a no-hitter? Had I walked anyone?" I knew I had never pitched a game where I hadn't given up at least one walk. And usually many more than that.

Now I asked myself, "Have there been any errors?" Questions like that kept creeping into my mind over and over again.

I recall Andy Carey sitting next to me on the bench, but he never said a word or even glanced my way. I also remember Mickey walking up and down the dugout several times, but he never stopped to talk to me or make eye contact. After our chat in the seventh, he wanted nothing to do with me.

I tried to think about who I would face in the ninth. The last batter had been Sandy Amoros. That meant the bottom part of the order would come up—Carl Furillo, Roy Campanella, and pitcher Sal Maglie. "No, he wouldn't bat," I decided. "They'll send up a pinch-hitter."

Thoughts about that were put behind me when I suddenly realized that I had to bat in the eighth. That was certainly something new. Normally, I would have been taken out for a relief pitcher since I rarely went the route. Or Casey would have pinch hit for me.

On this day, however, I would get a time at bat in the eighth. And that at bat is the most memorable one in my major league career.

It all started when I came out of the dugout. Even though I was in a daze, I recall distinctly the roar of the crowd as I made my way toward the on-deck circle. My ears almost hurt from the deafening sound, and it was hard to hold the tears back. Thick clouds of confetti blanketed the sky. I could barely see to get to home plate.

As I gazed across the field, I swear every fan in the ball park was standing. The crowd noise grew as I walked unsteadily toward home plate. It was only a bit short of 100 feet from the dugout, but it seemed like I walked a mile.

Roy Campanella said something when I entered the batter's box, but I can't remember what it was. Babe Pinelli seemed to be staring at me, looking for a reaction of some sort.

I remember there was also sort of a quizzical look on Sal Maglie's face. Here he had pitched a beauty of a game and was being upstaged by a pitcher who didn't have nearly the credentials he did.

I knew of course of Sal's propensity to brush back batters. What a perfect place to do it. Send me back on my heels and let me know that the Dodgers were still tough cookies who weren't going to crumble.

But somehow the look on Sal's face told me that wasn't going to happen. Pitchers have great respect for outstanding performances by other pitchers, and Sal knew that I had thrown a terrific game. Even though I realized he could deck me with one well-placed pitch, I tried to concentrate on hitting the ball.

I also believe that Sal might have thrown one up and in if the score hadn't been so close. After all, we only had a two-run lead, and Sal and the Dodgers figured they could still pull the game out. Three up and three down would provide them with that chance, and so Sal wanted me back in the dugout as quickly as possible.

Looking back, I'm sure I tried to hit the ball, but I can't remember anything about that time at the plate. I got a called strike, swung wildly and missed at the second pitch, took a ball that was wide, and then struck out swinging at a pitch I couldn't have hit if I had been Ted Williams. My feeble at-bat over, I headed back toward the dugout.

That at-bat was certainly the only time in my career when I was applauded by the crowd after I struck out. From the batter's box to the dugout, the fans hooted and howled until I finally disappeared into the dugout.

While most people remember what happened on that magical day in October, they don't recall that Sal Maglie struck out the side in the bottom of the eighth. After my futile attempt to get a hit, both Hank Bauer and Joe Collins went down on strike outs under the spell of Sal's magic.

What a game Maglie had pitched. He had only given up five hits and just the two runs. On any other day, he would have been a hero.

His performance in the bottom of the eighth meant that the slim 2-0 lead was all my Yankee teammates could give me as we headed to the top of the ninth. It would be the last chance for the Brooklyn Dodgers to throw a monkey wrench into my memorable day.

Although the cheering when I went to bat in the eighth was overwhelming, it couldn't compare with what I heard as I made my way to the mound in the ninth. I was rubbery-legged as I tried to make it across the fair/foul line without falling down and making a fool of myself. One of the infielders, either Martin or Collins, patted me on the back as they ran by. They may have said something but the din of the roar made it impossible to hear them.

At that moment, "The House That Ruth Built" had gone bonkers as fans joyously celebrated the anticipated showdown with history. In the radio broadcast booth, I found out later that radio announcer Bob Wolff had told his excited listeners, "applause is ringing to the rafters at Yankee Stadium."

─22─

The Miracle Ninth

At approximately 2:57 on October 8, 1956, records indicate Hall of Fame broadcaster Vin Scully told his international viewing audience: "Let's all take a deep breath as we go to the most dramatic ninth inning in the history of baseball." The Armed Forces radio commentator between innings said, "I'm going to sit back, light up, and hope I don't chew the cigarette to pieces."

I tried to do what Vin Scully had suggested to his viewers once I reached the pitching mound. I fiddled around with the rosin bag. It suddenly felt like it weighed 50 pounds. Then I walked around the back of the mound trying to calm myself. My stomach was jumpin' and my head felt like it was going to burst wide open.

I watched Joe Collins throw ground balls to Billy, Gil, and Andy. They seemed pretty nonchalant, but I knew they were nervous as hell. Martin bobbled an easy chance. I'll bet he hoped that wouldn't happen if a grounder was hit to him.

I glanced up near the press boxes. I was sure the sportscasters were trying to figure out what type of ending they would write for this day. Writing about a near-no-hitter was one thing. If I could get through the ninth, their story would be one to tell about for years to come.

As I mentioned, I later had to tell reporters that while I knew I had a no-hitter going, I never thought about what was called a "perfect game." I didn't really even know what that was. And I had just a two-run lead. I just hoped to finish the game, get the victory, and get the hell out of Dodge.

It was great to learn later on that in addition to the pressure on me, my defensive fielders, the managers, and the Dodgers' hitters, Vin Scully was nervous as hell. In a recent interview, he said:

> In the early days of television ... this was the fourth year for the Series ... the press always said the television announcers talked too much. During the Series, I therefore tried to talk sparingly.

Scully, who first debuted as a Dodger announcer in 1950, as a protégé of Red Barber, also remembered that he was restricted with what he could say about the potential for a no-hitter that memorable day.

"We talk about no-hitters all the time now, but not back then," says Scully, who is head and shoulders above all of his colleagues in that he has broadcast the astounding number of 15 no-hitters and three perfect games. He added:

> In 1956, we were afraid of garnering the wrath of the players and audience alike by talking about a no-hitter or perfect game. Therefore, I kept saying "that's the 22nd consecutive batter Larsen's retired" or something like that, but I never mentioned the no-hitter possibility.

Scully also recalled that the first few innings of the fifth game were rather dull. "Mel [Allen] didn't have much to say early on ... since there were only the good defensive plays and Mantle's home run."

The veteran broadcaster added:

> New York *Daily Mirror* writer Harold Rosenthal used to say he wanted to write a lead headline for a story. "It was a dull game ... everybody struck out," Scully recalls, "until the last couple of innings that's what we had, because not much happened offensively."

Scully also said he was afraid he'd make the mistake of mentioning the possibility of a no-hitter or perfect game and then be blamed if someone broke it up.

In the 1947 Series, Red Barber was given a lot of flak when he mentioned that New York Yankee pitcher Bill Bevens had a no-hitter and then it was broken up. I remembered that game and kept saying to myself, "Please God, don't let me make a mistake," especially when we reached the ninth inning.

After Game Five, Jesse Katz, a Philadelphia mathematician at the Remington Rand Univac Division of Sperry Rand compounded the probability of establishing the odds on my throwing a perfect game on October 8, 1956.

According to Katz, he used the *Who's Who in Baseball* record book to figure out how frequently men got on base against me. Apparently he found that 34% reached first base.

Using this statistic and others, Katz figured that before I threw the first pitch of the game, the odds were against me, 76,000 to one. After six perfect innings, those odds dropped to 41-1, and after seven, 11-1.

Katz told reporters that at the end of eight perfect innings the odds had dropped to 2½ to 1 against me pitching the perfect game. After one out, those odds switched to 13-10 against, and after two, the odds were finally 19-10 in favor of me retiring the final batter and pitching the no-hit/perfect game.

I was later told that before the Yankee infielders took the field in the ninth, Billy Martin took them aside and gave them a pep talk, saying "nothing gets through." I was too nervous to realize it at the time, but apparently Casey and Frank Crosetti were also shouting out instructions and flapping their arms wildly to signal Slaughter, Mantle, and Bauer to their respective positions in the outfield. Stengel later told reporters, "I had more managers helping me than I knew what to do with."

After the game, some sportswriters questioned why Casey didn't put in a replacement for Enos Slaughter, who wasn't as fleet of foot as in his younger days. I never did find out, but Casey was superstitious. Maybe he just didn't want to do anything to shake up things.

There's been a great many stories written about the tension in that ninth inning as I readied myself to pitch to the first Dodger hitter, Carl Furillo. One of the best I've ever read came from sportswriter Arthur Daley, who described what the atmosphere was like in Yankee Stadium as the two teams began the ninth.

> For almost four innings, wily Sal Maglie had matched Larsen putout for putout. Folks were beginning to wonder if this would be the first double no-hitter since Fred Toney of the Cincinnati Reds and Hippo Jim Vaughn of the Chicago Cubs tangled almost 40 years ago [Vaughn lost in the tenth].
>
> But then that precocious youngster, Master Mickey Mantle, tagged the ancient Barber for a homer in the fourth. Another run trickled in later. But the Barber, pitching far better ball than he had in his victory in the opener, was left holding an empty bag.
>
> Somewhere in the middle of the game the crowd seemed to get a mass realization of the wonders that were being unfolded. Tension kept mounting until it was as brittle as an electric light bulb. The slightest jounce and the dang thing might explode.
>
> Or perhaps it was more like a guy blowing air into a toy balloon. He keeps blowing and blowing with red-faced enthusiasm. But every puff might be the last. Larger and larger grew Larsen's balloon. It was of giant size at the start of the ninth.

Broadcaster Bob Wolff added, "You can hear the hum of the crowd in the background." Longtime Dodger publicist Irving Rudd was so upset, he jumped up on a table and yelled, "Get a hit … Get a f_____ hit!" Reserve Dodger outfielder Ransom Jackson told me, "I kept thinking there had to be a hit. Nobody pitches a no-hitter in the World Series."

Most of what happened in that incredible ninth is difficult to recall. I do remember that after I completed my warm-ups, I turned around and faced center field, and said to myself "Good Lord, I've got one more to go. Please get me through this."

Mickey Mantle described his feelings in the ninth in *My Favorite Summer 1956*:

> The crowd was on its feet and I was so nervous I could feel my knees shaking. I played in more than 2,400 games in the major leagues, but I never was as nervous as I was in the ninth inning of that game, afraid I would do something to mess up Larsen's perfect game. If I dropped a fly ball, it wouldn't stop his no-hitter, but it would end his perfect game, and that added to my nervousness.

In the ninth, every Dodger hitter looked like Joe DiMaggio. In fact, I might have felt better if Joe had been the batter, because when Carl Furillo took his place in the batter's box, his stare was enough to frighten me into surrendering a base hit to him on the spot.

Of all the Dodger hitters, Furillo was the most ferocious. Not the best, or the one with the most power, but a man whose very appearance made me uncomfortable. His half-shaven beard and steely demeanor gave me the creeps, and on this occasion his look seemed to say, "Larsen, I'm gonna stuff this ball right up your butt."

Why I looked at his face, I'll never know. But I did, and now my palms were sweaty and I hadn't even thrown the first pitch. Yogi looked out at me through his mask and I tried to concentrate once again.

"Throw strikes," I reminded myself, "throw strikes." But my brain was buzzing so much, and my arms felt heavy, and I wasn't certain whether I'd throw the first pitch five feet short of home plate or five feet over Furillo's head.

My warm-up tosses had gone by so quickly, I didn't even remember throwing them. Now Furillo was ready, and Umpire Babe Pinelli was ready, and Yogi was ready, and I was set to throw the first pitch toward home plate.

Despite the roar in my ears, I tried to concentrate on recalling how to pitch to the Dodger right fielder. Thinking back, I remembered that I had retired him on a fly ball to Bauer in the third and a pop-up to Billy Martin in the sixth.

Of all of the Dodgers, Junior Gilliam and Furillo were touted as the "smartest" hitters on the club. Known as a contact hitter who sprayed the ball to all fields, I remembered that Furillo liked the ball down and preferably on the inside part of the plate.

All day long, Yogi Berra had led me through the maze of Dodger hitters. This time he placed his mitt toward the high outside corner. I knew that he wanted me to keep the ball up to avoid Furillo's sweet-spot.

While I was paying attention, I'm sure if Yogi would have positioned the mitt ten feet outside the plate or over the batter's head, I would have tried to throw the ball there. I intended to follow Yogi's instructions all the way.

Carl Furillo was 5 for 17 in the Series. Once again I wanted to establish myself with a good first pitch that would let him and the Dodger hitters know I was still on track. While most reporters wrote that I threw a curve or two in the ninth, the truth is that they were all hard sliders. I think Yogi believed that my fast balls were my best pitches, and that we'd go with them until the Dodgers showed us otherwise.

I threw that first slider a bit lower than I wanted to, and I have no doubt that it would have been a ball. But Furillo was an aggressive hitter, and had decided he wasn't about to let the first pitch go by if it was close. My ability to throw several first-pitch strikes in the seventh and eighth innings no doubt contributed to his decision.

I think Carl could have handled the pitch, but he was a bit late on it, and fouled it away for strike one. My second pitch was another slider and it headed straight for Berra's mitt on the outside part of the plate. Furillo decided to try his luck on this one and fouled it off to bring the count to no balls and two strikes.

Once again, I was in the driver's seat. Should I waste a pitch or go right after Furillo? I think my brain may have told me to throw one away, but my arm was almost on remote and I was just throwing as hard as I could to somewhere near the center of the plate. If I got too cute, I'd make a mistake. Yogi had confidence in the hard slider and so did I. Give 'em your best and make them hit it, was my creed.

I threw the pitch, but it was high from ten feet out. Pinelli called it a ball, and Furillo backed away for a few seconds. The fact that it was high might have been a blessing. Calling that slider a curve was a misnomer, because it certainly didn't move much.

Yogi's signal for the fourth pitch to Furillo was a fast ball. It had a chance to be a called strike-three, but just at the last moment, Furillo fouled it off.

A good hard slider followed, but Furillo fouled it off as well. With the count now one ball and two strikes and the tension mounting with every pitch, I threw yet another slider. It was a tumbling pitch that moved across the lower part of the outside corner. Furillo liked what he saw and swung away. It was almost as if his bat was in slow motion, and I turned to see the ball sailing toward Hank Bauer in right field.

All of the fielders after the game told me how they felt as the game progressed toward the ninth. On the one hand they wanted the ball to be hit to them because they had confidence that they could handle it. On the other, they were scared shitless they'd screw up.

None of that crossed my mind as I watched the ball float in the blue afternoon sky. Would it fall for a base hit? Would Bauer catch it? Misplay it?

Judging the distance the ball would travel was difficult for me to do. The sound of bat to ball wasn't distinguishable because of the crowd noise. To my relief, it ended up being a routine play that anyone could have made. Hank Bauer was rock-solid steady as he coolly and calmly collected the fly ball into his glove for out number one.

The pitch of the crowd noise went up an octave. I saw arms waving and people grabbing each other. The fans were going crazy. Twenty-five consecutive outs on pitch number 89 had left me with two more batters to face to gain the no-hitter.

While I was a nervous wreck, the fans were delirious. In the ballpark that day was my boyhood chum Joe Medina.

> We sat behind home plate. Our mutual friends Charlie Graham and Clark Higgins were with me.
>
> The last two innings were really something . . . crowd on their feet . . . everyone knew Don had a perfect game. I kept score until the last two innings . . . then I got too excited.
>
> You keep thinking it's not going to happen . . . then each pitch . . . each out . . . it gets closer, more exciting. I could tell Don was a nervous wreck . . . You could see the pressure was really something.
>
> My buddy Charlie Graham almost cost himself a bundle of money. He kept telling the beer vendor to stand by because if Larsen pitched a no-hitter, he wanted to buy everyone in the house . . . all sixty thousand of them . . . a drink!

With Furillo retired, I started to think about Roy Campanella. I don't know if he was as nervous as I was when he came to the plate, but I'm sure he felt a lot of pressure as well.

The Dodgers were losing the pivotal Game Five of the World Championship, 2-0. If that wasn't bad enough, I hadn't given up a hit. Fifty-two World Series had been played before this one, and nobody had ever pitched a no-hitter.

And don't kid yourself, baseball teams *hate* to have a no-hitter pitched against them. It's bad enough to lose, but no team wants to think that a pitcher is that much better than they are on a given day.

Most times, when the no-hitter is still possible and the game gets into the late innings, the other team will try anything to scratch out a hit. Interestingly enough, nobody in the Dodger line-up tried to bunt on me. The Dodgers weren't known for their speed, but I was surprised they didn't try at least one bunt.

Of course, I knew that Roy Campanella wasn't going to do anything but try to get a solid base hit. I remember that Yogi and he exchanged words, and both had a good chuckle about something. There they were poking fun, and I was dying out there.

Our strategy with the great Dodger hitter was to pitch him inside, even though I had retired Campanella on two outside pitches in both the third and sixth innings.

This time around, I was determined to throw the pitches inside and keep the ball away from Campanella's power zone. My first pitch was a good fast ball in close. The crack of the bat scared me, but Campanella came around too soon and fouled it into the left-field stands for strike one.

Yogi called for a slider on the next pitch. Since this was the ninth inning and I was approaching 100 pitches, I wasn't sure how much "stuff" I had left. But Yogi was the boss, and so I set up to throw the slider. It was more of a fast ball and just a wee bit outside. I knew it would be ball one.

But while Roy Campanella was a very disciplined hitter, he decided that the pitch was hittable and swung the bat. Campanella said later he was trying to foul the pitch off, but instead the future Hall of Famer grounded the ball harmlessly toward an anxious Billy Martin who was positioned perfectly at second base.

There was never a doubt that Martin would handle the medium-speed grounder. Almost effortlessly, he scooped the ball into his glove, and threw easily to Joe Collins at first for consecutive out number 26 on pitch number 91.

Twenty-six up and 26 down. No runs, no hits, no errors, no walks, no passed balls, no wild pitches, no hit batters—nothing to spoil my day in the sun.

With just one more out standing between me and a no-hit, perfect game, it was difficult to know who was more nervous, Babe

Pinelli, the official scorers, my defensive teammates, Casey Stengel, the players on the Yankee bench, the Dodgers or yours truly.

Standing on the mound, I felt like I was in a dream world. I've heard players talk about the magic moment when something very special happens in a sporting event. It may be a great hit like Bobby Thomson's shot heard 'round the world, or The Catch in the NFC Championship Game by the 49ers' Dwight Clark, or the last-second shot by John Havlicek in the fifth game of the Celtics-Phoenix Suns playoffs in the mid-seventies. When players are asked to describe their feelings, most times they can't remember much, because they are so focused on the task at hand.

While the pressure had been building with every inning and every batter, I can honestly say that after I retired Roy Campanella, a bit of a peaceful feeling came to me. I had somehow reached a point where the challenge would be met, where I would find out if a miracle was truly going to occur. The stakes were clear now. If I retired the next batter, I would have a no-hitter and be the winning pitcher for the Yankees in the pivotal World Series game. Every athlete wants to be in a special situation like that, and I would get the chance.

The atmosphere on the field suddenly seemed in focus. Everything was moving in slow motion, but I focused and began to prepare for what I hoped would be the final batter.

The Yankee Stadium crowd had gone crazy after Campanella's out, but I would not allow myself to be distracted by them. I made up my mind I was going to focus on one thing—throwing strikes to whoever the Dodgers sent up to face me.

With that in mind, I kept my eyes peeled in the direction of the Dodger dugout. I knew Walter Alston would send up a pinch-hitter to bat for Sal Maglie. The Barber had pitched a great game, but Alston would want his best pinch-hitter at the plate so that he had every chance to not only break up my no-hitter, but come back and either tie up the score or hit me for a few runs and take the lead.

The choices to pinch-hit for Sal Maglie consisted of Dodger reserve third baseman Randy Jackson, outfielder/first baseman Dale Mitchell, outfield reserve Gino Cimoli, infielders Charlie Neal, Chico Fernandez, Don Zimmer, and Rocky Nelson, and catchers Rube Walker and Dixie Howell. Of those, the most logical was Mitchell, who ended up with a lifetime .300 plus average in ten seasons with Cleveland and one with the Dodgers.

From Colony, Oklahoma, the 6-foot, 195-pound, 35-year-old Mitchell, who had lazy gray eyes and close-cropped brown hair, first joined the Indians in 1946. A left-handed thrower and hitter, Mitchell had a number of good years with the club and led the American League with 203 hits in 1949.

In 1947, his first full year with the club, Dale hit .316, and in 1948 improved the average to .336. He played on the Indians' World Championship team that year along with Joe Gordon, Lou Boudreau, and Larry Doby.

In a career where he ended up with 1,244 lifetime hits, Mitchell batted .317 and hit 23 triples in 1949, the most in the American League since 1939. A .308 and .290 average followed in 1950 and 1951, but in 1952, Mitchell hit .323, second in the league to Philadelphia's great hitter Ferris Fain.

Dale Mitchell's prowess at the plate fell off in 1954 and 1955, and he was traded to the Dodgers during the 1956 season. With the Dodgers, he hit .292, most as a pinch-hitter in 19 games.

As I walked around the mound trying to ready myself, I saw that Dale was approaching the plate. I tried not to look at him too closely, but instead watched for Yogi to get in position. The break in the action had suddenly made my hands shake. I slapped the ball in my glove and tried to steady myself.

Later on, I'd read an interview with Umpire Babe Pinelli. He recalled the moments just before the first pitch to Mitchell in the ninth:

> When the last man in the ninth, pinch-hitter Dale Mitchell, stepped up, my blue suit was soaked with sweat. I noticed Commissioner Ford Frick in his box. He was pale as a sheet.
>
> With two out, Larsen was just one man away from immortality. As he prepared to throw, I took a firm grip on my emotions. Everyone else could sympathize with him—but not me. Refusing Larsen anything he didn't earn 100 percent was the hardest thing I'd ever done in baseball.

In Mickey Mantle's *My Favorite Summer 1956*, he described Mitchell and his feelings when the Dodger's pinch-hitter came to the plate:

> The Dodgers were down to their final out. It was Maglie's turn to bat, but Walter Alston sent up a pinch-hitter, Dale Mitchell, a veteran left-handed hitter. I knew him well. He had spent a little

over ten seasons with the Cleveland Indians and had a lifetime batting average of .312. He had very little power, only 41 home runs in 11 seasons, but he was a good contact hitter. He sprayed the ball all over the field and that made it impossible to defend against him....As Mitchell stepped in and went into his crouch, I shifted nervously in center field. "Please don't hit to me," I kept thinking. Then: "Please hit it to me." I worried about him hitting a sinking line drive or a bloop that would fall in front of me. I worried where I should play him. "Should I come in a few steps? Go into the bench for help", as an outfielder usually does in this kind of situation, but nobody was looking at me. They were leaving it up to me. They didn't want to be responsible if I should mess up. So I just stayed right where I was.

Writer Frank Graham Jr. wrote about Mitchell and my words to him (Graham) after the game:

Now Dale Mitchell was announced, pinch-hitting for Maglie. The Yankees knew the left-handed swinging Mitchell well; he had played against them often while he was with the Indians. They knew him as a threat to slash, slap or bloop a hit in any direction. Talking about it later, Larsen said, "He really scared me up there. Looking back on it, though, I know how much pressure he was under. He must have been paralyzed. That made two of us."

Yogi and I hadn't specifically discussed Mitchell that much, since he wasn't in the starting lineup. I'd faced him before in the American League and knew he was a good hitter.

Casting any strategy aside, I once again decided to throw the ball as hard as I could and hope for the best. While I was planning my attack, Mitchell told reporters after the game that he knew exactly what was at stake, but tried to focus on the importance of the outcome of the game. "My job was to get on base any way I could," he said. "It was still a 2-0 game, and if I could get on, I could bring the tying run to the plate. I was trying to look for a pitch I could handle."

As Mitchell readied himself by swinging two bats over his head like some sort of Neanderthal caveman, I looked at Yogi. I also took a deep breath, trying to somehow calm the nerves that threatened to blow my stomach apart. I read later that broadcaster Vin Scully told his viewing audience, "I think it would be safe to say no man in the history of baseball has ever come up to home plate in a more dramatic moment." He added "Yankee Stadium is shivering in its concrete foundation right now." So was I.

Umpire Pinelli positioned himself behind Yogi as Mitchell stepped to the plate for what would be 103 of the most exciting seconds in baseball history. Yogi signaled #1 for a fast ball, and at 3:05, I sent it spiraling toward the plate.

Mitchell, who stood slightly bent over when he batted, passed on the pitch, which was just a bit low and a little outside. The crowd loudly booed the call, but Pinelli was right.

Yogi next called for a slider, but for all practical purposes it was a fast ball. It had good velocity to it and caught the outside corner. The roar of the crowd drowned out Pinelli's call of "Stee-rr-rrike One" to even the count.

If Mitchell disagreed with the call, he didn't let Pinelli know. He simply resumed his batting position, and I stared down at Yogi. He fired the Spalding baseball back securely to my glove.

Seconds later, the rotund, barrel-chested catcher I'd come to love resumed his squatting position. He carefully flashed me the sign for another slider. I took my catcher's directive and buggy whipped the deceiving pitch. But its trajectory was low, and it certainly would have been ball two. No call was made on the pitch though, because Mitchell aggressively swung and missed on pitch number 95.

Looking back, I wonder whether the moment of truth really registered in my brain. One strike and I could go home with something every ball player dreams about—a no-hitter in the World Series.

Trying not to think about the possibilities, I prepared myself to throw what I hoped would be the most important pitch of my life. Up in the broadcast booth, Vin Scully's carefully chosen words added to the excitement: "Crowd's roaring now similar to the day Johnny Podres stood out last year. But there is so much more at stake."

If Yogi was feeling the strain, I couldn't tell. His eyes peered at me through the catcher's mask and his fingers indicated a fast ball.

Using my newly-discovered no wind-up delivery, I somehow calmed myself and threw a dastardly fast ball that wove in toward the inside back outer edge of the plate. Sensing strike three, Pinelli prematurely started to raise his hand to call the 27th and final Dodger batter out, but he wouldn't make the call. At the last possible second, Mitchell's powerful hands and arms lunged at the too-close-to-take fast ball and fouled it straight back of the plate. The crowd's thunderous "Ooooohhh" captured the moment.

A sudden gut-wrenching hush fell over the stadium as Pinelli dug a new baseball out of his umpire's bag and placed it in Yogi Berra's right hand. Mitchell stood just outside the batter's box nervously waving his bat at the sky. No doubt his mind was racing in tandem with the others as they all prepared to witness what I hoped would be a historic pitch.

They all expected me, the ol' Gooney Bird, to resume my position at the rubber and begin the sleight-of-hand motion that would deliver pitch #97. Every fan in the house that Ruth built craned their necks to get the best possible view, but I was just not ready. I stepped away from the rubber and off to the right side of the mound.

When I lifted up my left hand and took off my dusty blue hat with the fabled white *NY* emblazoned on the front, every eye in the stadium was on me. As the seconds ticked by, I wiped my brow with my forearm and then put my cap back on.

I was still not ready to pitch. I stooped down and picked up the half-full, dirt-smudged rosin bag that lay a foot to the right of the pitching rubber. Caressing it in my right hand, I jiggled a mist of white powder out of the thin bag and then peered down toward the ground.

For a few charged seconds, I just stood there, immobile. But then, I knew I was ready. I tossed the rosin bag, and after a quick glance toward center field, I turned and ascended the pitching rubber.

Behind me, the Yankee defense, forced to fidget in their respective positions as they awaited my next effort, now assumed their ready positions. Every Yankee player was determined not to ruin my chance at glory.

Catcher Berra, batter Mitchell, and umpire Pinelli returned to their respective crouched, close-knit positions surrounding home plate. Berra's eyes met mine, and the burly off-beat quipper and future Hall of Fame catcher ran through the regimen of pitch signs for what he hoped would be the final time.

Not unexpectedly, Berra signaled for a fast ball. Berra rose slightly from his deep crouch and positioned his catcher's mitt knee high and just to the outside lower position of the diamond-shaped plate.

The left-handed hitter Mitchell, sporting #8 on the back of his Dodger uniform, now assumed his crouched position deep in the batter's box. Babe Pinelli, umpiring for what would be his final time behind the plate after nearly a thousand games and 22 years as a man in blue, kneeled touch-close behind Berra. Pinelli later admitted that he was so short of breath that he felt faint.

Gasping for air in the frenzy, the overflow crowd now focused on the mound. I raised my hands and arms to shoulder length, all the while hiding my ball inside the worn Wilson-model glove that covered my left hand.

I propelled the tiny sphere on its intended trajectory toward Yogi Berra's mitt. While it took less than two seconds for that baseball to cut through the air and end up crossing the plate, those who witnessed my final pitch swore that time stood still.

I remember watching the ball turn over and over and head on a direct line with Mitchell's uniform letters. I saw Dale commit himself and make a futile half swing. He didn't connect and then I saw the ball pop squarely into Yogi's mitt.

Instantly, Dale looked back at Pinelli. I watched the umpire's mouth open, and he said something I couldn't hear. A second later, Pinelli's right arm pointed upward toward the sky.

Next thing I knew Yogi rose up out of his crouch. I saw Mitchell flail his arms and protest to Pinelli, but he was long gone. Without Pinelli or Yogi there, poor Dale looked rather lost. He was probably cussing at himself, wishing he'd either held up and taken a chance on a Pinelli ball/strike call or swung full-out at my pitch.

All the while Yogi was racing toward me with a huge grin on his face. When it registered that Pinelli had called strike three, I do not know. I didn't fully realize what had happened until Yogi leaped into my arms.

Two hours and six seconds from the first pitch of the game had elapsed. Later I'd learn that Vince Scully had memorialized the moment when he was kind enough to say: "Ladies and gentlemen, it's the greatest game ever pitched in baseball history."

—23—

Pandemonium

	1	2	3	4	5	6	7	8	9	10	R	H	E
Brooklyn	0	0	0	0	0	0	0	0	0		0	0	0
Yankees	0	0	0	1	0	1	0	0	x		2	5	0

WHEN YOGI BERRA JUMPED ON ME and grabbed me with the bear hug, my mind went completely blank. I was under friendly attack from the rest of my teammates as they danced with joy. Somehow I was swept into the dugout. Newspaper accounts said that several ball players all but carried me from the dugout runway to the clubhouse.

One reporter described the Yankee clubhouse scene this way:

The Yankee dressing room was bedlam. Players were yelling at the tops of their voices and sportswriters from all over the country were jamming into the room hoping to talk to the pitcher hero. Television cameras whirred and flash bulbs popped as Larsen climbed on a bench in the middle of the room to tell it like it was.

Those who couldn't get close to Larsen settled for the manager's office, including one rookie reporter who asked Casey Stengel, "Is that the best game Larsen's ever pitched?"

Off in a secluded corner of the Yankee clubhouse Don Larsen's catcher, a lonely figure, sat in front of his locker stripped to the waist and smoking a cigarette. One solitary reporter approached, and as he drew near, Yogi Berra looked up, and before the reporter could ask a question, Berra asked one. "What's new?"

Many articles were written describing my words and thoughts, but perhaps writer David Condon, in his column "In The Wake Of The News" the next day, gave the best account of the actions in the clubhouse just minutes after the game.

"Maybe," said the perspiring Larsen, as reporters and cameramen pressed him against his locker within moments after he entered the clubhouse, "it was as late as the seventh inning that he began thinking the no-hitter was there." Yes, he also knew he had a perfect game going. . . . Larsen smiled; he smiled and perspired almost continually as the shouting questioners bombarded him . . . . "About the eighth inning, I guess; I remembered how Floyd Bevens lost his no-hitter and I kept hoping it wouldn't happen to me," said Larsen. The photographers shouted for reporters to move away; the reporters fought back and bent heads toward Larsen. He spoke loudly. . . . "That Maglie pitched a helluva game, didn't he?" Larsen volunteered. . . . His lips showed touches of white as he chewed gum nervously. . . . Beads of perspiration dropped from his nose. . . . "I think it's the first time in the majors that I never walked anyone," said Don. . . . A reporter mentioned that in the first inning Larsen had run up a three-ball count on Pee Wee Reese, Brooklyn's second batter. . . . "I don't remember that," said Don. The crowd divided as Walter O'Malley, owner of the Brooklyn Dodgers, came up to congratulate the conqueror.

Larsen moved closer to O'Malley to oblige the photographers and the newsmen.

"Yes, I was nervous," Larsen said. "I was nervous in the last inning." There were shouts for O'Malley to remove his hat, for Larsen to hold up both hands, fingers in zero symbols to indicate the no-hitter and that no Dodger had gotten as far as first base . . . . What Dodger batter bothered him the most? "They all bother you," said Don. O'Malley edged away and now Dan Topping and Del Webb, co-owners of the Yankees, came forth to put arms around their pride. Topping might have embraced Don with more urging. "I'm still shaking," Larsen told Webb . . . "my knees were pretty shaky during that last   inning." What did Catcher Berra say to Larsen during the game? "He didn't say anything. Yes, I shook him off a couple of times, but that was just to confuse the Dodger batters. I came back with the same pitches I shook off," said Larsen. Don finally got off his white Yankee shirt; the undershirt was wet with perspiration. Yankee pitching coach Jim Turner wedged through, slapped Don's hip, and said, "You're my boy."

Foot by foot, Larsen edged across the clubhouse room to- ward a cooler where beer was on ice. He grabbed a can and took a long sip. A clubhouse attendant tried to hand him a cup, pleading "a beer can won't look good in the pictures"... "Who cares?" said Larsen. He raced ahead of the cameramen and reporters into the players' recreation room adjacent to the dressing quarters and plopped on a sofa beside Mickey Mantle. Mickey put his arm around Larsen's shoulder.... "In case anyone's interested," said the reporter, "Mickey said his home run was hit off a slider." No one was interested. Larsen sat and poured out the answers as the questions poured in. Yes, he had been close to a no-hitter before—when hurling for Baltimore against the Yankees in 1954; he thought that no-hitter was spoiled in the eighth inning. The year before, against Washington, he had one going until the seventh inning. A Yankee clothed only in droplets from the shower came in and said, "Hey, Larsen, break it up. Ya tryin' to take over our rec. [recreation] room. What's this excitement, the series isn't over yet."

Larsen this memorable afternoon pitched 97 baseballs at 27 Brooklyn batters in winning, 2 to 0. Each was delivered without a wind-up. "We were playing in Boston and I thought their coach, Del Baker, was swiping some signals. He's pretty good at that, you know, so I asked Jim Turner—our pitching coach—if I could experiment with no wind-up. We'd already clinched the pennant, and he told me to go ahead. It has worked out pretty well. For a while it confused the batters. Then, of course, I can cross them by winding up. But I didn't wind up once today," he said ....More bulbs popped; more questions came; more microphones were held under Larsen's mouth....The perspiration still dropped off; the back of the sofa was becoming as damp as his shirt....An usher came in and handed Larsen a baseball and fountain pen ....Babe Pinelli, the veteran umpire who this afternoon worked behind the plate for the last time in a career he is leaving when this series concludes wanted an autograph, a souvenir of the game that was the perfect climax to his own brilliant career. Larsen wrote his best wishes on the ball and signed it. Then he said: "That Pinelli called a helluva game."

The next day, *United Press International* would run a full length story of my version of the game. I remember talking to the reporter and I'm sure he must have helped me organize my thoughts:

My legs are still rubbery all over and I'm so nervous and excited I don't even know what day it is. Until today, the only thing I ever knew about a perfect game was what I read in a book. The last one was back in 1922, they tell me, and I didn't think I'd ever see one, much less pitch one.

If this story doesn't read altogether right, it's only because I still can't think straight. Honestly, in that last inning there I was so keyed up about the whole thing I almost fell down. Everything is still a little hazy but I remember striking out pinch-hitter Dale Mitchell on a fast ball for the final out. Just before I threw the ball I said to myself, "Well, here goes nothing." I'm not what you call a real praying man but once out there, in the eighth or ninth, I think it was, I said to myself, "help me out somebody." And I had plenty of help, too. That catch saved my bacon. And Andy Carey and Gil McDougald teamed up to pull me out of a hole when they robbed Jackie Robinson of a base hit in the second. The tightest squeeze I had was in the fifth on that ball Sandy Amoros hit. I was plenty lucky on that one. I thought it would be a homer and tie the game up but it curved foul, and I was tickled. Along about the sixth or seventh I realized I had a no-hitter but I never seriously thought about anything but winning the game.

I was especially anxious to make up for that lousy start I had against Brooklyn. You know the game in which I was six runs ahead and then was taken out in the second inning.

Casey Stengel has had a lot of faith in me this season—he sided with me when others didn't—and I just wanted to show him that his confidence wasn't misplaced.

Anyway, I hope my mom out in San Diego was watching the game on television. I think she was. Mom always tells me to be careful about how I pitch to Ted Williams. Ted wasn't swinging against me out there today but you know something? In that ninth inning, every one of those Dodger batters I faced looked like Williams to me.

Another fine sportswriter at the time, Will Grimsley offered this account entitled, "Don's Pins All Rubber In The 9TH."

"I was so weak in the knees out there in the ninth inning, I thought I was going to faint."

Big Don Larsen admittedly "in a daze," said he also mumbled a little prayer for help before he finally completed his perfect no-hit, no-run, no-man-to-first game against the Dodgers in the fifth World Series game.

Larsen said he realized in the seventh inning that he had a no-hitter going, but added: "I didn't get nervous—my main object was to win the game."

Then, he said, came the ninth, and he felt the full impact of his performance. "The thing I wanted to do was get out of the

ninth inning," he said. "Once I mumbled a little prayer to myself.
I said, "please help me get through this."

The towering right-hander from San Diego, Calif., said nobody on the Yankee bench mentioned that he had a perfect game
going.

"The only word said to me was by Yogi Berra," Larsen said.
"Yogi hit me on the seat of the pants and said, 'go out there and
let's get the first batter.'"

The Yankee dressing room—the dressing room of the "old
pros"—was bedlam for the first time during the Series.

Yogi grabbed Larsen around the neck. Mickey Mantle, normally quiet and retiring let out a resounding war whoop.

"Beautiful, beautiful," said Casey Stengel, the Yankee manager,
his creased face breaking into a broad smile. "This kid is a good
pitcher."

Walter O'Malley, the president of the Brooklyn Dodgers came
in.

"You beat us and I'm not happy about that," he said, elbow-
ing his way through a crowd around the beaming pitcher. "I have
to congratulate you—do me a favor will you? Sign this ball."

Larsen, who came to the Yankees in December, 1954, as an
insignificant part of the 19-player deal with Baltimore which
brought the Yankees Bob Turley, said Berra's crafty signal calling
and the Yankee's fine defensive play deserve equal credit for his
feat.

"I was pitching fast balls and sliders mostly," he said. "But
mainly I had pretty good control. I only shook off a couple of
Yogi's signals, but he stuck with them, so I went ahead and pitched
what he called. I'm glad of it."

The 6-foot-4, 225-pound Californian said his heart sank when
Sandy Amoros, the Brooklyn left-fielder, hit that shot in the fifth
inning which went foul by inches into the right field stands.

"I thought sure he had it," Don said, "and I also thought Duke
Snider's long foul in the fourth also might have gone in. I was
relieved when the umps motioned 'foul'."

Larsen was lavish in his praise of third baseman Andy Carey,
who before Monday had been the "goat" of the series with fielding errors and impotence at bat.

"That was a great stop Andy made on Jackie Robinson's hot
liner in the second inning," he said, "and he made a beautiful play
on Gil Hodges in the eighth. They saved the game for me. And
also Mickey Mantle's fine running catch of Hodges' hard-hit ball
to left center in the fifth."

When Larsen caught his breath, he said there was a bit of
irony in Carey's helping him to his perfect pitching performance.

"In 1954, when I was with Baltimore, I had a no-hitter going against the Yankees until the eighth inning," he said. "And you know who spoiled it for me—that guy, Carey."

Larsen said he changed his delivery about two weeks ago to eliminate the windup. The absence of the routine pitchers' windup was a unique part of his delivery, as the 64,519 fans and the millions of others on television may have noted.

"I just decided I could pitch better without it," he said. "Nobody gave me the idea. I figured I could get better control. And I believe I can."

Larsen simply puts the ball in his glove, faces the batter and lets fly.

Regarding my emotions when the game was over, I apparently told a reporter that I didn't cry when it was all over, but I did have a tear or two in my eyes when Yogi [Berra] came rushing at me....Then when Mr. O'Malley [president of the Dodgers] asked me to sign a baseball for him, my hand was shaking so much I could hardly write.

Dodger manager Walter Alston probably summed up the feelings of the Dodgers when he told reporters: "Larsen pitched a helluva ball game." That was quite a statement from the scholarly Alston, who added "and don't forget that Maglie pitched a great game too."

The Dodger skipper went on to say,

All the Dodgers were on their own at the plate all day and never was bunting discussed.

We thought we'd get some hits. We just kept swinging. Nobody tried to come up with any suggestions on how to break up Larsen's rhythm without a wind-up but I don't think that no wind-up business is what did it for him. He simply had great control and great stuff.

Pinch-hitter Dale Mitchell was right when he told writers that he made it a point to talk with me the day after the perfect game. He also said that he "would never be convinced that the last ball thrown wasn't outside."

Mitchell said, "I asked Larsen about the pitch being wide, but Don wouldn't admit anything. I should have figured that umpire Babe Pinelli would be calling anything close to the plate a strike." He added with a note of regret, "I guess I should have swung."

I tried to stay out of the controversy. Yogi Berra answered Dale Mitchell's claim that the last pitch thrown was a ball. Yogi told reporters:

> The third strike on Dale Mitchell was absolutely, positively a strike on the outside corner. No question about it. People say it was a ball and that I rushed the mound to hug Larsen to make the ump think it was a strike. Nonsense. It was a perfect strike.

After the game, Babe Pinelli described Dale Mitchell's last at bat:

> Larsen's first pitch looked good up to the last instant. Then it broke too high. "Ball", I said. Next, Mitchell took a swinging strike.
> Pitch number 3 was a steaming fast ball a fraction outside. "Ball two" I croaked.
> A foul ball followed. The quiet in Yankee Stadium was so deep I could hear the rasp of Larsen's breathing. If he'd heaved the next one into the grandstand, I wouldn't have been surprised.
> He let it go [Larsen told me later he didn't remember throwing it]. He hid the ball behind his glove so well I didn't pick it up until it was two-thirds in. It was his fast one. To the outside corner. At waist height. It clipped the corner without swerve or dip. Mitchell lunged, but for reasons I'll never know held back. We all stood frozen.
> "The third strike," I said, "and out."
> The first perfect World Series game was in the books and the whole country was going crazy.
> What did Larsen "have" as I saw it? Great courage and a great catcher, Yogi Berra, who directed all 97 of his pitches without a mistake. Plus a radical new no-wind-up style that speeded up his pitching pace, confusing the Dodgers. Mostly though, Larsen showed as sharp-breaking a curve as I've ever watched. And he threw it up at varying speeds. That's important. You can master everything else, but you're not a pitcher until you've mastered the change-up curve ball.
> It was the greatest game I ever worked in ... And it was also my last behind the plate. Yes, I'm through after this series. Boy, what a way to bow out.
> It's unbelievable ... simply unbelievable. What a game, what a game. I never saw anything like it before. I umpired four no-hitters in regular season play but none of them compared to this ... The strange thing about those no-hitters is that all were previously pitched by Dodger pitchers. Now I work a no-hitter pitched

against the Dodgers—and a perfect game at that. Boy, I'll have something to talk about and remember to my dying day. What a thrill. Nothing I ever saw could ever hold a candle to this one.

Pinelli also recalled the last pitch in this interview:

It was a fast ball ... It was right over the middle. It was an easy call. He was simply great ...That change of pace, particularly to the right-handed hitters, was great. It kept curving away from them. Seven or eight of them were swinging like at a ping-pong ball.

Sportswriter Dick Young of the *New York Daily News* also interviewed Pinelli for a column entitled: *Pinelli Calls His Last— And Greatest Game.*

"You gotta believe there's a guy up there calling the shots, when something like this happens to you." Babe Pinelli said it in the quiet of the umpires' cubicle as he shed his chest protector. He had just worked behind the plate in Don Larsen's historic perfect game—the last time Babe ever will work behind the plate.

It was as though this thing had been planned for him; as though this whole immense happening was a special going-away gift, he thought. Babe Pinelli is retiring from baseball at the conclusion of this World Series.

He has worked almost 1,000 games behind the plate during his 22 years as a big league umpire—and the last was to be the only perfectly pitched game in World Series annals; 27 batters up, 27 down.

"What a way to bow out!" he said happily. He fumbled around the floor of his locker, excitedly searching for something. "I gotta send a baseball to Larsen and have him sign it for me," he said.

Babe stripped down to reveal a dull bluish splash of color beneath his wishbone. It was the mark left by a wicked line drive that had struck him the day before.

"I'm a pretty lucky fellow," said Babe. "I might have been hurt bad, and would have missed this one. That would have been a shame. I haven't missed one since I came up to the National League in '35; and this was the greatest one of them all."

The younger men in the room smiled as Babe spoke. They were the other umps, and seemed to be enjoying the sight of a man who is to be 61 next week acting like an excited boy.

"You were pretty near perfect yourself," said Larry Napp, who umpired at third base.

"They only talked to me about one pitch," said Babe proudly. "Yogi asked about the one to Amoros. He thought Sandy had struck out. He said 'low?' and I said, 'yeah, it was low.' It wasn't really a complaint. He was just asking."

"Key-ripes" exclaimed Hank Soar, who worked first base, "the day you don't get a guy saying something, that will be the perfect game."

"He was uncanny," Babe said of Larsen. "He had pin-point control. They both did. Don't forget about Maglie. He was great, too. He was better than in the game he won in Brooklyn—only then, they got him some runs."

"He [Larsen] was just missing in Brooklyn," said Soar who had been the plate umpire for the second game.

Ed Runge, the ump stationed down the right-field foul line, was asked how far foul Sandy Amoros's hooking drive into the right-field seats had gone in the fifth.

"That much," said Runge, and he spread his thumb and index finger about four inches apart.

"That was a break for the kid," said Pinelli, "but you've gotta get a few breaks to pitch a game like that. That was a helluva call too," Babe said to Runge. "It shows how valuable it is to have a man down the line in these games. If I gotta call that one from the plate, I go the other way."

Frank Graham, Jr. in his *Sport Special*, described what he had seen in the ninth inning when I faced Mitchell.

The crowd sent up a groan as Larsen's first pitch went wide. Don came back with a slider and Babe Pinelli, umpiring his last big-league game behind the plate, called it a strike. Larsen, firing hard, his nonchalance gone and the game taking on a dream-like quality, got a fast ball over and Mitchell swung at it and missed. Trying to over-power the hitter now, Don threw another fast ball and Mitchell fouled it into the stands. It was Larsen's 96th pitch of the game and by now the crowd was screaming on every one he threw. Peering in through the haze, Don caught Berra's signal for still another fast ball. He mumbled a brief prayer to himself: "Please get me through this." Then he pitched.

It was on the outside corner and Mitchell cocked his bat, then held up. When Pinelli thrust his right arm up into the air, it was as if he had pulled a lever which set free a torrent of tumult and shouting. Berra rushed out to the mound and hurled his stubby body into Larsen's arms. The other Yankees poured out of the dugout to bury their hero under an avalanche of hugs, slaps and violent handshakes. Frenzied fans tumbled down from the stands to get in their licks at the beleaguered pitcher before he disappeared down the steps of the Yankee dugout. Pinelli, having called the third strike, had turned and rushed for the umpires' dressing room, his last decision at the plate his most memorable one. Mitchell stood in the batter's box, making his feeble protest to a world that had suddenly lost interest in him. Looking back now, I certainly do have an opinion about that last pitch. Over the years, so-called baseball experts have questioned the last strike call. All I can say is that they are plainly mistaken. That pitch caught the strike zone. Besides, Dale Mitchell had taken a half swing and went around. It was plainly strike three. Yogi's right and Babe Pinelli was right.

Yogi also said I made only one bad pitch in the game.

"That was the pitch to Gil Hodges in the fifth inning," the Yankee catcher said. "Hodges hit it to deep left center and it took a great running catch by Mickey Mantle to grab it . . . It was a slider which hung—when they hang, it's dangerous." Right, Yogi, absolutely right.

Interestingly enough, Dale Mitchell became famous more for what happened in the last at-bat against me than he did for his other baseball achievements. He commented later, "Here I average better than .300 for a career, get more than 200 hits in a season twice, play on three pennant winners, and all people remember me for now is that I took a called third strike to give Don Larsen his perfect game in the World Series."

What a difference a day makes. Before the game, no one seemed too interested in what I had to say about pitching techniques. Now I was some sort of expert on the subject.

My new no wind-up and theories about pitching were now of paramount importance to every reporter. Trying to keep a straight face, I told them:

"Just call it my new delivery," grinned the six-foot-four right-hander just before shoving off for a movie after today's World Series game with Brooklyn was postponed because of rain.

"This idea of pitching without a wind-up came to me about 10 minutes before I went out to face the Red Sox two weeks ago," he added. "So I went out and tried it and I beat them, 2-1, on a four-hitter.

"It worked out so good that I decided to use it against Boston the last time I pitched a week ago."

In that one, the unpredictable Larsen blanked the Red Sox on three hits during the seven innings he worked.

"Look," Larsen reasoned, "you don't have to be a big brain to know that all batting is in rhythm. So is pitching. So it's up to a pitcher to upset a batter's rhythm. When you don't wind up, the hitters have to be ready faster. Doesn't that make sense?"

I really enjoyed reading the accounts of different players' thoughts about the game. Duke Snider admitted that he had a tough time with the no wind-up.

You wait for Larsen so long and then he goes ahead and throws it. You can't tell when he's going to let it go. And while you're waiting there, maybe you drop your elbow or something and before you get set again the pitch is there ... I guess we should have stepped out more on him like Robinson did.

The most gracious of all of the Dodgers in defeat was my mound opponent, losing pitcher Sal Maglie. For a fierce competitor like Maglie to lose as he did, in spite of a great performance, had to have been devastating for him. Nevertheless, he made it over to congratulate me and talk with reporters about the game.

Described by one writer as "a sad and dejected athlete who had pitched a superb game himself," Maglie told reporters, "I'm glad he got it [perfect game], as long as we had to lose."

Apparently Maglie, after striking out the side in the bottom of the eighth, had left the field and gone down the steps and through the dugout without pausing. Sal sat on a runway wall for a minute or so with his head bowed and his hands clasped in front of him.

Maglie then returned to the dugout and watched the final three Dodger outs in the game. Later, in the clubhouse, Sal discussed the Yankee runs and told reporters that "everyone who hit a breaking ball got a hit. The one to Mantle was a curve that broke ... right over the middle of the plate." The exhausted Maglie also told the writers that "we were in the wrong ballpark. But we not only got no hits, we got no runs, and nobody could do anything about that."

In the Yankee clubhouse, Sal Maglie joined me in talking to reporters. He told them:

Everybody might have been cheering for you, Don, in the ninth, but I felt sorry for you because I know what was going through your mind. Had the same experience a few weeks ago, remember? Gee, it's tough in the ninth. Can't make a mistake, watch your control, remember what the "book" says about each batter. Hope a blooper doesn't drop in or a topper along the foul line or an accidental hit off a bat or a million and one things that can ruin you. I really felt sorry for you, Don. But you were the best and there was nothing we could do about it.

Gil Hodges echoed Sal Maglie's comments about the difference there might have been if the game had been played in Ebbets Field. Hodges' long drive to left center field in the fifth inning, which Mickey pulled in after a long run, probably would have been a home run in Brooklyn.

"Mickey would have had to have climbed mighty high if he'd have caught that one in Ebbets Field," Hodges said.

Pee Wee Reese apparently told Sal Maglie after the game, "I was beginning to think both you and Larsen never would allow any hits and this thing would be called on account of darkness in about the seventeenth inning."

Casey Stengel had some advice for those who felt every pitcher would copy my revolutionary new pitching form. Sportswriter Frank Graham, Jr. in *Sport* wrote about this issue and captured Casey's response:

There is the possibility that Larsen's perfect game may have an effect on the pitching motion of the future, but this is highly debatable. Immediately after the game there was speculation that Don's new delivery, minus the traditional wind-up, might have thrown the Dodger hitters off stride. As most good pitchers operate on the theory that to win they must keep the hitters off stride, it was reasoned that Larsen, in discarding the wind-up to improve his control, might have stumbled on the secret weapon that would nullify the lively ball in the eternal struggle of pitcher versus hitter. When Stengel was asked about it later, he delivered one of his penetrating monologues: "He pitched a perfect game, a no-hitter, and everybody says that's the way to do it. Well, he didn't wind up, and so I guess you got to say it worked, but in the second game of the Series last Friday he can't get the ball over the plate, walks four men, and I get second-guessed for taking him out of there. No winding up wasn't the way to do it last Friday."

I have no idea how long it took for me to answer all of the reporters' questions, but I would have stayed there all night if need be. I was so very proud of my performance, and I wanted to make sure that I credited my teammates, Casey, and the coaches for all their help.

After the last of the reporter's questions, I finally showered and readied myself to leave Yankee Stadium. My intention was to return to the hotel and celebrate with a few friends. That was not to be.

I must admit my recollections of that celebration night are a bit fuzzy. Fortunately, Frank Graham, Jr. of *Sport* described the evening:

Finally the last flash bulb had been popped and the most diligent reporter had drifted away to immortalize Larsen's performance in the next day's newspaper, and Don was free to dress and walk up 161st St. to the Concourse Plaza Hotel where he lives alone when the Yankees are at home. If he expected to spend a moment in solitary meditation before setting out to paint the town, he was in for a rude shock. He opened the door to find his room as packed with visitors as the Yankee clubhouse had been. "How the hell they got in there," Larsen said, shaking his head, "I'll never know."

He found out they were mostly people who couldn't force their way past the clubhouse guards. They had found the door to his hotel room a less impregnable barrier. They wanted interviews and endorsements and appearances, and Don's head would have been swimming at any unusual time of day had not his agent, Frank Scott, been there to handle the requests. Scott, a former Yankee traveling secretary who entered the more lucrative business of handling the outside affairs of big league players, had added Larsen to his stable some time before, but not until now had the arrangement been profitable to either party. Now the Scott-Larsen partnership was in business, and those who wanted something of Don had to wait their turn. Anyone trying to reach Don's room by telephone for the rest of that evening was invariably greeted by a "busy" signal.

Not one to linger long over business matters, Larsen soon disappeared from the room, taking a couple of friends from San Diego with him. "I'm going to the same places I always go," he told them, making it clear that fame and glory had not gone to his head. One of the places he always goes is a bar on 57th St. owned by Bill Taylor, the ex-Giant outfielder. The place was jumping that night and Don, who had whiled away so many evenings there in the past at his own expense, was now the agreeable recipient of more free beers than he could handle.

Later Larsen was joined by Artie Richman, a close friend who is a sports reporter for the *New York Daily Mirror*. [Don, an ardent admirer of his friend and fellow-townsman, Ted Williams, does not completely share Ted's loathing for newspapermen.] With a couple of girls who are members of a singing group called the "Bon Bons," Larsen and Richman began making the rounds. Like most of his thirsty clan, Larsen regards eating as a waste of time when there is serious drinking to be done, and so on this evening, when the free ones were coming one after the other, dinner could not be fitted into the schedule.

The party finally arrived at the Copacabana, one of Manhattan's biggest [and most expensive] night clubs. Larsen asked that the management refrain from introducing him, but no self-respecting night club proprietor could pass up such an opportunity. Comedian Joe E. Lewis, the star of the show, summoned Don up to the microphone for a bow and a bit of one-sided banter [by Lewis]. "It was just as if President Eisenhower had walked in the place," Richman said later. "The customers cheered for five minutes."

Afterwards the customers lined up for autographs and many of them brought over the club's photographer to have their picture taken with the new hero. Larsen and his party then sat around with Lewis until the place closed. Presumably none of Don's many admirers there was willing to send over drinks at Copacabana prices because when the bill was presented Larsen and Richman turned white. Lewis, however, saved the day [it was indeed almost daylight] by picking up the tab.

One thing that was great about the perfect game was that I read articles in the newspapers the next morning quoting my family. I really wish they could have been there to see the game, but according to the articles, they'd enjoyed it just the same.

My father, James, had watched the game in Berkeley.

"I didn't realize I had prayed that hard." That was the reaction at Berkeley of James H. Larsen to the first perfect World Series game which his son Don pitched today in his 2-0 victory over the Brooklyn Dodgers.

"Yes, sir," said Mr. Larsen, "I got down on my knees last night and prayed for Don. No, I didn't pray for a no-hitter, I just asked God to help Don beat those Bums."

Larsen recounted that he sweated out his son's every pitch after the fifth inning when he first realized he had a chance for a no-hitter, but was confident Don would make it.

A former semi-pro player, Larsen recalls that his son "always wanted to be a professional player when he was a prep diamond and basketball star in San Diego." Young Larsen first signed a contract with the St. Louis Browns, but "he wasn't a bonus player," said the beaming father.

In San Diego, my mother Charlotte did just the opposite— she didn't watch, but apparently for my own good. A newspaper reporter gave this account of her reaction to the perfect game.

Don Larsen's mother "kept a rule" and helped him win his perfect World Series game today.

Mrs. Charlotte Larsen, 61, a housekeeper at a La Jolla home for retired people said:

"I make it a rule never to watch Don when he pitches. Seems like every time I watch him, he loses. So I just don't do it."

She added, happily: "I didn't today and see what happened."

"I just couldn't bear to watch," Mrs. Larsen admitted. "If I had, I'm afraid I probably would have torn out my hair and everything else."

Mrs. Larsen nervously followed her son's progress through second-hand reports from friends. But she had no inkling he was pitching a perfect game and a no-hitter until the contest was over.

"Every couple of minutes somebody would come and tell me how Don was getting along," related the distinguished-appearing, gray-haired woman who made headlines of her own two years ago when she was lost four days in the Santa Rosa mountains. "But I had no inkling of the no-hitter. For some reason, that was never mentioned."

The pride my mother and father took in my performance meant a lot to me. We all want to give that to our parents at least once in a lifetime.

I've always cherished the thoughts after the game from the great Joe DiMaggio as well. In his column for *International News Service*, with the headline "Best I've Ever Seen," Joe wrote:

What can an "expert" say about a perfectly pitched baseball game?

Not an awful lot, particularly when he knows that every sports reporter and columnist in the country is commenting today on the beautiful job that Don Larsen turned in at the Stadium in the fifth World Series game.

So I'll merely content myself with saying that this was absolutely the best pitched game I've ever seen as player or spectator and that takes in some great pitchers and some wonderful pitching performances.

I was in center field when Monte Pearson threw his no-hitter against Cleveland and on the other side of the score when Bob Feller pitched that no-hitter for Cleveland against the Yankees right after the war. Great as they were, however, they were eclipsed by the game Don Larsen put together at the Stadium yesterday.

Joe's comments are very special. Having a Hall of Famer hitter like him talk about my pitching performance is something I'll never forget. October 8th, 1956, was a mystical trip through fantasyland. Sometimes I still wonder whether it all really happened.

—24—

The 9th of October

IN ATTENDANCE THAT MAGICAL DAY in New York was Al "Sandy" Cederholm of Fond Du Lac, Wisconsin. Sportswriters and broadcasters may have attempted to visually repeat the game for their readers, viewers, and listeners around the world, but Sandy has unforgettable memories of that October day.

Monday, October 8, 1956, was a school day, but when my mom said she had a ticket for me to Game Five of the World Series, I thought little of the possible punishment for skipping school. Her only directions were that I dress up and behave myself, and while I didn't much like getting dolled up, I put on a shirt and tie.

I got to Yankee Stadium real early, and I found my seat about fifty rows up and directly behind the Dodger dugout. I decided to head for the lower seats along the left field line to watch the outfielders catch batting practice fly balls. To my surprise, one of those hits glanced off the left field fence facade and right into my hands, providing me with the first miracle of the day.

Proud as hell of my new World Series souvenir, I headed up to my seat, but then I noticed that a bunch of kids were huddled around a ballplayer down by the Dodger dugout. Quickly, I scampered toward them, and holy shit, who should be sitting there big as life but Joltin' Joe DiMaggio. I patiently waited my turn, and then Joe took my ball and autographed it while I smiled from ear to ear. Two miracles down, and the best was yet to come.

I remember the close play on Jackie Robinson by Gil McDougald and Mickey Mantle's home run, but as the innings

went by the crowd got quieter and quieter as Don Larsen continued to set down the Dodgers in perfect order. From the sixth
inning on, people were literally holding their breath as the pressure mounted.

When the ninth inning came, I decided I wanted to be part
of history if Larsen was successful. I sneaked down by the Dodger
dugout and huddled near the fence. With the count one and two
on Dale Mitchell, I readied myself, and as Larsen threw the pitch,
I leaped onto the field. Either I'd be one of the first to pat Larsen
on the back or the security men would cart me away.

When the crowd roared, I knew I'd guessed right, and I raced
lickity-split for the mound. Other delirious fans were headed
toward Don Larsen, but I swear I touched the back of his shirt
only a second or two after Yogi Berra leaped into his arms.

The perfect game was my third miracle, and the next day's
Journal American featured a picture of me right there with Don,
Yogi, and the rest of the crazed Yankee fans.

When I picked up the *New York Daily Mirror*, which was
only *four cents* in New York City, and *five* elsewhere, I saw the
banner headline: "Larseny in the Bronx! Don Wins Perfect Game.
No-hits Dodgers 2-0." The *San Francisco Chronicle Sporting
Green's* headline was "No hits. No runs. No errors." The *New York
Daily News* called me "Zero Hero." Other papers around the country featured similar headlines.

I couldn't believe my perfect game had made news around
the world. Perhaps more than anything else though, was what a
difference one magical day made in my life. Three days before, I
was a dejected young pitcher who had let himself and his teammates down in Game Two. I had just hoped to hell that Casey
would give me another chance in the Series to redeem myself.

Now I had pitched a perfect game against the Dodgers and I
was the toast of the universe! Suddenly all of the reporters knocked
each other down trying to interview me. After the game, I told reporters "Before yesterday, no one knew I was alive . . . Today, everyone is telling me they went to school with me."

After celebrating the night before and waking up to realize
the perfect game wasn't a dream, I found myself glued to the comments made by the ball players, managers, coaches, and sportswriters regarding my performance and those of the other players who
participated in the game.

Newspapers as famous as the *Mirror* and as little known as
the Laporte, Indiana, *Herald-Argus* (near my   hometown of

Michigan City, Indiana), attempted to tell their readers how I'd pitched the perfect game. They exalted the performance and tried to put into perspective for their readers the significance of the achievement.

You could buy the *Argus* for 30 cents a week, one dollar a month, five dollars for six months, and eight dollars for a year in 1956. Their managing editor Donald Benn, aptly described most people's feelings about me that morning after Game Five. He wrote:

> A good many baseball fans said who's Larsen? When the listening and watching world learned about 3 o'clock EDT Monday that a New York Yankee pitcher by that name pitched a no-hit, no-run game which was also a perfect game, 27 men up and 27 men down. The answer, of course, is that Don Larsen is a big, strapping guy who has never became a top flight pitcher for the Yankees although he has shown flashes of greatness . . .

David Condon, the well-respected writer for the *Chicago Tribune Press Service*, found another way to laud the perfect game:

> Don Larsen, the New York Yankee's prodigal of spring training, became the darling of the baseball world this magnificent October afternoon with the most memorable world series feat ever accomplished in the big stadium that has seen Babe Ruth, Joe DiMaggio, and other Yankee heroes at their best . . .

Oscar Fraley, in the *Stars and Stripes* called me the "Towering Larsen, a modern Rube Waddell with all the talents of the old mound master," and the *San Francisco Chronicle* described me as "madcap Don Larsen, a carefree soul who breaks automobiles, likes bright lights, reads comic books, . . . and is just about the last person in baseball who might be expected to pitch a perfect game."

Shortly after the Series, baseball writer Al Hirshberg wrote an even more personal article entitled, "When Larsen Isn't Pitching."

> There have been hundreds of fun-loving rovers cavorting on and off big league baseball diamonds down through the years, but few were as fun-loving or as roving as Don Larsen of the New York Yankees. The tall, amiable right-hander set conventional training methods back a century when he pitched himself into baseball's gallery of the gods with the first perfect game of World Series history, against the Brooklyn Dodgers last fall.

It couldn't happen to a nicer guy, nor to one with less on his mind. Larsen lives as though there's no tomorrow. A restless, enigmatic soul with an insatiable appetite for the good, clean fun that is available in large cities between the hours of midnight and five a.m., he meanders endlessly in and out of favorite haunts looking only for something better to do than go to sleep. He is an insomniac who came from nowhere and, until the afternoon of Monday, October 8, 1956, when he pitched the game, appeared to be going nowhere. Up to then, he was accepted in baseball circles as a friendly eccentric who might have been a great pitcher if he ever put his mind to it. Since then, he has become a national institution.

Hirshberg also wrote:

He [Larsen] is a somewhat baffling personality, a man of many friends and few intimates, a loner who, paradoxically, hates to be alone. He has an easy-going warmth which draws people to him. It is amazing how many claim to be his close friend, yet know so little about him. But he is well-liked by those who have come into contact with him, and those who claim to know him best accept him for what he is—a good companion who rarely gets angry at anyone.

My Yankee teammates also got into the act when reporters asked them about me.

One player, who apparently kept his identity anonymous, told writer Will Grimsley that, "He's [Larsen] been typed as strictly a playboy ... you get the idea he is a wild roustabout who goes around busting up beer joints. That's not so at all. He has a devil-may-care attitude. He's really a swell-friendly guy."

Mickey Mantle devoted part of his daily newspaper column on the Series for the *New York World Telegram* and *Sun* to summing up his thoughts about me. Mantle wrote:

"He [Larsen] is a dry sort of humorist . . . and can make the rest of us Yankees forget about nerves. If a manager had 25 Larsens on a team he would never hear an argument."

I probably achieved the ultimate compliment for that day and age, however, when a baseball writer reported the contents of a conversation he had with a harried TV agent as he rushed around the clubhouse trying to find me after the game. "Forget Elvis Presley" the agent told him, "this guy Larsen is the hottest thing in the country right now."

In the *LaPorte Herald-Argus*, Donald Benn tried to put the perfect game in perspective:

> The perfect game in baseball is the equivalent of a sixteen foot pole vault, a 3.57 mile run, and a 300-foot pitch with the javelin. It is an utterly fantastic performance which combines skill and an unbelievable compounding of circumstances and are called breaks.
>
> Like the no-hit game itself, the perfect game has proved to be beyond the reach of generations of great pitchers in the major leagues. There have been some near misses but always circumstances combined to cheat the great hurlers and keep their names from this highest elevation of glory.
>
> To the baseball-wise it was not so surprising that the achievement, when it came, was the workmanship of a pitcher who has not achieved stardom and who may never reach that category. So often mediocre twirlers have pitched no-hit games, only to be forgotten by the next month. This does not in any sense diminish the wonder of it all, or the fact that a man using his arm and his brain, and backed up by eight teammates of varying skills, can occasionally produce an effort that is called perfect.
>
> That Larsen did it in a World Series game when the pressures are great and the stakes are high places his achievement on a pinnacle that will shine high above the greatest achievements in any competitive sport anywhere, anytime.

While these were words I would treasure, so were the ones from Frank Graham, Jr., who wrote in *Sport* that:

> The perfect game which Don James Larsen pitched that Monday afternoon had consequences on many levels. It was important to baseball, because the game's history, like a nation's, is brought to life mainly by the tales of heroes and their mighty deeds. Larsen's game which was the most brilliant single pitching performance in baseball history, now took its place alongside a handful of the greatest individual achievements, like Johnny Vander Meer's successive no-hitters, Babe Ruth's 60 homers, Joe DiMaggio's 56-game hitting streak, and Lou Gehrig's consecutive-game record.

Those who had participated in the classic game were sought out by every reporter. Duke Snider told reporters "He gave me only two curves ... the first one I hit way out to right field and the second one I hit hard, foul. He didn't give me any more curves."

Pee Wee Reese told reporters he figured the no wind-up helped me but it was more than that.

> If anyone deserved to pitch a perfect, no-hitter, Larsen did. His control was perfect. He had a good, live fast ball. The fact that he didn't take any wind-up might have gotten the ball up on you quicker.

Sandy Amoros called the game "perfecto," and right-fielder Carl Furillo talked about Amoros's drive being "foul by a foot" and added that "Larsen may have been faster in the second game of the Series, but he had nothing like the control he had today."

My Yankee teammates were also enthusiastic in their praise about my performance for the press. Joe Collins told reporters, "How about that. Unbelievable. Just unbelievable," and my room-mate Rip Coleman admitted, "I was so excited the last couple of innings I almost threw up."

Pitcher Bob Grim was warming-up in the bullpen "but I quit to watch the last couple of hitters . . . I still can't believe it."

Third baseman Andy Carey, who had broken that no-hitter I had going with Baltimore in 1954, told reporters, "It's something to be part of, isn't it?" Coach Bill Dickey said, "I've never seen this club so excited as it was in the ninth inning and that goes for me too."

Pitcher Bob Turley told reporters, "I just couldn't look." Reserve outfielder Bob Cerv said he had "stomach butterflies."

Mickey Mantle said, "Well that's one time my homer won't make headlines. Wasn't he terrific?" He also went on to say, "Larsen gave us all butterflies . . . and if there was any trick to the no-hitter it was the fact that Larsen could get a first strike on almost every hitter no matter what pitch Berra called for."

Whitey Ford was warming up in the bullpen during the game and told the *American Press,* "But don't tell Casey I stopped and began peeking from the seventh inning on. I couldn't heat up because of the goose pimples."

Pitching coach Jim Turner tried to give reporters his reasons for my success. Turner told them, "He's always known how to pitch but it was consistency he lacked. He was our best pitcher in September. His last four games all were four-hitters, you know."

Catching partner Yogi Berra told writers, "Don threw only one fat pitch, the one to Hodges and Mickey got it. That's right. What Don said about us not talking to each other was right."

When Berra was asked if he talked to any Dodgers during the epic, he replied, "Only to one guy." Yogi recalled, "Furillo and I started a conversation. I told Carl, 'This guy's stuff is real good today.' And Furillo, I think answered, 'You can say that again.'"

Yogi Berra also told the throng of reporters that:

> Larsen would never have done it if the score had not been so close, 2-0. If it was 9-0 he would have been paying little attention . . . It was close and he had to be extremely disciplined. He was. At the start of the ninth I didn't say a thing about how well he was throwing. I went to the mound and reminded him that if he walked one guy and the next guy hit one out the game was tied.

In a separate interview with Casey Stengel, reporters said that:

> Stengel, for the first time in his 66 years was speechless but only for a minute. Then the Ole Professor released his emotions in spasmodic expressions.
>
> "Terrific! Terrific!" Casey started in low tones and then he rocked the house with, "I've never heard of such a thing! He had his control and when Larsen has his control he can deceive you!"
>
> "The difference in Larsen, as I see it," he said, "is that he used to be too careful with his pitching. Today he had perfect control. He threw three called balls to only one batter—Pee Wee Reese in the first inning. That was the difference. When you got control you can pitch to the batters' weakness."

Casey Stengel also said he got some unwanted help in the eighth and ninth innings.

"I never had so many assistant managers," Casey Stengel said later. "On every pitch, the guys on the bench were hollering out to the fielders, telling them where to play the hitter." He also told radio broadcaster Bob Neal, "the difference today was that Larsen got the ball over the plate and found out the Dodgers couldn't hit home runs off of him. The other day he was too careful."

Writer Joe King of *Sport Magazine* somehow caught up with Stengel and got him to describe the game as only Casey could. Under the banner "Larsen Story in Stengelese," King wrote:

> I am a wise guy because I leave this fellow in there long enough to pitch the no-hitter but I am fortunate because I didn't leave him in there in Brooklyn because then I wouldn't be able to start him so soon.

In Brooklyn he has six runs of a lead and I tell him look they can't get ahead if they hit four home runs so go ahead and throw the ball, but if you play that dart game, aiming the ball and walking them, I am going to get enough of that.

What I always say about this fellow is the quality is always there but like any—you have to see it come out. As with everything I am willing to go three shots with a fellow to see what he has to give but when it gets to be five shots then I am the one who is getting abused.

This fellow pitches good enough as you saw but he can also handle a bat which you saw when he bunted on the third strike. He had to swing the first time because when you let them know you are going to bunt, these defenses are getting so good that they knock off your head man. Crosetti put the bunt sign on and took it off and I put it on again because that is the kind of batsman I have up there.

What I don't like is all the rest of these kids on the team are forgetting all about that money and getting excited over this no-hitter and I don't think they ought to get excited because we have to win to get ahead. When Mitchell comes up I am so excited that I am arguing with some of those kids about how to play him but he is hard to play anyway the way he hits. Once when Carl Furillo chipped one down the right-field line I said "Oh my, this is what he did to Reynolds," but I can't see where the ball goes because everybody is jumping up in front of me. I can tell it didn't go in but I ask them boys was it close and they jump up and down like cheer leaders and tell me not a chance.

Lemme tell you no matter how good our fellow was that Maglie was so good I am glad he didn't get the two runs first and I am also glad they didn't tie us for him because then we would wind up with a no-hit pitcher who wouldn't be helping us much.

When my big man comes up there with a man on third you figured he is in there to get the fly ball but this Maglie looks at Mantle the way he does and instead of getting two or three runs and putting them out of it I am out of the inning.

It looks as if this Maglie and the other fellow on first base has had a dress rehearsal for this play because this Hodges grabs the ball on first base for one out and don't even think before firing it to the plate because he has me figured out and knows I gotta send the man in. I don't know how this fellow can be beat at first base not the way he can throw it like he plays a little jai-alai.

Anyway, this fellow of ours shows he has the quality and we are back in business and I don't mean only the Yankees but all the baseball people. He gives us something to say against the pro football and the college men who are in the papers and we can get some news about baseball.

Regarding his true impressions of the game, Stengel said in the same *Sport* article:

"I've seen no-hitters before, too, but never a perfect game, either, and never a game like this under such pressure in the World Series.

"There are no words big enough to use on the fella," said Stengel, who often backed up Larsen this season when the front office wished him censured. "I've never seen anything like he did out there today in my life."

The kind words from so many people I respected meant a great deal to me. For days and months following October 8th, I would continue to read media accounts of the game and treasure the moments once again.

There was even a song written and performed with an accompanying guitar about the perfect game. I've never been able to trace down the singer's name, but this is how it went:

Come and gather around me people, and in song I will relate,
The story of Don Larsen, it was October 8th.
In 1956, and in old New York town,
The day that young Don Larsen pitched to twenty-seven down.

Don Larsen was his name,
But he wasn't near his fame,
When he pitched perfect baseball,
In the great World Series game.

He started in the minors, the St. Louis called his name,
To Baltimore one season, where his pitching was a shame.
They traded him to the Yankees, in the 17 player swap,
No one dreamed that young Don Larsen was slated for the top.

He was cool and temperamental, with his wife and he apart,
He even thought of quitting, with a sad and aching heart.
But the old gray fox stood by him, Casey Stengel patient man,
Put young Larsen into action when the big Fifth Game began.

After seven perfect innings, every Dodger knew the worst,
Not a man had hit on Larsen, not a man had walked to first.
Larsen said a prayer to heaven, and his shaking legs stood
still,
And the angel of the pitchers stood beside him on the hill.

Seventy thousand fans were breathless,
Came the ninth to bring him down,
Every player left the dugout,
Larsen paused there on the mound.

From Berra he got the ball,
With no windup let it fly,
And Dale Mitchell, the pinch-hitter,
Watched the third strike go on by.

Way high above the bleachers,
In that gallery in the blue,
There was Ruth, and Christy Mathewson,
And the Big Train watching too.

And I know that they were pullin,'
For that kid upon the mound.
The day that young Don Larsen,
Pitched to twenty-seven down.

Don Larsen was his name,
And he wasn't near his fame,
When he pitched perfect baseball,
At the great World Series game.

Imagine, a song written about me. Then imagine all the grief
I took from Yankee teammates when the song was played. They
were brutal, but I love every one of them.

Epilogue

IN SPITE OF THE EXCITEMENT AND HOOPLA surrounding the perfect game, there was still the 1956 World Championship to be decided. One and perhaps two games remained, and the Series returned to Ebbets Field where we had lost our last five games.

We now led three games to two, but Casey warned us that the Series was far from over. Coming down to earth after the craziness of Game Five would be no easy task. When our club sent "Bullet" Bob Turley to the mound to start Game Six, no one was quite sure how their players would react.

Turley, of course, had been a major part of the big trade with the Orioles that brought me to the Yankees in 1955. If he could sew up the Series, then Stengel and George Weiss could boast that they'd traded for two players who ended up winning the last two games necessary for the club to become World Champions.

After nine innings of Game Six, however, neither team had produced any runs. That meant that in the last 18 innings played between the two clubs, a total of two runs had been scored. Many people wondered whether Sal Maglie and I had put the players' bats to sleep in the Fifth Game, but Bob Turley and Dodger Clem Labine were no less effective in Game Six.

Clem Labine told me recently his performance is one that people forget, but I certainly never will. He'd only started three games all year, and he really came up strong for the Dodgers. Ten innings of seven-hit shutout ball. What an achievement, especially when your team is one loss away from losing the Series.

In that game, sportswriters questioned whether Casey Stengel went too far with Bob Turley when he allowed him to pitch the tenth inning. He had only given up three hits until the ninth, but when he walked Junior Gilliam to open the tenth, most people thought Casey would bring in one of our relievers.

But Casey stuck with Turley, and when Pee Wee Reese laid down a perfect sacrifice, and then Turley intentionally walked Duke Snider, the bases were full of Dodgers with no one out. At this point, another critical decision faced Stengel, one that immediately reminded me of the ninth-inning situation in the fifth game.

Using today's managerial strategies where the emphasis is on the "specialized player," there is no way that the slow-footed, 40-year-old Enos Slaughter would ever have been playing left field in the final inning of Game Five. Without question, a younger, more agile outfielder would have replaced Slaughter for "defensive purposes," and no one would have been surprised.

However, Casey Stengel didn't manage that way. He played hunches and was not inclined to switch a winning line-up in midstream. Therefore, just as Slaughter was positioned in left field for the last innings of my perfect game, he was there as Bob Turley faced Jackie Robinson.

Jackie Robinson brought back images of his great days of old when he hit a blue-dart liner straight at Slaughter. Enos would later explain that he didn't see the ball well off the bat, but for whatever reason, he took a fatal step forward before realizing the ball was headed over him for the outfield wall.

When he finally caught up with Robinson's hit, it was too late, for Gilliam raced across the plate with the winning run to tie the Series at three games apiece.

Bob Turley had pitched brilliantly, but in a losing cause, which unfortunately happened to him far too often during his career. In fact, after the game, Casey told reporters: "I can't figger out that fella [Turley] . . . He don't smoke . . . He don't drink . . . He don't chase around none . . . But he can't win as good as that misbehavin' fella you know about that was perfect!"

I wonder who Casey was talkin' about.

Of course, Slaughter's miscue caused an avalanche of controversy with everybody second guessing his judgment on the play and that of Stengel for leaving him in. Apparently Billy Martin really gave it to Casey as only he could, telling his mentor that he'd better get Slaughter out of left field for the Seventh Game before Enos blew another game for us.

My own thoughts differed from those of Martin. I could see very clearly the shot by Robinson from the dugout, and I don't fault Slaughter at all. Jackie's hit was really smacked and the ball seemed to rise a bit as it headed over Gil McDougald's head. Even if Enos had picked up the ball earlier, and sped backwards, I doubt very much whether he could have caught it.

Whether Slaughter should have been in left field is a valid question, but no one will ever get me to criticize Casey Stengel on his choice of players. Ninety-nine times out of 100, he was right on the beam.

With the Series now squared up at three games apiece, our club prepared for the deciding Seventh Game. My head was still spinning from all the attention I was getting about the perfect game, but I readied myself as well, because I was prepared to go out and throw in relief if need be.

In that Seventh Game, the pitching match-up seemed at first glance to be a mismatch. Walter Alston chose Don Newcombe, the big right-hander who'd gone 27-7 during the regular season. To face Newcombe, Casey had a difficult choice to make between Tom Sturdivant, who'd pitched so well in Game Four, Whitey Ford, and Johnny Kucks.

In making his decision, Casey apparently dismissed the idea of using Ford, since left-handers had such a tough time in Ebbets Field. Sturdivant, who had pitched on October 7th, would have to have pitched with only two full days of rest. Jim Turner and Stengel apparently decided that was not enough.

Johnny Kucks, who had pitched in Games One and Two, got the call. The hope was that he could go four or five innings and then turn the game over to our "bullpen by committee," as they call it now, that could finish off the Dodgers. As was his custom, Stengel never let Johnny know he'd be the starting pitcher until the team arrived at Ebbets Field on the morning of Game Seven.

When he took the mound for that monumental Seventh Game, Johnny Kucks was a 22-year-old, second-year pitcher who'd exceeded everyone's expectations during the regular season by winning 18 games. He'd toiled 224 innings, and while he wasn't a strikeout pitcher, Kucks had good control. He walked only 72 men in all those innings. When his sinker was working, Johnny was unhittable.

While his young age and inexperience would be against him, the fact that he was a sinker-ball pitcher made Johnny the right pitcher to face the Dodgers. Coming off two games where Bob Turley and I threw high velocity fast balls and breaking balls, Casey felt that Kucks' sinker might keep the Dodger hitters off-guard.

While Casey showed a lot of faith in starting Kucks, Johnny must have wondered what the devil was going on when he saw Tom Sturdivant and Whitey Ford warming up *before* he threw the first pitch of the game. Kucks told reporters after the game that he knew the hook would be a quick one if he had trouble early in the game.

The pressure on Kucks subsided some however, in the very first inning when Yogi Berra clobbered a two-run homer off Don Newcombe to give the Yankees a 2-0 lead. There's something about being up a couple of runs before the first pitch that instills immediate confidence in a pitcher, and Yogi's blast allowed Johnny to take a deep breath.

Kucks held the Dodgers scoreless in the first two innings and then Yogi helped his pitcher out again with his second two-run homer to give us a 4-0 lead. A gentle quiet suddenly came over Ebbets Field after Yogi's home run as the Dodger faithful realized that a second consecutive World Championship was slipping away.

Johnny Kucks, of course, went on to pitch a masterful three-hit shutout and we kicked the Dodgers' butts all the way out of Ebbets Field with a 9-0 whitewash to win the World Series four games to three.

A footnote to that game is that whatever Billy Martin must have said to Casey stuck, because in the Seventh Game Elston Howard played left and hit a home run! Moose Skowron, who had been disappointed to have played first base all season only to be replaced by Joe Collins for most of the Series, also contributed with a spectacular grand slam.

In fact, Hank Bauer recalled recently that while Moose was at bat, Casey gave out one of his famous whistles. "Moose told Campanella Casey was gonna take him out," Hank said. "Campy says no, just go see what he wants. Moose comes over and Casey says, 'Take a couple of shots to right.' Next pitch, Moose hits a low slider into the left field stands. When Moose comes back to the dugout, Stengel says, "Way to pull the ball, Moose."

Kuck's pitching and strong support won the day. Besides pitching the perfect game, I now had a championship ring on my finger.

The celebration was a non-stop affair, and October 10th would rank with October 8th as two of the greatest days of my life.

If we hadn't won the World Series, much of the luster of the perfect game would have been lost. To not only be a part of my first World Championship team, but to pitch the perfect game as well was almost too much to comprehend.

I was named the Most Valuable Player in the Series. With all the great performances in those seven games, I was genuinely surprised and absolutely overwhelmed that the sportswriters covering the Series would grant me such an honor.

When I look through the roll call of Most Valuable Players in the World Series and see names such as Sandy Koufax, Bob Gibson, Whitey Ford, Frank Robinson, Roberto Clemente, Reggie Jackson, Pete Rose, Johnny Bench, and Willie Stargell next to mine, it is quite a thrill. To think that I was selected over Yogi Berra, or Duke Snider, or Tom Sturdivant, or Clem Labine, all of whom had a great Series in 1956, makes the award even more special.

Sport Magazine presented me with a brand new Corvette. I loved that baby. I also appeared on the Bob Hope Show and made numerous other personal appearances over the next year.

A short time after the World Series was over, I received a very special letter. It read:

Dear Mr. Larsen:

It is a noteworthy event when anybody achieves perfection in anything. It has been so long since anyone pitched a perfect Big League game that I have to go back to my generation of ball players to recall such a thing—and that is truly a long time ago.

This note brings you my very sincere congratulations on a memorable feat, one that will inspire pitchers for a long time to come.

With best wishes,

Sincerely,
Dwight D. Eisenhower

That letter meant so much to me. I remember carrying a copy of it around with me for days and showing it to everyone I knew.

Although there are few baseball fans who haven't heard about the perfect game, there are many who don't realize that I went on to play another ten years in the major leagues before retiring in 1968. Baseball was an incredible experience for me, and I cherish its memories to this day.

I'm not sure what people expected from me after the perfect game. Those who managed me, or coached me, or played with or against me must have had certain expectations, and perhaps I disappointed some of them by not living up to their standards. When I look back over those final ten years in the majors, however, I am damn proud. God gave me the talent to pitch in the major leagues, and to pitch a perfect game, and I know in my heart that I gave baseball every ounce of effort I had every time I went between the lines.

After the perfect game, Casey Stengel said a lot of things about me, but the one I'm most proud of is that he said I was "always a hard worker." I may have been called "Gooney Bird" and even less flattering nicknames, but any manager I ever played for will say he got 100% from Don Larsen.

In 1957, the Yankees again trained in St. Petersburg. From day one, everybody talked about the perfect game. That was all right. I enjoyed the limelight and talked to reporters as often as possible. Autographs were in demand too.

I knew Casey expected a solid season from me, and I won the opener in Washington. That season I ended up 10 and 4 in 27 games with a 3.73 earned run average.

We won the pennant again and faced the Milwaukee Braves in the Series. They were a powerful club that featured Joe Adcock, Red Schoendienst, Johnny Logan, and Eddie Mathews in the infield; Hank Aaron, Andy Pafko, and Billy Bruton in the outfield; Del Crandall behind the plate, and a murderous pitching staff that included Warren Spahn and Lew Burdette.

I relieved Bob Turley in Game Three, and garnered a "W" when Tony Kubek hit two home runs. In that game, I pitched two consecutive scoreless innings, making it eleven straight counting the

'56 streak. That's still a record today. My long-time friend Johnny Logan broke up the streak with a dinky single. He says I glared at him on first base and cussed a blue streak, but I don't remember doing that. The Series went the full seven games, and I started the final one against Lew Burdette.

Unfortunately, the Braves hit me hard early and I was replaced in the third inning. We lost that game 5-0, and the Series. Our reign as World Champions lasted only one short year.

Nineteen fifty-seven was a celebrated year in other ways however, since during the All-Star break, I met Corrine Bruess, who would become the love of my life. Corrine was a flight attendant for TWA, and we started dating after I ran into her on a flight out of Kansas City.

Casey Stengel really took a shine to Corrine. In fact, after he learned that I'd met her on an airline flight, he told us, "That was a great thing Eddie Rickenbacker did—inventing aviation."

On December 7, 1957, Corrine Bruess, born and raised in Sleepy Eye, Minnesota, became Corrine Larsen.

Marrying Corrine was the best thing that ever happened to me. She and I spent time with the other Yankee couples, and while I still liked having fun on my own, bringing Corrine along made it more complete somehow.

An elbow injury limited my participation to just 19 games in 1958, but I ended up winning nine games and losing only six with a 3.08 earned run average. Sal Maglie joined the Yankee club that year. He and I never did sit down and talk about the battle we'd had on October 8, 1956. That sounds pretty odd, but it just never happened.

We won the American League pennant and faced Milwaukee once again in the Series. The Braves won the first two games, 4-3 and 13-5. I started Game Three, and together with relief help from Ryne Duren, we whitewashed the Braves, 4-0.

Warren Spahn then beat us 3-0 in Game Four to give the Braves a seemingly insurmountable 3-1 Series lead. Bob Turley started Game Five for us and turned the tables on the Braves with a strong 7-0, five-hit outing.

Game Six then went to extra innings, but we evened the Series with Milwaukee when we scored two runs in the tenth, and Turley came in to retire Joe Torre with the tying run on third base.

I played in five World Series, and all of them went to the seventh game.

When I had started Game Seven against the Braves in 1957, I had felt tremendous pressure. I knew the world was watching, and that my teammates were hoping I'd carry them along so that they at least had a chance to win.

The fact that I was hit pretty hard in that Seventh Game, and lost to Lew Burdette 5-0 was a stinging disappointment to me. My performance in Game Three in 1958 gave me some redemption and caused Casey to start me in Game Seven of that Series. I pitched the first two innings, (giving up one run), and to one batter in the third.

Bob Turley relieved me and went on to pitch the final six and two-thirds innings. Bill Skowron's three-run homer in the eighth led us to a 6-2 win that made us the first team since 1925 to come back and win the World Championship after being down three games to one. I had my second World Series championship ring, something I treasure to this day.

The year 1958 was a great time for Corrine and me. We lived in a rented house over in New Jersey across the George Washington Bridge from New York City. Art Ditmar, Mickey Mantle, Tom Sturdivant, and Bobby Schantz and their wives lived nearby. All of us chipped in fifty bucks and we bought a '49 dark brown Packard. Since Tom Sturdivant loved to drive, he was our chauffeur. I remember bouncing across the bridge en route to Yankee Stadium in that Packard. It weighed almost as much as a tank, and ol' Tom would gun it across the bridge like there was no tomorrow.

In 1959, the Chicago White Sox won their first American League pennant in 40 years. Our club hit rock bottom in May when the team fell to dead last. The White Sox went on to beat the Indians by five games. We finished third.

Bob Turley and I both struggled that year with losing records. I never could find my control on a consistent basis, and finished 6-7. Bob went 8-11. Whitey Ford was the only pitcher to win as many as 16 games for our club.

In the winter of 1959, I got a second dose of the news that every ball player expects, but dreads. I loved playing for the Yankees, and so the news that I had been traded to Kansas City hit me doubly hard.

I can't say that the trade was completely unexpected, because a player always hear rumors that something may be up. I hadn't exactly set the world on fire in 1957 and 1958, and so when the Yankees had a chance to pair Athletics slugger Roger Maris with

Mantle, they jumped at the chance and traded me, Hank Bauer, Marvelous Marv Throneberry, and Norm Siebern together for Maris, Kent Hadley, and Joe DeMaestri.

The trade was even tougher on Hank Bauer. I don't know if he ever forgave Casey or the Yankees for trading him. Hank had given the club some great years and everything he had every time out. I think it hurt him more than any of us to be cast away by the very club he was so loyal to.

For Corrine and me, the trade meant a house-hunting trip to Kansas City where she had many friends from her days with TWA. I hated leaving the Yankees, but if I had to be traded, at least it was to a club that was in a great place like Kansas City.

Charley Finley owned the Athletics at that time, and in 1960, I joined them at the age of 30. The team trained in Palm Beach, and I got to know players like Dick Williams and Whitey Herzog that I'd played against for years.

Our team ended up in the basement with a 58-96 record. I didn't help them much, losing 10 of 11 decisions. I hurt my arm that year and was sent to Dallas to rehabilitate it, but I never got any consistency going and struggled along with the losing ball club.

Playing for a last-place club after being with a contender like the Yankees all those years was really tough on me. No one who hasn't experienced losing as many games as we did can really know what it's like to endure such an experience.

All ball players deal with losing in different ways. Some rationalize the losses and blame them on injuries, or bad luck, or poor management, or whatever. From my point of view, baseball is a team game, and you win as a team and lose as a team.

Besides me, the 1960 Athletics had several former Yankee players on the team who were used to winning. Hank Bauer, Jerry Lumpe, Andy Carey, Norm Siebern, and Bob Cerv all did their best to help keep a positive attitude on the club, but our pitching was mediocre, the hitting weak, and we never recovered from a bad start.

Nineteen sixty-one featured Roger Maris' 61 home runs. I started the season with the Athletics, and won one game before being traded along with Ray Herbert and Al Pilarcik and Andy Carey to the Chicago White Sox for Wes Covington, Bob Shaw, Gerry Staley, and Stan Johnson.

Again I renewed some old friendships and got to play with Nellie Fox, the best second baseman I ever saw, as well as Luis

Aparicio and Minnie Minoso. Al Lopez managed the fourth-place White Sox that year, and I pitched well for him, going 7-2, with two saves on a pitching staff that included Early Wynn, Billy Pierce, and Juan Pizarro.

In 1962, I was shocked when I was traded out of the American League for the first time along with Billy Pierce to the San Francisco Giants. Alvin Dark managed a solid club that year, and I had the privilege of being able to watch the great Willie Mays in action all year long.

The Giants would go on to win the National League pennant that year, the same year the expansion Mets, under my old boss, Casey Stengel, lost a record 120 games. With Mays, Orlando Cepeda, Harvey Kuenn, Willie McCovey, and Felipe Alou in the line-up, we had plenty of power.

The pitching staff for the Giants in 1962 was one of the best I've ever seen. Jack Sanford was almost unhittable that year, winning 24 while losing only seven, and Billy O'Dell, Juan Marichal, and Billy Pierce backed him up.

I pulled my weight for the Giants by appearing in 49 games, going 5-4, and saving a career-high 11 games. I liked the role of stopper, and Al Dark showed a lot of confidence in me.

The Dodgers led our club in the last month, but could only win three of the last 13 games they played. Willie Mays had 49 home runs that year, and we closed fast to gain a tie with the Dodgers and force a playoff.

I got credit for the win in the final game of the playoffs, when the Giants came back from 4-2 down in the ninth to win 6-4. Now our club would be facing the Yankees, who had beaten the Twins by five games behind the American League's Most Valuable Player, Mickey Mantle.

Our two clubs split the first two games in San Francisco and then we boarded the plane and headed for Yankee Stadium. I had always hoped I'd get back to New York, and I was thrilled at the chance to step one more time between the lines at my old park.

When I replaced Billy Pierce in the seventh inning of Game Three, I received an ovation from the Yankee Stadium fans that I will never forget. Their appreciation was heart warming, and it brought back fond memories of my years with the team.

Being on the same mound where the perfect game occurred was something that's difficult to describe. Even though I was nervous as hell, I took time to look around that great old stadium and remember back to that incredible day six years earlier.

New York won Game Three 3-2, but Pierce got the loss. I picked up a win in the Fourth Game when I relieved in the sixth inning just before the Giants plated four runs on Chuck Hiller's grand slam. For whatever reason, the Good Lord had allowed me to return to Yankee Stadium one more time. I topped it off by gaining a victory against my old club. It happened on the sixth anniversary of the perfect game.

The Series went the distance, and then Yankee pitcher Ralph Terry pitched his masterful shutout in Game Seven. Our club almost pulled it out in the bottom of the ninth, but Bobby Richardson speared Willie McCovey's hard liner to end the game with the tying and winning runs on base.

Besides playing in the Series, I had another reason to call 1962 a great year. On October 5th, just three days shy of the sixth anniversary of the perfect game, Corrine presented me with our son, a baby boy named Don Scott Larsen. Years later, he and his wife Nancy gave us a grandson, Justin.

I began 1963 with the Giants at their spring training facility in Phoenix. The team was loaded with the same powerful line-up as the previous year, but the pitching staff didn't live up to pre-season expectations.

Juan Marichal won 25 games, and Jack Sanford 16, but in August our team cooled off, and we finished just 14 games over .500 at 88 and 74. I appeared in 46 games for the Giants that year, and ended up 7-7 with a good E.R.A. of 3.05.

I started the season with the Giants once again in 1964, but then was traded in the second month of the season to the Houston Colt .45's. The very man who traded for me that year was general manager Paul Richards, who had dealt me away from Baltimore to the Yankees in 1954.

Now 34 years of age, I played on a Houston team that included Jim Wynn, Rusty Staub, and a 20-year-old future Hall of Fame second baseman by the name of Joe Morgan. We would finish 66-96 that year under Harry Craft and Lum Harris and ahead of only the lowly Mets who lost 109 games under Casey Stengel.

The fabulous Astrodome opened in 1965. I started against the Yankees in a pre-season game that was part of a round-robin tournament to mark the opening of the Dome. Just after the regular season began however, another irony occurred when Paul Richards traded me again, this time back to the Baltimore where my major league baseball career had first begun.

Under the tutelage of my old Yankee buddy Hank Bauer, I appeared in 27 games and won one while losing two with a 2.67 earned run average. The Orioles, with such outstanding players as Boog Powell, Brooks Robinson, and Luis Aparicio, featured a pitching staff that included Steve Barber, Milt Pappas, Stu Miller, and 19-year-old future Hall of Famer Jim Palmer.

I pitched decently well in Baltimore, and got to watch the great Robin Roberts, who at 38 was winding up a brilliant career. I also enjoyed playing for Hank, who brought home a winning team (94-68). We finished third behind league champion Minnesota, whose Mudcat Grant won 21 games, and the Chicago White Sox.

Just as every ball player knows there is the potential that they will be traded, I also knew that there would be the day when I would be released. When I began the 1966 season in spring training with the Orioles in Miami, I knew the odds of making that ball club were slim.

Hank Bauer and the Orioles were poised to contend for not only the league title, but the World Championship as well. In fact, the team went on to beat Minnesota by nine games for the pennant, and then crush the Dodgers in four straight to claim the World Championship.

During spring training that year, I tried my best to prove that I could still pitch in the majors. Unfortunately the handwriting was on the wall, and I could tell that Hank was struggling with what to do.

Ballplayers always hope that the manager or the general manager (in this case Harry Dalton), will meet with them, face to face, and give them the news. That's the class way to handle such an emotional moment, especially for a veteran who knows he may be getting his last shot at the major leagues.

Maybe there was a mix-up or lack of communication, but I heard about my release from the team from Clay Reed, the clubhouse man for the Orioles. I didn't appreciate that, and I've always wondered why Harry or Hank didn't tell me themselves.

After the release, I pitched in the minors in Hawaii and Phoenix. In 1967, I did well enough to get called up for a last hurrah with the Cubs, who were managed by Leo Durocher. Ernie Banks, Ron Santo, Randy Hundley, Billy Williams, and Ferguson Jenkins were members of that third-place team.

I got into three games with the Cubs, but I was so damn nervous that I just couldn't get the ball over the plate. I guess Leo must have gotten tired of seeing my act, and I was sent down to Dallas-Ft. Worth.

I didn't pitch too badly there and decided to give it one more try in 1968. Unfortunately, my body wore out, and I finally decided to hang up the uniform when I was released by San Antonio during spring training.

After that, I took a job in the corporate world, spending 25 years with a paper company on the west coast as a manufacturer's representative before retiring in 1993 to Idaho.

People wonder why a ball player hangs on and on, even when he should probably quit. After playing in the major leagues and experiencing the thrill of the sport at that level, it's hard to let it slip into the past. When I quit I was very disappointed that I could no longer do the job I knew had been designed for me. Of course, I knew my body was going to wear out sometime, but I wanted to show everyone that I could still pitch.

When I think about my baseball career, I try to put things in perspective. My major league record may be 81 and 91, but I had 14 years in the big leagues. I played on two World Champions, five pennant winners, and in five World Series, all of which went to that exciting seventh game.

During my career, I played with Mickey Mantle, Willie Mays, Yogi Berra, Ernie Banks, Whitey Ford, and against Ted Williams, Duke Snider, Roy Campanella, and Stan Musial, some of the greatest players ever to play the game.

Besides the players, Corrine and I made lifelong friends we'll never forget, and enjoyed a great relationship with baseball fans all over the world. Baseball may be just a game, but it brings people together like nothing else I know.

I still miss the enjoyment of being with my teammates. There's a family atmosphere around a ball club, a close personal relationship that transcends the game. I also miss the competitiveness. It's fun to be out there on the field competing against other teams.

Feeling that I'd contributed to the ball club in even the smallest of ways was pure delight.

As for the perfect game, it's still hard for me to believe that it really happened.

Of course, I know it did, and I think about it probably at some time or another every single day. Just as with other significant days in history when something of great consequence happened, people come up to me and can tell me where they were on October 8, 1956. They may have watched it on television, or heard the game on the radio, or been there, but most people can recall more details about that game than I can.

To have pitched the perfect game against the Dodgers, Sal Maglie, and their powerful line-up, means a lot to me. They were the defending World Champions and the second best club in the world that year, maybe one of the best of all time. From Gilliam on down the line-up, there wasn't a slack hitter in the group.

In some ways, it's probably good that the perfect game happened because people remember it, and not all of the other mistakes I made during my career. And believe me, I made just as many when I was with the Yankees as I did with other clubs. But with the great Yankee team behind me, there was always a chance to catch up and still win some games.

My regrets are few with the Yankees, but I do have one.

I was extremely disappointed that they did not give me a bonus for pitching the perfect game. During the winter, I tried to get a thousand dollars that I needed for my mother, but George Weiss refused.

Despite their slight, I had special plaques made up and sent them to all of the club executives, the Yankee players, coaches and manager, the umpires, league officials, and friends to commemorate the game. I gave my uniform to the San Diego Hall of Champions and had my ball, glove, hat, and shoes silvered.

As I travel around to baseball card shows and make special appearances, I'm often asked whether my perfect game performance is the greatest game ever pitched. If I had been a spectator at that game, I would probably say yes, but being the one who pitched it makes me have to rely on what others say.

Looking back, though, I still wonder why I was chosen to pitch the miracle game on that autumn day. Maybe the good Lord wanted to show all of the underachievers in the world that with His grace, we are capable of anything. I never was possessed with the most talent, and just two short years before the perfect game, I lost twenty-one games and won only three. But I never gave up hope. I never allowed myself not to believe that great things could happen.

All I can say is that I'm very thankful to have done one thing while I was on this earth that is considered perfect. I may have had an up and down baseball career, but no one can ever take away that October afternoon in 1956 when I threw the only perfect game in World Series history.

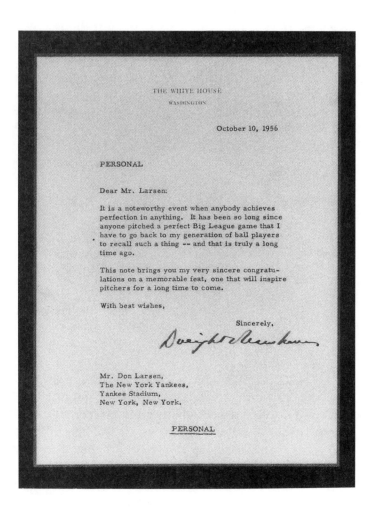

THE WHITE HOUSE
WASHINGTON

October 10, 1956

PERSONAL

Dear Mr. Larsen:

It is a noteworthy event when anybody achieves perfection in anything. It has been so long since anyone pitched a perfect Big League game that I have to go back to my generation of ball players to recall such a thing -- and that is truly a long time ago.

This note brings you my very sincere congratulations on a memorable feat, one that will inspire pitchers for a long time to come.

With best wishes,

Sincerely,

Dwight Eisenhower

Mr. Don Larsen,
The New York Yankees,
Yankee Stadium,
New York, New York.

PERSONAL

Postscript

Don Larsen's Place in Major League History

Commentary by Mark Shaw

UNDOUBTEDLY THE PERFECT GAME pitched by Don Larsen is one of the most stunning events in the history of sport. Until another hurler surpasses Larsen's performance by pitching a "better-pitched" perfect game at a "more significant" moment, Larsen's achievement stands by itself as the greatest game ever pitched.

There are those who would disagree with such an assessment. They usually point to four pitching performances that offer stiff challenges to Don Larsen's lofty position in baseball history.

Just six World Series games before Larsen's miracle, 24-year-old Brooklyn Dodger southpaw Johnny Podres had battled his team's never-having-won-a-World Championship demon in the Seventh Game of the 1955 Series. Facing the all-star laden New York Yankee team, Podres stepped to the mound in Yankee Stadium on October 4, 1955, against Yankee counterpart Tommy Byrne.

Don Larsen was a spectator in his first year with the Yankees when Johnny Podres attempted to do what no other Dodger pitcher had done before—bring home a World Championship for his beloved Bums. In 1941, 1947, 1949, 1952, and 1953, failure had been the buzz-word for the "wait 'till next year" Dodgers.

Johnny Podres' lackluster 9-10 won-lost record in 1955 made him an unlikely hero like Don Larsen. His 9-4 in 1953 and 11-7 record in 1954 didn't reveal a "big-game" pitcher. However, when

Dodger ace Don Newcombe sustained an arm injury prior to Game Three after the Yankees had won the first two, Manager Walt Alston called on Podres who pitched a seven-hit, 8-3 Dodger win that gave his "loser-labeled" team new life.

When Carl Erskine and Roger Craig beat the Yankees in Games Four and Five, the Dodgers suddenly were within a step from a World Championship. Unfortunately, they couldn't beat Whitey Ford's four-hitter in Game Six and the Series suddenly was headed for the like-no other pressure-packed Seventh Game.

Yankee left-hander Tommy Byrne would be Podres' mound opponent, but the Yankee team that Podres faced was missing a key player in the starting lineup.

Yankee slugger Mickey Mantle had suffered a torn leg muscle and would only pinch-hit. The Dodger line-up, however, was also weakened since Jackie Robinson's twisted knee prevented him from playing.

After the loss of Game Six, Podres had boldly informed startled Dodger veteran Pee Wee Reese, "Don't worry, Pee Wee, I'll shut them out tomorrow."

Before the Seventh Game, Podres's confidence was still evident when he told third-string catcher Dixie Howell during warm-up, "Dixie, there's no way that line-up can beat me today."

Through three innings, the game was scoreless, but in the fourth, the visiting Dodgers broke through for a run on a Roy Campanella double and Gil Hodges's single. A second run came through for the Dodgers in the sixth, and Podres now had 12 outs left between him and a place in the heart of every loyal Dodger fan since the beginning of time.

Johnny Podres's future and that of the Dodgers would have gone south, however, if it had not been for the famous miracle catch by Dodger left-fielder Sandy Amoros. In the bottom of the sixth, Billy Martin walked and Gil McDougald reached first on a perfect bunt. Two men were on with no one out, and up to the plate stepped Yogi Berra.

With a pitch that Podres later described as "high out over the plate," Berra launched a spiraling, slicing ball toward the left field line. If the ball found safe ground, one run would score and maybe two.

After the game, the Cuban-born Sandy Amoros would tell reporters, "I dunno ... I just ran like hell," in answer to their questions as to how he made the difficult catch. Whatever the explanation, the left-handed Amoros raced toward the ball, extended his gloved hand to a couple of feet away from the left field corner and made a great catch.

Besides saving a run and maybe two, Amoros was somehow able to hear Pee Wee Reese's screams of "Give me the ball," and he threw the ball on a line drive to Reese who then fired to first baseman Gil Hodges to double up McDougald. When Hank Bauer grounded out, the devoted Dodger fans put their hearts back in their chests.

The Dodger seventh passed quickly for Johnny Podres. We got out of a jam in the eighth, and when "Moose" Skowron and Bob Cerv were retired in the ninth, the Yankees' first black player, Elston Howard, stood between Podres and his destiny. Utilizing his bullet-like rising fast ball and a deadly change-up, Podres forced Howard to hit a ground ball to Pee Wee Reese who threw quickly to Gil Hodges for the third out as the Dodgers and the city of Brooklyn went bonkers with their first World Series championship.

Thirty-eight years before Podres' Seventh Game victory, two National League hurlers were participants in a baseball game like no other in the history of the sport. When the Cincinnati Reds faced the Chicago Cubs on May 2, 1917, little did the fans at Chicago's Weeghman Park know that Fred Toney and James Vaughn would exhibit pitching performances that surely never will be repeated.

Since major league baseball history indicates that a no-hitter is pitched once about every 12,500 games, the odds that two would be pitched in one day must be astronomical. When Toney and Vaughn took the mound against each other, neither pitcher knew that they were destined for baseball immortality.

Cincinnati Reds' right-hander Fred Toney was a giant of a man at 6-feet 6-inches and 245 pounds. He would win 20 games twice in a career that saw him record 137 victories in 13 years in the majors.

The 6-foot-4, 215-pound Chicago Cubs' southpaw James "Hippo" Vaughn was as well known for his girth as for his proficiency. A five-time 20-game winner, he would win 178 games in 13 seasons in the majors.

Ironically, the most famous man in this unparalleled game was neither Toney nor Vaughn. Waiting for his chance to make a mark in this miracle game was none other than the man the King of Sweden once called, "The Greatest Athlete in the World," Jim Thorpe.

How Jim Thorpe made his presence known only occurred after Toney and Vaughn had exhibited pitching gems through the first nine innings of the game.

"Big" Fred Toney, who was credited with the longest no-hitter in major league history when he pitched 17 hitless innings for Winchester, Kentucky, in the Blue Grass League, quietly retired the Cubs' hitters throughout the first nine innings. His rival pitcher Vaughn did likewise against the Cincinnati hitters.

Of the two, Vaughn had pitched the "better" no-hitter, having struck out ten and not allowing a Reds' hitter past first base. Only one close call occurred for either team. Cub first-baseman Fred Merkle was retired on a great catch by Manuel Cueto of a ball hit to the base of the left-field wall.

Having dazzled the afternoon crowd with their pitching magic and officially recorded no-hitters by blanking their opponents for nine innings, the two hurlers now headed to the tenth. Pitching a no-hitter against a no-hitter was remarkable in and of itself, but more remarkable was that neither pitcher had achieved a "W" for their phenomenal effort.

In the tenth, Cincinnati Reds' shortstop Larry Kopf led off with a single, spoiling "Hippo" Vaughn's no-hitter. When Chicago center fielder Cy Williams next misplayed Reds' first baseman Hal Chase's high fly ball, the Reds suddenly had men at first and third and one out.

The 1912 Olympic decathlon champion and former All-American football player Jim Thorpe now stepped to the plate for the Reds. Never much of a batter in his major league days, Thorpe proceeded to hit a high chop just off the plate that Vaughn caught but had no play at first base.

Kopf scampered home with the only Reds' run, and when Toney 1-2-3'd the Cubs in the bottom of the tenth, he had a no-hit victory that has never been equaled to this day.

Johnny-John Samuel (The Dutch Master) Vander Meer from Prospect Park, New Jersey, ended his 13-year major league career with a record of 119 wins and 121 losses. A 6-foot-1, 190-pound, left-hander, Vander Meer would nevertheless make his mark in Major League history because of his performance for the Cincinnati Reds on June 15, 1938.

Sporting a machine-gun fast ball and plenty of confidence, the 22-two-year-old Vander Meer had experienced a pitcher's dream just four days earlier on June 11th when he no-hit the Boston Bees. On the following Wednesday, Vander Meer would once again take the hill for the Reds and attempt to become the first man in baseball history to throw consecutive no-hitters.

The Reds were pitted against the Brooklyn Dodgers, who were playing their very first night game. Evening baseball was new in those days, but better than 38,000 Dodger fans showed up not only to be a part of the team's history, but to see the vaunted Reds' left-hander try to duplicate his earlier achievement.

With catcher Ernie Lombardi behind the plate, Vander Meer continued his pitching mastery by holding the Dodgers hitless through six innings. To aid his effort, first baseman Frank McCormick popped a three-run home run.

Despite two walks in the seventh, Vander Meer kept on course by mixing a sharp curve ball in with a darting fast ball. The eighth was smooth sailing, and with the never-before total of 17 no-hit innings behind him, Vander Meer faced incredible odds against performing another no-hitter when he went to the ninth.

That ninth would almost be more than the packed Ebbets Field could stand. Bowing to the pressure, Vander Meer suddenly lost his control, and with one out, walked in succession catcher Babe Phelps, third baseman Cookie Lavagetto, and first baseman Dolph Camilli.

Manager Bill McKechnie now strode to the mound to calm his pitcher down. Outfielder Ernie Koy was the next Dodger hitter, and after two pitches, Vander Meer induced Koy to hit a grounder to third baseman Lew Riggs who threw to Lombardi at home plate for out number two.

In order to make Vander Meer's anticipated achievement even more memorable, the final Dodger batter that day would be none other than future Hall of Famer Leo "The Lip" Durocher. The Dodger shortstop in 1938, Leo now strode to the plate determined to break up Vander Meer's attempt at glory.

With the count ball one and strike two, however, Leo could produce only a soft fly ball to center field. When Harry Craft easily fielded the ball, Johnny Vander Meer had pitched the only back-to-back no-hitters in baseball history.

Milwaukee Braves pitcher Lew Burdette won 21 games and lost 15 in 1959. Backed by a slugging lineup that included Hank Aaron, Eddie Mathews, Joe Adcock, and Del Crandall, who combined for 131 homers, Burdette was a model of consistency. His previous two seasons had produced 37 wins.

When Burdette took the mound in Milwaukee's County Stadium on May 26, 1959, he and the Braves were highly favored to defeat the Pittsburgh Pirates even though their roster included such veteran ball players as Dick Stuart, Bill Mazeroski, Dick Groat, and Hall of Famer Roberto Clemente.

Roberto Clemente and Groat did not play that cool evening in Milwaukee, but the rest of the Pirates took on the Braves behind a 33-year-old, pint-sized, 5-foot-9, 170-pound, left-hander named Harvey Haddix. Nicknamed "The Kitten" because Haddix reminded his former Cincinnati Reds' teammates of Harry "The Cat" Brecheen, Haddix was definitely the underdog pitcher against the formidable, fireballing Burdette.

Born in Medway, Ohio, Harvey Haddix began his major league career with St. Louis in 1952. He spent five seasons with the Cardinals and won 20 games in 1953, 18 in 1954, and 12 more in 1955.

At Philadelphia in 1956 and 1957, Haddix went 12-8 and 10-13, respectively before joining Cincinnati for the 1958 season where he got his new nickname and won eight and lost seven. In 1959, he joined the Pittsburgh Pirates and was part of a pitching staff that included Roy Face (18-1) and Vernon Law (18-9).

When he took the mound on May 26, 1959, Haddix was in the midst of a season where he would finish at an even .500 (12-12). Lew Burdette on the other hand had won seven of the first nine games of the 1959 season.

In what proved to be a monumental pitching duel, the two hurlers who threw from opposite sides of the mound completely dominated the Pirates' and Braves' hitters. The hardest hit ball over the first few innings was a line drive by Braves' shortstop Johnny

Logan, which was speared by the Pirates' fine fielding shortstop Dick Schofield.

Inning after inning, the batters were mowed down, and while Burdette was giving up a base hit here and there, the willowy Haddix went to the bottom of the ninth having retired 24 men in a row. Three outs stood between him and a no-hit, perfect game, which would come less than three years after Don Larsen's masterpiece in the 1956 World Series.

With the score still 0-0, Haddix, who swore he didn't realize how close he was to immortality, faced the bottom third of the Braves' order: Andy Pafko, Johnny Logan, and Burdette himself. With nearly 20,000 fans screaming wildly, Haddix nonchalantly struck out Pafko, retired Logan on a fly ball to left field, and then whiffed Burdette, who looked at a called third strike.

Twenty-seven men up and 27 down meant Haddix had pitched with perfection, but unfortunately, the hard-working Pirates' hurler had no victory to show for his stupendous efforts. His Pirates' teammates had failed to score against Burdette, and so the teams headed for extra innings.

Using a still-buzzing fast ball and a knock-'em-dead curve, Haddix retired six straight Braves' hitters to pitch the longest perfect game in the history of baseball. Thirty-six Braves had gone down, but after 12 innings the unlucky Haddix was still locked in a scoreless duel with the cunning Lew Burdette.

After the Pirates had been retired in the top of the thirteenth, Haddix's perfect streak finally came to an end. A throwing error by third baseman Don Hoak permitted second baseman Felix Mantilla to be the first Braves' base runner. Then after Eddie Matthews sacrificed him to second, Hank Aaron was walked to set up the double play.

Harvey Haddix's second offering to outfielder Joe Adcock was his undoing. The Braves' slugger hammered it just over the fence in right center field. A mix-up in base running reduced Adcock's apparent three-run homer to a run-scoring double and cost the Braves two runs, but it made no difference as Haddix saw his no-hitter, his perfect game, and his chance at victory all vanish with the crack of Adcock's bat.

Johnny Podres's clutch Seventh Game World Series victory, the double no-hitter pitched by Fred Toney and James Vaughn, Johnny Vander Meer's second successive no-hitter, and Harvey Haddix's incredible 12-inning perfect game stand along Don Larsen's World Series perfect game as the greatest games ever pitched in major league baseball history. Which is the best of all time may be subject to debate, but when all the important factors are considered, Larsen's effort stands by itself.

While the double no-hitter, Vander Meer's achievement, and Haddix's incredible performance are often stacked up against Larsen's effort, Johnny Podres's pressure-packed victory seems the chief challenger to Larsen's perfect game.

Coming as it did in the Seventh Game of a World Series was reason enough, but Podres also pitched knowing that the hearts and minds of every Dodger fan were with him since his Dodgers faced the stigma of having never won a World Championship. This sets his game aside from Haddix's since the Pirate hurler faced the Braves in a regular-season game where the pressure did not match that of a World Series game.

To be sure, Harvey Haddix did retire 36 straight men, nine more than Don Larsen. No one can doubt the magnitude of that achievement, but the atmosphere under which Larsen performed sets it aside from Haddix's game and all of the other performances.

In the book, *Baseball's 50 Greatest Games,* author Bert Randolph Sugar explored the facts and circumstances surrounding not only Don Larsen's game, but the other four mentioned above. Sugar, whose incredible writing describes each of the 50 games with perfect visual clarity, places Larsen's pitching performance ahead of any other with the conclusion that, "It was the greatest single pitching performance in the history of baseball."

Lowell Reidenbaugh, in *The Sporting News* selected baseball's 50 greatest games. He rates Larsen's game as the second greatest game in the history of baseball behind Bobby Thomson's "The Shot Heard 'Round the World,' and ahead of any other pitching performance.

Based on the competition faced, the stakes of the game, and the totality of the performance, Mr. Sugar and Mr. Reidenbaugh's words of praise are correct. The quality of Larsen's opponent, the defending World Champion Brooklyn Dodgers, the fact that it was a pivotal Fifth Game of the World Series, and the overpowering, pinpoint control pitching performance by Larsen elevate the game to its number one position.

If this be the case, the most mystifying question regarding Don Larsen's achievement is how in the world the Yankee right-hander was able to pull it off. Was it Larsen's no wind-up delivery, his pinpoint control, or the Dodger team's poor batting ability that day that was responsible for the perfect performance?

Bert Sugar wrestled with this question in his book, and his argument is not only great prose, but quite compelling. He wrote:

> Dodger batters thinking there was less in Larsen's delivery than met the eye, tried to time their swing, when they swung at all, and found themselves out of sync with the arrival of the ball. Coupled with his no wind-up delivery, Larsen dealt in a form of insincerity known only to great pitchers, which he was on this, day of days. When he promised one thing, he delivered another. The total effect had the Dodger bats rustling, almost sighing at the ball.

Besides sportswriters, the Dodger and Yankee ball players had their viewpoint as to why Larsen was so damn effective. Sal Maglie's battery-mate, Roy Campanella, told the Associated Press, "Larsen had great control," a comment echoed by Dodger third-base coach Billy Herman who said, "Larsen was ahead of the hitters all after-noon ... his control was perfect."

Yankee pitching coach Jim Turner told reporters, "He [Larsen] could get any pitch he threw over ... He had a good curve, slider, and his fast ball burst upon the hitters." Yankee catcher Yogi Berra compared Larsen and his control to that of former Yankee great Ed Lopat, "Don's control looked like Lopat's, who was the easiest pitcher I ever caught. Right away, I knew he could get it over where he wanted it, any pitch he threw and that was good enough for me."

Regarding the no wind-up delivery, Dodger first baseman Gil Hodges commented:

> He got the corners all afternoon ... with everything he threw ... fast ball, slow curve, or hook. I for one didn't feel disturbed by his short wind-up, after the first time at bat, it shouldn't bother a hitter.

Third baseman Jackie Robinson told writers, "Larsen's game was the finest pitching performance I ever saw ... That he didn't wind-up didn't bother us. It was the stuff he had on the ball."

Besides Yogi Berra, the man who had the best seat in Yankee Stadium was Umpire Babe Pinelli, who had a lifetime of memories all rolled into the magic game. After he caught his breath, an exhausted Pinelli told reporters that he felt Larsen's success was due to "that change of pace, particularly to right-hand hitters . . . It was great . . . kept curving away from them. Seven or eight of them were swinging like at a ping-pong ball."

Certainly Larsen kept the Dodger hitters off guard. Of the 97 pitches he threw, 70 were strikes and just 27 were balls (72%). He was behind the hitters only three times and threw a strike for a first pitch *17 times*. In all, he threw only 97 pitches, just 16 above the minimum (based on three pitches per batter) for a nine-inning game.

In addition to the logical explanations for Larsen's perfect game, there are other practical thoughts. The Dodgers weren't able to hit Larsen's few "mistake" pitches, there were at least three great fielding plays made by the Yankee defense, and perhaps the game was meant as a "going away present" for the retiring Pinelli.

Less logical reasons center on such things as Larsen's premonition about a no-hitter made the night before the game even though he didn't know he would pitch the Game Five. Third Baseman Andy Carey's dad's purchase of a mock newspaper bearing the headline, "Larsen Pitches No-Hitter," also adds to the intrigue.

Whatever explanation may be offered as the reason why Don Larsen was able to pitch the perfect game in 1956, his achievement will always be subject to opinion and conjecture. Regardless, there is no doubt that on October 8, 1956, Don Larsen pitched an unbelievable, incomprehensible, it-could-have-never-happened ball game that is the greatest miracle in baseball history.

Appendices

Miracle on the Mound

The 97 Magic Pitches

Inning #1

Batter	Pitch #	Ball/ Strike	Result
Gilliam	1	Ball	
	2	Strike	Foul
	3	Ball	
	4	Called strike	
	5	Called strike	Strike out
Reese	6	Strike	Foul
	7	Ball	
	8	Called strike	
	9	Ball	
	10	Ball	
	11	Called Strike	Strike out
Snider	12	Ball	
	13	Strike	
	14	Ball	
	15	Lined to right fielder Bauer	Out

Inning #2

Batter	Pitch #	Ball/ Strike	Result
Robinson	16	Called strike	
	17	Lined off Carey, rolled to McDougald, throw to 1st, Robinson out by less than a step.	Out
Hodges	18	Ball	
	19	Strike	
	20	Called strike	
	21	Swinging strike	Out
Amoros	22	Strike	
	23	Strike	Foul
	24	Ball	
	25	Ball	
	26	Popped out to Billy Martin	Out

Inning #3

Batter	Pitch #	Ball/ Strike	Result
Furillo	27	Called strike	
	28	Fly to right fielder Bauer	Out
Campanella	29	Ball	
	30	Called strike	
	31	Strike	
	32	Swinging strike	Strike out
Maglie	33	Lined to center fielder Mantle	Out

Inning # 4

Batter	Pitch #	Ball/ Strike	Result
Gilliam	34	Grounder to second baseman Martin	Out
Reese	35	Tap to second baseman Martin	Out
Snider	36	Ball	
	37	Ball	
	38	Strike	Foul
	39	Called strike	
	40	Strike	Foul
	41	Called strike	Strike out

Inning #5

Batter	Pitch #	Ball/ Strike	Result
Robinson	42	Ball	
	43	Strike	Foul
	44	Strike	
	45	Strike	Foul
	46	Fly deep to left fielder Slaughter	Out
Hodges	47	Called strike	
	48	Called strike	
	49	Ball	
	50	Ball	
	51	Fly to Mantle deep left center field, one-handed catch	Out

Amoros	52	Ball	
	53	Called strike	
	54	Strike	Foul
	55	Ball	
	56	Grounder to Martin	Out

Inning #6

Batter	Pitch #	Ball/ Strike	Result
Furillo	57	Srike	Foul
	58	Fly to Martin in short right	Out
Campanella	59	Pop to Martin in center field	Out
Maglie	60	Strike	
	61	Strike	
	62	Ball	
	63	Strike	Foul
	64	Strike	Foul
	65	Ball	
	66	Swinging strike	Strike out

Inning # 7

Batter	Pitch #	Ball/ Strike	Result
Gilliam	67	Called strike	
	68	Ball	
	69	Strike	Foul
	70	Grounder to shortstop McDougald	Out

Reese	71	Strike	Foul
	72	Fly deep to center fielder Mantle	Out
Snider	73	Ball	
	74	Fly to left fielder Slaughter	Out

Inning #8

Batter	Pitch #	Ball/ Strike	Result
Robinson	75	Called strike	
	76	Strike	Foul
	77	Grounder to Larsen	Out
Hodges	78	Called strike	
	79	Ball	
	80	Swinging strike	
	81	Ball	
	82	Lined to third baseman Carey.	Out
Amoros	83	Called strike	
	84	Fly deep to center fielder Mantle	Out

Inning #9

Batter	Pitch #	Ball/ Strike	Result
Furillo	85	Strike	Foul
	86	Strike	Foul
	87	Ball	
	88	Strike	Foul
	89	Strike	Foul
	90	Fly to right fielder Bauer	Out
Campanella	91	Strike	Foul
	92	Grounder to second baseman Martin	Out
Mitchell	93	Ball	
	94	Called strike	
	95	Swinging strike	
	96	Strike	Foul
	97	Called strike	Strike out

| 97 pitches | 70 strikes | 27 balls | (72% strikes) |

Larsen's Professional Pitching Record

Year	Club	League	G	IP	W	L	Pct.	SO	BB	ERA
1947	Aberdeen	Northern	16	71	4	3	.571	38	31	3.42
1948	Aberdeen	Northern	34	211	17	11	.607	151	77	3.75
1949	Springfield	Three-I	18	74	4	4	.500	55	25	4.38
	Globe-Miami	Arizona-Texas	7	29	2	4	.333	22	24	5.27
1950	Wichita	Western	21	106	6	4	.600	47	38	3.14
	Wichita Falls	Big State	9	44	3	3	.500	23	16	5.93
1951	San Antonio	Texas	(In Military Service)							
1952	San Antonio	Texas	(In Military Service)							
1953	St. Louis	AL	38	193	7	12	.368	96	64	4.15
1954	Baltimore	AL	29	202	3	21	.125	80	89	4.37
1955	Denver	American Assoc.	13	100	9	1	.900	74	43	3.69
	New York	AL	19	97	9	2	.818	44	51	3.06
1956	New York	AL	38	180	11	5	.688	107	96	3.25
1957	New York	AL	27	140	10	4	.714	81	87	3.73
1958	New York	AL	19	114	9	6	.600	55	52	3.08
1959	New York	AL	25	125	6	7	.462	69	76	4.32
1960	Kansas City	AL	22	84	1	10	.091	43	42	5.36
	Dallas-Ft. Worth	AL	5	39	2	1	.667	42	12	2.31
1961	Kansas City/ Chicago	American Assoc.	33	89	8	2	.800	66	40	4.15
1962	San Francisco	NL	49	86	5	4	.556	58	47	4.40
1963	San Francisco	NL	46	62	7	7	.500	44	30	3.05
1964	SF/Houston	NL	36	114	4	9	.308	64	26	2.45
1965	Houston	NL	1	5	0	0	.000	1	3	5.40
	Baltimore	AL	27	54	1	2	.333	40	20	2.67
1966	Phoenix	Pacific Coast	35	119	8	5	.615	64	42	2.50
1967	Phoenix	Pacific Coast	6	9	0	0	.000	4	3	6.00
	Dallas-Ft. Worth	Texas	35	65	5	0	.556	46	13	2.35
	Chicago	NL	3	4	0	4	.000	1	0	9.00
1968	Tacoma	Pacific Coast	6	7	0	0	.000	3	1	3.86
	San Antonio	Texas	9	13	0	4	.000	9	5	6.23
	Minor League Totals		215	887	44	44	.577	574	330	3.58
	American League Totals		277	1278	65	71	.478	681	617	3.87
	National League Totals		135	271	16	20	.444	168	106	3.36
	Major League Totals		412	1549	81	91	.474	849	723	3.78

Larsen's World Series Pitching Record

Year	Club	League	G	IP	W	L	PCT.	SO	BB	ERA
1955	New York	AL	1	4	0	1	.000	2	2	11.25
1956	New York	AL	2	10.2	1	0	1.000	7	4	0.00
1957	New York	AL	2	9.2	1	1	.500	6	5	3.72
1958	New York	AL	2	9.1	1	0	1.000	9	6	0.96
1962	San Francisco	NL	3	2.1	1	0	1.000	0	2	3.86
World Series Pitching Totals			10	36	4	2	.667	24	19	2.75

World Series Batting Record

Year	Club	League	G	AB	R	H	2B	3B	HR	RBI	SB	AVG.
1955	New York	AL	1	2	0	0	0	0	0	0	0	.000
1956	New York	AL	2	3	1	1	0	0	0	1	0	.333
1957	New York	AL	2	2	1	0	0	0	0	0	0	.000
1958	New York	AL	2	2	1	0	0	0	0	0	0	.000
1962	San Francisco	NL	3	0	0	0	0	0	0	0	0	—
World Series Batting Totals			10	9	2	1	0	0	0	1	0	.111

Compiled by Robert M. Browning, National Baseball Library, August 27, 1993.